Journey to a Closed City

With the

International Executive Service Corps

Russell R. Miller

Science & Humanities Press
Chesterfield, MO 63006

Copyright

Graphics Credits:

Graphics Credits:
Cover by Dr. Bud Banis. Based on photos and graphics with text and enhancements by Dr. Bud Banis.

Publication date January, 2004
ISBN 1-888725-94-X Regular print Science & Humanities Press Edition
ISBN 1-888725-95-8 large print (16pt) MacroPrintBooks Edition
First Printing, January, 2004

Library of Congress Cataloging-in-Publication Data

Miller, Russell R., 1928-
Journey to a closed city with the International Executive Service Corps / Russell R. Miller.
p. cm.
ISBN 1-888725-94-X (pbk. : alk. paper) -- ISBN 1-888725-95-8 (pbk., large print (16 pt) : alk. paper)
1. Ivano-Frankivs§k (Ukraine)--History--20th century. 2. Miller, Russell R., 1928---Travel--Ukraine--Ivano-Frankivs§k. 3. International Executive Service Corps--Ukraine. I. Title.
DK508.95.I82M55 2004
914.77'9--dc22
2004000776

Science & Humanities Press
PO Box 7151
Chesterfield, MO 63006
(636) 394-4950
sciencehumanitiespress.com

Dedication

To the Family

Elsie

Cheron, Mike, and Paul

Mark, Margaret, and Cindy

Timothy and Melinda

Ray and Azeline

Acknowledgement

In acknowledgement of the good guys with their helping hands:

Don Arnold, Ms. Barnes, Bill Bratton, Bob Bowen, Jim Collier, Capt. Nation (ComNATSPac), Lou Nofrey, Chuck Sindelar

Contents

The Ukrainians

Anatoly Kuvika	General Director
Bogdan Goodzak	Marketing Manager
Kapitolena	Executive Secretary
Lydia	Sasha's intended
Medvid (the bear)	Communist party boss
Misha	Disco manager
Sasha	Interpreter and liaison
Svetlana Mizina	Department Chief
Tanya	Liberian
Valentina	Laundry lady
Valerie	College student and interpreter
Vladimir Ivanov	Union boss

Chapter 1

The Silent Generation

As the 747 strained to rise above O'Hare field, the familiar thud of "wheels-up" sent a shudder through the airplane signaling the pilot's confidence that we were truly airborne. For me, the sound served notice another overseas trip had begun. There had been many of these over the last 20 years, but this one promised to be considerably different from the rest.

In the past, my typical stay away from home was two weeks rather than the two months this assignment would require. Before, such a long journey would have been a burden for my family. Now I was retired, the children were grown, and my wife had long ago become accustomed to my frequent absences.

An even greater difference from previous trips, however, was my destination. The Ukrainian town I was traveling to was one of the former closed cities of the Soviet Union. For many years, the residents of Ivano Frankivsk were sealed-off from the rest of the world and could neither come nor go without the express and infrequent permission of their Soviet authorities. The reason for their enforced isolation was concealed in the nearby Carpathian Mountains where the Russians had installed batteries of intercontinental ballistic missiles aimed at their enemies in the West, in preparation for a war that never occurred.

When the rusting Iron Curtain finally crumbled, the entire Soviet system splintered into separate independent states. This left the newly established Ukrainian government without its traditional source of financial support, and its struggling defense industry without access to the gigantic Russian military complex that was its only customer.

This economic dislocation was creating considerable hardships for the new government and its inexperienced administrators who were attempting to adopt democratic principles and adapt to free market policies. The process of transformation from the old to a new economy was creating increased unemployment and was resulting in a growing dissatisfaction with the new capitalistic system.

Many of the international development agencies in Europe and the United States were attempting to ease the burden on the new nations by assisting them in their transitioning effort. One of these was the Stamford, Connecticut based organization I was to represent in Ukraine. My role was to advise the management of the Karpaty Amalgamation in converting a part of their operation from the production of highly sensitive guidance and control systems to more commercially acceptable products. The amalgamation's management knew they could no longer exist as they had in the past but was experiencing considerable difficulty in turning their electronic swords into more mundane but marketable ploughshares.

Although I was traveling in response to a Ukrainian request for an economic adviser, there was something sinister and foreboding about closed cities whenever I read about them in the press. The term "closed" sounded even more ominous as a description of the place where I would live for the next two months.

I wondered what the town would be like, and how its residents would react to a lone representative from a former political enemy. From my own experience, I know change becomes more difficult with age. It is always hard to accept regardless of how it occurs. When it is the result of failure it becomes an even more difficult task. I could only imagine how hard it must be for old-line communist managers, and their "red directors," to reject an economic system they had devoted their entire careers to promote.

This would also be my first time traveling for the senior citizen's equivalent of the Peace Corps, the International Executive Service Corps (IESC). I had never worked before as an unpaid volunteer with no personal stake in the success or failure of a project. Before I retired as head of international marketing any trip I made could affect the profitability of my department. Without that incentive, and lacking any personal consequences, I wondered if it would be a challenge to perform, and what obstacles I would encounter in the days ahead. My concern about my destination and my assignment eventually gave way to the anticipation that always accompanies a journey to an unfamiliar place.

Long airplane trips provide a fertile opportunity for reflection; sometimes focused on the future, other times centered in the past. On this particular flight my thoughts drifted back to the beginning of my own personal journey and how closely it mirrored the experiences of many in my generation who grew up during the turbulent years of the 1930's and the 1940s.

As dusk began to fall, I watched the emerging clusters of miniature lights encircle the cities along our route. How different these places were from the small town where I was raised.

Iowa Falls is a Christmas card community along the cliff-lined banks of the Iowa River. The small town, with its 1890 style buildings, provided an almost ideal setting for a young boy growing up in the 1930s. Yet, the setting was in stark contrast to the depressing economic conditions of the time. Children were largely sheltered from the serious concerns of their parents who were fearfully watching the closing of banks and the foreclosure of farms.

My father was in one of the banks required to shut its doors when the owners were unable to support their failing loans with personal funds. I was still too young to sense the fear that accompanies a lost profession and the need to find new ways to support a family. For me, no explanation was necessary when he no longer went through the large marble entrance of the bank, but instead climbed the darkened stairs to a small office on the second floor of a building further up the street. This is where he sold insurance to the few former clients and friends who had enough remaining assets to worry about their possible loss.

Throughout the country, similar circumstances had a searing effect on a generation of fathers who, slightly over a decade before, had fought for their country in the First World War. These difficult economic conditions also left a less tangible but, never the less, indelible impression on the developing consciousness of their children.

The Midwest is an area of extremes, with stifling summers and withering winters. The residents long ago became accustomed to such severe conditions. Some offer the dramatic temperature changes as the reason for their strength of character and independence. My own recollection centers on warm summer days and firefly nights. Fall was pheasant hunts and football games, while winter provided the opportunity for ice skating with equally weak-ankled companions on the nearby river. Spring meant a new beginning for the farmers who worked the rich land that supports a large share of the surrounding population.

After school, my friends and I would hurry home to turn on the radio and tune in the latest adventures of *Jack Armstrong the All-American Boy*, *Captain Midnight*, *The Lone Ranger,* and *Little Orphan Annie* with her secret decoder ring. My favorite program was *Terry and the Pirates.* I listened anxiously as young Terry and his friends relentlessly pursued the exotic but unscrupulous Dragon Lady through a series of Far Eastern adventures. The program created an enduring interest in the orient for this avid young listener.

Following supper, my parents would set aside their own concerns while they listened to the unrelenting problems of *Lorenzo Jones and His Wife Bell, Easy Aces,* and *One Man's Family*. Later in the evening we would all laugh at the escapades of Jack Benny, Fred Allen, and Fibber McGee and Molly.

Since television was not yet available, my friends and I turned to reading as our major means of recreation. The 1930's were arguably the most productive period for American writers. We progressed up our own literary ladder from comic books and Captain Marvel to the big-little books and pulp magazines featuring the exciting adventures of Doc Savage, Flying Aces, and the diabolically clever Dr. Fu Manchu.

As our reading tastes developed we eventually encountered a new view of the world through the written words of Hemingway, Fitzgerald, Steinbeck and other novelists of the time. These writers, with their vivid descriptions of life outside of the Mid-west, provided the beginning of an abiding interest in distant places for me and many other youngsters who were previously exposed to only small town life.

In these communities, families are close to one another, having sometimes lived in the same area for several generations. I played with friends whose parents were playmates of my own father and mother. Some of my teachers, years before had taught my parents when they were young. In such towns, the adults watch out for each other's children as if they were their own. These firm intergenerational ties, along with a strong sense of community, enabled economically troubled Iowa parents to provide an ethical anchor for their children and raise independent and resilient offspring.

Then came the event that forever changed the lives of Americans in the small towns and big cities alike. On December 7, 1941 Japan attacked Pearl Harbor and the world was never the same again. Brothers of my friends, and sons of our neighbors, suddenly left home, some never to return. Boys that grew-up hunting the cornfields with twenty-two rifles and four-ten shotguns entered the service and quickly became proficient with M1s and bazookas.

The government believed the geographically and philosophically isolated Midwest needed to be involved in the war as quickly as possible. To bring the war closer to home, the 34th Division, with men from Iowa and the surrounding states, was one of the earliest units activated. These young men were briefly trained and quickly sent to fight in the African campaign. Later, the same division was part of the Anzio landing and fought through the hell that was the Italian theater of operations. A gold star in a neighbor's window, signifying the death of a son or husband, became an all too familiar sight in many of our neighbor's homes.

The war immediately became the defining element for all of the country. My family listened nightly for news of previously unheard of places like El Alamein, Bataan, Wake Island, and wondered if any of our friends were serving there.

On the home front, everyone was involved in the war effort. Adults bought war bonds, and children saved their coins to buy saving stamps. To conserve scarce material, woman's skirts became shorter and less full while men gave up wearing vests, spats, and cuffs on their trousers. The government issued ration books to adults and children alike. Coupons were required to purchase even limited amounts of gasoline, tires, and shoes; as well as necessary foodstuffs such as meat, coffee, sugar, and flour. Each time a person went to the store they took along the required ration stamps with their purse or wallet.

The farms of the region became the defense plants of the Midwest, and provided even more food than before for the country's troops and overseas allies. Because the military badly needed rope, some farmers converted their less productive fields to growing hemp. Processing plants dotted the landscape, and later these abandoned facilities were converted into the dancehalls and roadhouses for post-war Iowa.

In spite of the dedicated efforts of the people, I remember a level of melancholy hanging over America during the early 1940s. The news from the war zones was not encouraging. Although the anxieties of the depression had largely disappeared, new concerns for family members and friends in the service took their place.

But this was also the era of the big bands. The music of Dorsey, Miller, Goodman, and Artie Shaw helped to lift the mood of the men and women at the USO clubs, and the people at home. The orchestras were widely popular in America, and we listened to the swinging strains of *In the Mood, String of Pearls,* and *Dancing at the Savoy*. Their vocalists focused on lyrics telling of lost love and loneliness. Songs such as *I Walk Alone* and *Sentimental Journey* reflected the emotions of the times.

The "swing" music of the big bands also produced the syncopated rhythms that inspired the young "jitterbugs." As my more rhythmically adept friends spun and dipped their bobby-soxed dates at the school dance, I relied on the more sedate and less demanding steps of a timeless fox-trot.

High school, with its mixture of social life and classes, was much the same as before the war. The weight given to each aspect of school life varied considerably with the individual student. Summer jobs were plentiful because of the absence of older men who were now serving in the military. My friends and I would work in the fields (for fifty cents and hour) when the farmers needed extra hands to harvest the crops.

My principal summer occupation was lifeguard and swimming instructor. First working at the new WPA built city pool, then at Father Foley camp in Minnesota. During the winter, ushering at the theater and selling shoes provided extra spending money for the movies, sodas, and a growing collection of records.

For high school boys, entrance into the service was the inevitable consequence of graduation. This future could have been depressing, but many viewed it with more anticipation than dread. For me, there were two principal goals in high school. One was lettering in football and the other was graduation. Academic achievement was never an important element in my own educational equation, but I did manage to achieve both of my objectives with little notable accomplishment in either.

Suddenly, the war was over with the dropping of the atomic bomb on Hiroshima and Nagasaki. This was a cause for celebration for the people who were dreading the invasion of Japan. Everyone was acutely aware of the casualties produced at Normandy and they believed the invasion of Japan would result in even grater losses. The abrupt end of the war brought considerable relief, and there was little concern over the devastation produced by the powerful new weapon as people focused on the many lives that were saved.

I graduated from high school the following spring. Both Germany and Japan had surrendered, but the draft continued. Six of my friends and I devised a clever plan to avoid serving in the Army. We enlisted in the Navy. There was one problem, however.

I am quite nearsighted and it seemed unlikely I could meet the physical standards of the Navy. Memorizing the eye chart at the recruiting station proved to be the solution. Like most things in the service, the chart was standard issue and was the same each time it was necessary to recite the wiggly letters to a disinterested Navy corpsman. Looking back, I recall little personal concern for the consequences that might arise from a squinting recruit reciting a totally different combination of letters than those displayed on the corpsman's chart. For 17 year olds, there is no such thing as consequences.

San Diego boot camp was a kaleidoscope of the cultures that made up the fabric of America during the 1940s. The ethnic and geographic diversity of the recruit training command was a revelation to young men from a small town suddenly thrown together with the different accents and attitudes of the East Coast, South and Southwest.

The predominantly Protestant Johnsons, Olsons, Hummels, Simpsons, Morks, Elliotts, and Millers from the Midwest mixed quickly with the Murphys, Imperias, Rubens, and Lopezs' from the rest of the United States. Boot camp lasted for twelve exhausting weeks while the new recruits learned to salute, shoot, and march in endless cadence-called close-order drills, under a searing San Diego summer's sun.

Then it was time for more permanent duty assignments.

Each morning, the new seamen stood stiffly at parade-rest on an asphalt grinder, with new white hats squared, while the Chief Petty Officer barked the day's roster. When your name was called it could be a free ticket to any place in the world where the Navy had a ship or shore station. Every morning I dreamed of a different exotic location only to return dejectedly to the barracks for another day of waiting and nervous anticipation.

When my name was finally called, it was not for some far-off port with a strange sounding name but instead for a specialist school on the other end of the base. I shouldered my seabag and trudged across the grinder to begin 12 weeks studying the Navy's detailed administrative systems and practices.

After graduation, I was assigned to the staff of the Commander of the Naval Air Transport Service in the Pacific (ComNATSPac), headquartered at John Rodgers Field in Honolulu. The Hawaiian Islands are not as exotic now as they were then but, at that time, they had the same romantic attraction that Fiji or Tahiti might provide the young people of today.

The base serviced the four-engine propeller driven Mars flying boats. Their noisy approach would cause the enlisted personnel to rush to the windows each time the huge seaplanes glided to a watery landing on their way to Guam, the Philippines, or Shanghai. Then shortly leaving in their wake visions of even more distant ports of call.

The only sea this sailor saw was between San Diego and Honolulu, but serving in the Navy may well have been the single most influential event of my life. The service provided members of my generation with an increased sense of self-reliance and direction that stayed with them for the remainder of their lives.

Returning home, there was a summer job available as a section hand on the Illinois Central Railroad. Many years before, my grandfather worked on the first train to come to our small town, bringing with him the Irish half of my American heritage. I wondered if he were still alive what he would think of his gandy dancer grandson? If there had been any doubts about going to college they quickly dissolved with the drudgery of the job.

Like many other returning servicemen, the educational benefits offered by the GI Bill were hard to refuse. They included payment for tuition, books, and a living allowance of $73 per month. I attended Ellsworth Junior College in Iowa Falls where my parents had gone many years before.

It was difficult to return to the classroom after a two-year absence, but this time I had a different outlook and knew what I wanted to do. I wanted to work for a large corporation and become *The Man in the Gray Flannel Suit*. According to contemporary magazine articles, a grade point average of at least 3.0 out of a possible 4.0 was the necessary threshold to qualify for consideration by the leading companies. This was considerably higher than the gentleman's C I carried in high school, but if better grades were necessary, then better grades I would get.

Then it was on to the University of Iowa. Attending a post-war university was a singular experience. Most of the male students had been in the military, and were very serious about their education. Their attitude substantially altered the University culture that had existed before the war.

Some of the older veterans had married and were living with their new families in cramped university supplied Quonset huts. Instead of adopting the styles of the time, these khaki clad dads were intent on getting an education and saved their modest living allowance for food and formula.

Several of my fellow Navy enlistees and I lived in rented rooms in an off-campus house. The independence available in this type of housing was preferable for the "old salts" to the enforced regimentation of a college dorm, or the required sociability of a college fraternity.

All of the students wanted to complete their education as quickly as possible and get on with it--whatever the individual "it" might be. They were not as eager as later generations to change the world. Perhaps because many of them already had.

I made the grades demanded by the corporations. It was a period when jobs were plentiful and businesses were expanding to make up for the lost war years. The University had a well-established placement center and many of the county's major corporations made a point of recruiting there. Several offers came my way and I accepted a job--inexplicably with the Clandestine Section of the Central Intelligence Agency.

The desire for adventure obviously overwhelmed good sense. The CIA was making a transition from the wartime Office of Strategic Services (OSS) to an organization that would be better equipped to meet the requirements of the newly defined cold war. The Agency's one-year training program consisted principally of parachute jump school and ranger training to prepare their recruits for service behind the Soviet and Chinese borders.

After I accepted their offer, I wondered what might cause this usually sensible person to trade his pinstripe suit for a parachute. I never found out. Before graduation, the Agency called to say they were cutting their budget and there would be no new hires. (A year later the CIA re-contacted me in Chicago but, by then, I had lost any taste for a cloak and dagger career.)

By the time the CIA retracted its offer, all of the major corporations had filled their staffing requirements. Miss Barnes, the implacable head of Iowa's placement service took the Agency's abrupt reversal as a personal affront and immediately went into action. She was one of the first of many people who, through the years, went out of their way to provide a helping hand when it was badly needed.

The result of her effort was a job with the Long Lines Division of AT&T beginning at $78 a week. If I wanted to be part of a large corporation, AT&T certainly met that criterion. This began an occupational odyssey through corporate America lasting over forty years, which included seven companies and nine different cities.

With an offer in hand and future presumably plotted, my wife and I were married shortly after AT&T's management training program began. Our marriage fit the generational pattern of the time. Elsie was a 21-year-old elementary school teacher I met while we were in college. I was a 24-year-old graduate with a new job and no money. This began our life-long partnership, or perhaps more accurately our joint venture, with Elsie taking care of the home while I provided the income.

The Long Lines Division was converting its basic technology from open wire stretched between tall wooden telephone poles to the more reliable coaxial cable buried underground. At the same time, in other areas of the country, the company was installing new microwave transmission towers to facilitate high-density communications that would alter the business architecture of America during the coming years.

AT&T's management training program was based on the Navy's personnel policies and practices that relied on continuous reassignment and relocations. After four years with four different assignments in four different cities, a friend who had previously left AT&T helped me find a job with a company I had never heard of, making a product that I never really understood. The company was the newly formed Univac (now Unisys), and the product was the revolutionary electronic digital computer.

Univac was a descendent of the legendary ENIAC computer, fathered by the pioneering efforts of John William Mauchly and J. Presper Eckert. Sperry Rand purchased their small Pennsylvania company, and married it to Electronic Research Associates, a developer of large-scale computers in St Paul, Minnesota. The resulting offspring were room sized binary coded behemoths, fed by thousands of heat generating vacuum tubes. Their data processing speed was in milliseconds, and their memory capacity was less than is now found in the average handheld computer.

New technology was rapidly becoming the engine driving economic and societal change throughout the country. As technology advanced, management concepts attempted to keep pace. The result was constant change as companies attempted to adapt their philosophies to the swiftly shifting demands of an expanding technology driven global economy.

One of the more profound of these changes was the traditional attitude toward lifetime employment. Before the depression and the Second World War, it was typical for a worker to join a company and remain until retirement or death. This attitude changed considerably in the new economy.

As the computing business grew, a management cycle began to emerge that remains in many high-tech industries today. In the beginning there were the founding technocrats who were well grounded in the sciences, but had little business management experience. When the desire to expand the business increased, marketing people replaced the wizards. This usually resulted in the desired expansion, but often at the expense of operating profits. Increased sales and declining profits ultimately paved the way for the rise of financial experts who attempted to inject greater fiscal constraints into the corporate operating culture.

The revolving organizational structure created a new class of corporate condottiere who, like their mercenary predecessors, drifted faultlessly from one corporate patron to another. The new management style placed considerable strain on traditional family ties and the entire social structure of the country by eliminating the sense of community cohesiveness that had existed during previous generations.

Dramatic changes were also taking place in corporate culture. In the post-war period, executives who had survived the depression and the war possessed the maturity, integrity, and experience required to succeed. Their management approach was patterned on their service experience where a leaders first responsibility was to the "troops." With the passage of time, these men were gradually being replaced with younger managers whose priorities, learned in the classroom, placed a more singular emphasis on the profitability of the bottom line, and whose sense of responsibility was more self-centered.

Our family was swept along on the tide of change. After Univac, I worked for the General Electric Computer Department in Phoenix, during GE's brief foray into large scale computing systems.

Then back to Univac, this time in New York, where the retired General Douglas MacArthur and the rest of the Sperry Rand Board were attempting to alter the management structure to better compete with IBM and the other main frame giants dominating a fast growing industry. A major business magazine of the day described Univac as a company with the unfailing ability to snatch defeat from the jaws of victory. The company seemed determined to live up to its reputation.

The next move was from New York to Los Angeles with Ampex Corporation. From there, after four years, it was North to Seattle to join the Boeing Company as Manager of Business Planning for the Commercial Airplane Group.

One cloudy Seattle morning I recall watching the excitement among Boeing employees as the huge 747 strained to become airborne on it first flight. Their achievement marked a new era in air transportation that would significantly contribute to America's position in an expanding global economy. Yet, within a few months many of these same enthusiastic people would be searching for a new employer as Boeing laid off 70,000 people in the next year and a half.

It was at this time some Washington wit erected a billboard on the outskirts of Seattle displaying a glowing light bulb with a dangling pull-chain. The caption read "Will the last person leaving Seattle please turn off the lights." I made sure I was not that person.

Fortune smiled again in the form of an old friend offering a job at Zenith Electronics in Chicago. After a year and a half I became Vice President of International Marketing. The companies I dealt with ranged in size from tiny outlets in Bermuda and Jamaica to massive organizations owned by the politically powerful Riady family in Indonesia, the Bicardis' of Puerto Rico, and Jardine Matheson the storied "Noble House" of Hong Kong. The work involved traveling to over 100 countries, meeting interesting people, and learning about diverse cultures. It was a fascinating experience for someone who grew up in a small Midwestern town.

But, the wheel continues to turn, seasons change, a young man grows old, and after 20 years it was time to leave. During my career, along with other members of my generation, I had the opportunity of working in the communications, computing, commercial aircraft, and consumer electronics industries. All of these were technologies that had a significant impact on the daily lives of most Americans, and transformed the way the country conducted business.

It was also a period of profound cultural transformation. During the 1960s and 1970s, old values were abandoned and few values took their place. I left my first job to find greater stability for my family and unwittingly entered a world of constant and continuing change.

During this turbulent period, Elsie and I raised and educated three children. I once heard "the two most important things parents can give their offspring are roots and wings." I believe we unwittingly accomplished this. Our roots grew deep within our own family rather than in a particular location. While none of us learned to embrace change, we all learned to cope. As a result, our children eventually became independent, resilient, and productive adults.

Years ago, "Time Magazine" editorially christened our generation *the silent generation (1925-1942)*. So designated, presumably, because of our lack of a cause and our search for security. *Time's* youthful writers may not have understood that arising from the depression and WWII our focus was on stability and the desire to establish a career that would protect our families from the economic consequences of a depression and the hardships of another war. In attempting to achieve this, I believe we did contribute to considerable social, technological, and economic change that substantially benefited this country, and helped advance its position in the world.

Retirement is never easy. The rapid transition from intense work to extreme leisure is radical and traumatic, and requires considerable adjustment. Perhaps the most dramatic changes in a person's life come through graduation from college, marriage, first-time parenthood, and eventual retirement. When I retired, I joined other members of my generation who were searching for a way to remain productive while still enjoying the luxury of leisure.

Many of them were devoting more time to their investment portfolio and improving their golf game. Some had taken up hobbies or returned to the classroom. Still others were contributing their expertise to charitable and educational institutions with the singular purpose of "paying back" or "doing good." I was interested in finding a way I could use the skills I had acquired from a lifetime in business, while still enjoying the benefits of retirement.

The Cold War was over. The Soviet Union had collapsed. Left in the rubble was the broken promises of an advanced egalitarian society. In its place was the reality of a bankrupt government that had relied on massive militarization to control a once awesome empire. Its individual countries were now attempting to make a troubled transformation from a Soviet style central planning system to a free market, competitive economy.

Competition was something with which I was very familiar. Like many others, I volunteered my services to the International Executive Service Corps as a means of using my experience and occupying my time while learning to adapt to a new type of life. Now I found myself on a night flight to Europe in route to Ukraine.

As a splinter of first light penetrated the dark horizon I was able to finally doze thinking about the wife I left behind, and wondering what might lie ahead.

Chapter 2

City of Sorrows

The huge tires of the 747 squealed in protest as they forcefully encountered the rain-drenched runaway of Frankfurt's Rhein Main *flughafen*. The airport is a favorite hub for international travelers. Rhein Main and Amsterdam's Schiphol airports have become the crossroads of the world's new economy. Their waiting lounges are filled with tired, sprawling passengers wearing kaftans from Kuwait, dashikis from Africa, Saris from India, and men in their suits and regimental ties from Great Britain.

I planned to spend the night in Frankfurt before taking the early morning flight to Kiev. Some travelers take pride in their ability to spend long hours on a plane and still hit the ground running. I was never one of those.The loss of sleep on a long flight, even for a young person, can cause memory loss, mood swings, attention lapses, reduced reaction times, and impaired decision making. I found as I grew older the adverse effect of lost sleep increased exponentially, so the older I got the more value I placed on a good night's rest.

Although my days of critical meetings were behind me, I was glad to take advantage of the non-connecting flight schedules and overnight in Frankfurt. The airport Hilton provided a familiar convenient location, a clean room, and an elegant early morning buffet. I usually avoid a large breakfast, but knew I would not be able to have such a selection of meat and fruit for many days to come.

I awakened early, still partially on Chicago time, and headed for the hotel dining room. Even at the early hour, the room was already beginning to fill with businesspeople from around the world. The chef had attempted to provide a breakfast buffet that would appeal to a variety of the world's early morning eating habits. Pancakes, eggs, and an assortment of cold cereal for Americans; bangers (sausages) and potatoes for the Brits; cheeses, cold meats, and croissants for the Europeans; and an array of rice dishes tailored to mid-eastern tastes. Accompanied by coffee, Coca-Cola and tea.

I arrived at the Lufthansa counter well ahead of schedule, and took advantage of a leisurely check-in and coffee in the wood paneled frequent flyer lounge. The International Herald Tribune is one of the world's best papers and I was pleased to see there were copies available for the guests, even at the early hour. This would be the last paper I would see for two months and I eagerly placed a copy in my already bulging briefcase.

International flights typically require at least a two-hour check-in before departure to allow for increased security and custom regulations. A friend took this requirement too casually in Maricaibo and arrived for his flight to Bogota only thirty minutes in advance of departure. Although there was ample time before take-off, the Televensa agent refused to let him board. The plane left with vacant seats and without my friend, who spent two more days in Venezuela waiting for the next scheduled flight. After his experience, I always made sure I was at the check-in counter well ahead of schedule.

As the 737 took off for Kiev, I remembered other flights I had taken from Rhein Main Airport. One of my frequent destinations was Tel Aviv where, for many years, I worked closely with our Israeli licensee. Because of previous hijackings, the German airport authorities take their security duties even more seriously on flights leaving for Israel. There was a separate building for departures to only Tel Aviv. Here the security people carefully go through each passenger's luggage, opening bottles and testing all electrical appliances by plugging them into a nearby outlet to insure there are no detonators or explosives concealed in a traveler's personal belongings.

Once security is satisfied, armed guards lead the travelers to busses waiting to take them to their plane. Prior to boarding, the passengers must again identify each item of luggage to make sure there are no suitcases without an accompanying passenger. If a bomb is to explode in flight, it will at least take its owner with it.

The plane to Tel Aviv is parked on an isolated airstrip, away from the central terminal and surrounded by soldiers and an armored personal carrier. The mobile unit follows the departing aircraft as it rumbles down the runway. I was never sure what their role was, but assumed it was to shoot the wheels off in case of an emergency.

However, that was another time, traveling to another place. This departure was more relaxed. The sky over Frankfurt was unusually clear and the take-off uneventful. The plane was crowded but the Lufthansa staff went about their tasks with typical German efficiency. No motion was wasted as magazines were distributed to those who wished them, seat belts were checked, and the flight attendants made sure there were no bags obstructing the aisles or emergency exits. Since the plane would not be flying over water, we were spared the unintelligible instructions for donning and inflating life vests in the event we would have to ditch the aircraft. The attendants quickly completed their routine tasks and assembled in the back of the plane to prepare for breakfast service.

Settling in for the three-hour flight I heard, "going to Kiev are we?" Turning, I looked at the man sitting next to me. He was a tall scholarly looking person, wearing a tweed jacket, who looked as if he might be equally at home in an university classroom, or hunting grouse on the Scottish uplands. His gold Rolex, however, suggested he was not an academic.

He introduced himself, "my name is Trevor Gunn and I am with British Tobacco." I told him my name, and added

I was traveling for the International Executive Service Corps.

"How long are you planning to be in Ukraine?" he asked, peering through his thick lenses.

"Two months."

"Too bad" he replied. I'm going to be in the country only a week and damned glad of it. This is one of the most fouled up places I have ever seen—with the possible exception of Africa.

I had heard the same reaction from a German chemist on the flight from Chicago to Frankfurt. He had been visiting clients in the Midwest and was returning home. When I told him I was going to be in Ukraine for two months he replied "two months-that long-too bad." The scientist added, " in Germany many people are still concerned about the lingering effects of Chernobyl. Now the threat of nuclear fall-out is even greater than before. Ukraine is running out of money for everything including the maintenance of their nuclear reactors."

"He has reason to be concerned", Trevor said. "I come to Ukraine often but leave as soon as possible. Not because of the threat of radiation as much as the general condition and attitude throughout the government."

This was not what I wanted to hear. "What's wrong with the country?"

Trevor seemed all too eager to tell me. Taking a sip of tea, he said, "the bureaucrats have done a really first-rate job of mucking everything up. I was formerly with British Intelligence. After thirty years, I upped sticks to go with British Tobacco. Now I am in charge of security there. My job is to make sure the operations in our overseas plants are as secure as possible. We have to protect ourselves from theft, fire, and occasional terrorism. BT is setting up factories in several former Soviet countries but Ukraine is the most difficult. The government is constantly changing their regulations, and everyone has their hand out."

Trevor loosened his seat belt, took another sip of tea and continued. "One of our new plants is a joint venture in Eastern Ukraine. These former Soviet countries are a great new market for us. The people are heavy smokers and the Russian cigarettes are very bad so there is great growth potential. But there are also many management problems. Between inexperienced management and constantly changing government regulations I am not convinced our investments make good business sense."

The Lufthansa attendant brought our breakfast. Spreading a thick layer of marmalade on his cold toast, Trevor continued. "To make things worse the country is virtually bankrupt. The Soviets concentrated all of their energy on defense products and ignored anything that wasn't needed by the military. You will see when we land in Kiev. There is usually some old Russian made Tupelo aircraft on the airfield. If we taxi close to them, you can see the Plexiglas on the underside of their nose section. That is so the Russians could quickly convert their commercial aircraft back to military use, if they needed to."

Contrary to the traditional British demeanor, my traveling companion was becoming increasingly agitated. Punctuating his remarks by tapping his black Mont Blanc pen on the edge of the table Trevor continued. "The Soviets constructed their highway system throughout Ukraine with the idea of moving troops from one location to another, and for temporary landing strips. Because of these misplaced priorities, there were not enough transportation facilities to get crops and produce to market. In some cases, communities in one area of the country were going hungry while in other places there would be more food than they could use. The communists spent all their money getting ready for war and none on taking care of their people. The same *nachalniks* as before are running Ukraine, only these petty bosses are now wearing free market suits.

I had to agree with Trevor. I traveled in Russia and Eastern Europe while the iron curtain was still in place. It was immediately apparent there was almost no production of consumer goods in any of the countries. When products that people needed in their daily lives were occasionally manufactured, it was necessary to wait hours in long lines before the customers could buy whatever was in stock on any given day. If what they bought turned out to be nothing they could use they would buy it anyway and trade it with their neighbors for something they needed.

After the Soviet military machine became bankrupt, industry in Russia and the other newly independent states lost their only paying customer. The companies had no experience producing goods people actually needed. Since the companies were never involved in businesses governed by the market their managers lacked marketing and distribution skills, and had no idea how to react in an uncontrolled economy.

The Soviet system began to unravel and quickly assume the characteristics of a Russian matryoshka doll. As each level peeled away the economies became smaller and smaller. Hidden in the political center, not apparent to inexperienced observers, was a cancerous core of corruption that was difficult to access, and it was now threatening the future of the entire democratic process.

These problems were the reason western aid organizations were attempting to provide advisers to help the new countries move from a command economy to one governed by market forces. The agencies were assigning advisers to reform the banking system, while others had the responsibility of establishing a new rule of law. Still others were assigned to help the cities clean up pollution, as other advisers directed their attention to providing incubators for small business. Then there were people like me, who were hoping to help the large industrial companies convert their resources toward commercial production.

Now that Trevor and I had analyzed the world's geopolitical problems, we turned our attention to exchanging travel tales like two old fishermen comparing their catch. The recollections of jeopardy linger longer than remembered pleasure, and it was the risks of travel that dominated our conversation.

"Do you know how to tell when you are in a really dodgie town?" Trevor began. He proceeded to tell me without any encouragement. "It's when people remove their windshield wipers after parking their cars, then store them in the boot, or take them along with them."

He was right. I had often seen that done in several cities in South America, and it was common practice in Nigeria.

I chuckled and told Trevor that "one of the most intimidating places I ever visited was Medellin, Colombia."

"I've heard of the place," Trevor said. "Isn't that the home of the cocaine cartel?"

"That's right. Medellin is also believed to be the murder and kidnapping capital of the world. The two facts are not exactly unrelated."

I continued telling Trevor about a business arrangement I had with two brothers. They bought parts from Zenith and then built color television sets to our specifications. I had to travel to Medellin several times a year to discuss business, but was afraid to stay overnight. The usual schedule was to fly into Bogota and spend the night at the Tequendama hotel, then early the next morning I would fly to Medellin. Their airport was an hour outside the city, and it was necessary for a car to travel into town through the mountains, over a dangerously narrow, winding road.

Instead, I would take a helicopter service over the Andes. Looking down, you could see the large haciendas belonging to the drug lords, each with its own immense swimming pool. It was a scene directly out of Tom Clancy's "Clear and Present Danger."

The brothers would have a car and armed guards waiting at the heliport. We would discuss our business through an interpreter. When it was time for lunch, each would reach into a desk drawer and remove one of a matched pair of highly polished Berettas. Stuffing the guns into the back of their belts we would leave for the restaurant where the bodyguards would occupy one table while we sat at another. In the evening after our discussions had finished, I would retrace my journey over the mountains with considerable relief, back to the relative safety of Bogota.

Trevor had never been to South America. Most of his travels were in Africa and Asia. In return, he told me about the time in Sierra Leone when he went missing. He and his driver were traveling on a remote road when bandits stopped their car. They were both beaten and robbed. His office finally sent out soldiers to find them, or they might be lying there still.

I told Trevor "in all of my travels I never really experienced any physical harm. There was a time, however, in Dakar when I became worried and thought I was being followed."

"That has happened to me several times," You have to depend on your intuition" Trevor said, tapping his head with a forefinger. "The human body has an excellent early warning system. Whenever I feel threatened I can feel the hair on the back of my neck begin to rise. When it does, I know I had better pay attention."

I continued with my story. "I was coming back from a meeting in Lagos, Nigeria and decided to stop in Dakar, Senegal. I arrived late at night and traveled alone in an old taxi through the dark narrow streets of the sleeping sultry African city.

"When I awoke the next morning, I looked out my window and saw a bright African sun shining through the limbs of a huge tree next to the hotel. My gaze focused on the large black pods hanging from its branches. As I looked more closely, I saw the strange objects were actually huge bats sleeping upside down.

"After breakfast I met with the Commercial Attaché' at the U.S. Embassy. Following our meeting, I decided to look around town. The day was hot, as only an African city can be in mid-day. The shops were closed, and I drifted toward the waterfront with its cooling breezes and unloading freighters. There was a faint scent of salt in the air partially masking the odor of decaying fish.

"As I walked, I began to sense someone trailing behind me. I circled a corner filling station to see if my unwanted African companion would follow. He did not, but was waiting on the other side. I was able to get a better look at the man. He was taller than I and had a large scar across his right cheek. If this were Nigeria, I would have thought it was a tribal marking. In Senegal, I attributed its origin to bad luck.

"I began to walk again. So did he. The afternoon air, heavy with heat and humidity, became even more oppressive as I grew more apprehensive.

"We approached a large intersection where five roads met like spokes in a wheel. As we entered the middle, both of us were isolated in the hub. I whirled and approaching him said in my deepest voice, "if you don't stop following me I'm going to rip your head off." I turned and quickly walked away. Much to my relief my shadow hesitated briefly and walked in the opposite direction."

"If he hadn't" I told Trevor "I would have probably fainted."

Laughing Trevor said, "sometimes bravado beats brawn-and occasionally brains." He was right. It wasn't too bright but, on the other hand, I didn't want the man on my tail when we entered a more secluded area.

The seatbelt sign reappeared while the attendants collected the breakfast trays. As our plane taxied toward the terminal Trevor pointed out the window, "there-those are the Russian planes I told you about."

We began gathering our belongings. Leaving the plane, Trevor had one more word of advice. "Have a good stay, and remember pay attention to the back of your neck. Some of these people can get pretty rough." He then disappeared in the crowd.

Kiev's Boryspil airport is old and rundown. The sweating incoming passengers moved slowly along the long lines waiting for passport check. The customs agents went through each page of every passport looking for what, only they knew.

Young soldiers in ill fitting uniforms patrolled the area, supervised by officers in their pie-plate hats left over from the Russian Army. Although the Ukrainian government was now independent, it lacked money for new uniforms, and typical of service organizations throughout the world, the big fellows had been issued the little guys' outfits.

Finally, I finished with customs, and went to reclaim my luggage. The airport is one of a few that has yet to install some type of baggage carousel so I had to locate my bags among many others stacked on several waiting luggage carriers. With my bags finally in hand, I began to look for the person I was to meet.

Soon, I saw a large man holding a small sign above his head identifying himself, and the IESC. Standing next to him was a couple approximately my age. We apparently had been on the plane together and, as I later learned, were traveling to a town in the same oblast (province) as Ivano Frankivsk. The man and woman were both well dressed and had the easy assurance of people who have often traveled together.

The man with the sign was well over six feet tall and was dressed in a bright red running suit people of the region seem to favor. In addition, to his size, he displayed a well trimmed but ferocious looking black beard. He was not the type of person you could easily miss in a crowd.

As he began collecting our luggage, I was pleased to see the couple had more gear with them than I, including a large steamer trunk the driver was struggling to move.

Once he had the trunk under control, the sweating Ukrainian began maneuvering his new charges through the baggage check area. The customs officials wisely seemed reluctant to interfere with our forward momentum.

Our driver stored the bags in the trunk of his chalky gray Lada and tied the steamer trunk precariously on its roof. Finishing his task, he folded his large frame behind the wheel, while my companions and I took our seats. The car's engine sputtered and, with a great belch of exhaust, jerked away from the curb. To celebrate his accomplishment, the driver lighted a foul smelling Russian cigarette and headed out on the Karkhiv highway for the 39km drive to Kiev's city center.

As we rode, the couple introduced themselves as Dave and Marlene Levine from Portland Oregon. Dave had been a professor at the University there for many years, and later entered private business as a consultant in municipal planning. Marlene was a social psychologist. They were both retired but still wanted to find a way to do something useful with the knowledge they acquired over their lifetime. When they learned the IESC was recruiting seniors with specialized skills for overseas assignments they decided this would be an opportunity for them to "give back". At the same time, they could travel to a part of the world they had not seen.

The Levines approached the IESC the same way I had. After reading about the organization in a local paper, they sent a resume to the Stamford, Connecticut headquarters. Shortly afterward, they received a blue application form to fill out which, when completed, described their work experience and personal interests.

The IESC office then coded the information and added it to the 12,000 applications already stored in their computerized skill bank. When a requirement came into Stamford matching Dave's set of skills, one of the 40 volunteer recruiters contacted him to see if he was interested and available. A month later the Levines were on a plane to Kiev.

The driver handled his car well, but spoke little English. Dave and Marlene made up for his notable lack of conversation. While the Ukrainian pulled on his cigarette Dave talked of their travels and their children. One of their daughters lived in Alaska and had an Eskimo husband and child. Dave asked if I was married. The car was quickly filling with dark clouds of particularly foul smelling smoke. Through the gathering haze, I admitted I was, "45 years in fact."

I had quit smoking 20 years before and now remembered why. Cracking open the car window I added. "I have three grown children. One of them lives in Bermuda at the opposite end of the Celsius scale from your daughter."

Tapping my shoulder, Marlene said, "You know the IESC would pay for your wife's travel and living expenses along with yours."

"Yes I know, but she decided she would rather not come. She traveled with me to Russia, the Czech Republic and Hungary so she is familiar with the communist countries. She thought they were interesting to see but two months in a remote Ukrainian town, with nothing to occupy her time, seemed too long."

"She could be right", Marlene admitted. "I worry about that myself, but I hope I can find some type of volunteer job where I can use my experience. The IESC office here promised to help."

The day was clear and sunny—a good day for a ride. There were only a few other cars on the road, and the driver was going at a slow pace. The white-birch forests began to meld into the outskirts of Kiev. Large factories started to appear. Surrounding each were mammoth gray housing blocks that typify the outskirts of all Soviet cities. Dave seemed to be paying particular attention to the apartment complexes we were passing.

Finally, he spoke "Have you ever heard of Babi Yar?"

"No" I replied "never." I noticed the driver glance in his rearview mirror when Dave mentioned Babi Yar.

"Not many Americans have" he went on. "Marlene and I are more aware of what happened there because we are Jewish. It was in September of 1941, just after the German invasion of Kiev. The Nazi troops occupying the city rounded up the city's Jewish population and herded them into the Babi Yar ravine. They were shot and buried there. People believe the Germans massacred over 100,000 Jews in just two days.

Between 1942 and 1943, the Nazis used Babi Yar as a concentration camp. They called the camp Syrets after the name of the suburb where it was located. Later the Soviets filled the ravine with concrete and used it for the foundation of some of these hideous apartment buildings they love to build."

"Kiev has a sad history", Marlene said. "During the German occupation, over 40 percent of the city was destroyed. The retreating Russian troops caused much more destruction by blowing up many of the historic buildings, including the famous Dormition Cathedral. By the time the Red Army regained the city, hundreds of thousands of the citizens had lost their lives."

When Marlene paused, Dave continued. "The reconstruction under the Soviets consisted mainly of war memorials and these unimaginative concrete buildings. Now, Kiev is almost two cities, one that is old and attractive and the other that is new and drab."

The Levines were like many couples who have been together for a long time. Any lengthy story becomes a joint undertaking. Each one sensing when to pause, and the other when to continue. Apparently, however, they both knew their history very well.

We continued our ride in silence.

In spite of its somber past, Kiev remains a rather attractive place with many parks. It is built mostly on the hills overlooking the Dnipro River, which divides the city. The old section of town is on the right bank of the river and includes hills surmounted by churches and the remains of ancient castles and fortifications. The new section of the city is on the left bank of the river and its buildings have been built primarily after World War II. As we passed a large and ornate cathedral, the driver made the sign of the cross and pointing said "St. Sophia."

Shortly after his extensive sightseeing commentary, we pulled into the driveway of the Hotel Dnipro. Stopping, the driver motioned me to get out and for Dave and Marlene to stay.

Waiting inside the hotel was a young English speaking woman from the local office of the IESC. She explained I would be staying here and the Levines would be staying at another hotel. She spoke in Russian to the unsmiling desk clerk as he gravely examined each page of my passport. Because of frequent travels, there were numerous accordion folded supplements to the original pages. It quickly became obvious that the hotel clerk's careful scrutiny of my bulging passport was going to take some time.

I began to look around. The Dnipro was a typical Intourist-style Soviet hotel with all of the architectural allure of a gigantic concrete box. The central lobby was dark and unattractive with worn furniture, and a small kiosk squeezed into a dimly lighted corner. I looked through the kiosk's window and could see only a few items available for sale, and no one behind the counter.

The desk clerk finally concluded I was no immediate threat to national security and motioned me to sign in, but retaining my passport for more careful scrutiny by others. Miss IESC had become nervous by the delay. Quickly scribbling an office telephone number, she said I was to meet with the country director the next day. The driver would pick me up at ten. To avoid having to wrestle with my luggage for a single nights stay, I took my overnight bag from the car and sent the larger ones to the office with the driver.

Soviet hotels follow the communist principle that it is demeaning for one worker to serve another. As a result, there are no bellboys in the hotels or redcaps at the airports or train stations. This can make things difficult for a traveler with aging limbs and heavy bags.

I collected my key and started for my room. It was on the fourth floor, down a dark hallway, past the traditional *dezhurnaya* dozing at her desk. These floor ladies appear to have all trained at the same school. Throughout the Soviet Union they look and dress alike while projecting a similarly dour demeanor. Their responsibility is to act as a receptionist for individual floors, while more importantly keeping an eye on the guests. They can also be helpful, if they are so inclined, by providing an iron, ordering a taxi, making a wake-up call, or relinquishing an additional blanket when the central heating is off.

My room was small, and had the decorative style of the small midwestern hotels my father and I stayed in during the 1940's. After the depression, he had taken a job with the Federal Land Bank. The Bank owned many repossessed farms and was eager to sell them to new owners.

My father's territory was Iowa and southern Minnesota, and I would occasionally travel with him during vacation. Since he was on the road much of the time this was a good opportunity for us to be together. Fifty years later, my cramped room in Kiev brought back many pleasant memories.

After showering, I took a walk. It was the middle of the day, and as I walked I soon became aware of the unusually large number of working age people on the streets. They were reasonably well dressed, but in yesterday's style. Many of the younger women were making a fashion statement with skirts two inches less than long enough. Others wore spandex tights, reaching the knee and trimmed with white or black fringe. Their clothes were in marked contrast to the drably dressed babushkas operating the many sidewalk stands.

Most of the younger women were blonde; however, some favored orange, green, or purple hair. It was astonishing to see such a kaleidoscope of coiffures vividly displayed along the dreary streets of Kiev. I hesitatingly concluded the young women's appearance must surely be a declaration of independence rather than a statement of fashion.

The most popular men's fashion was a denim jacket with U.S. Army embroidered in gold letters.

Popular among both men and women were T-shirts prominently displaying the city of Phuket, Thailand. Obviously some industrious Asian businessperson had discovered a profitable outlet in Ukraine for his overstocked goods.

One thing not common on the streets of Kiev was smiles. In an hours walk I failed to see a single one. The people on the street were unhurried, almost loitering, and most appeared very disconsolate.

Returning to the hotel, I found the dining room was already beginning to fill. The hostess led me to a small table and a large menu. Leaving, she advised my choice that evening was between roast pork and stroganoff.

The dining room was well lighted and contained an odd mixture of west and east European business people, along with what I suspected were Ukrainian bureaucrats. There were also several tables with attractive well-dressed young women. In contrast to the women on the street, these looked very chic and seemed somewhat out of place with the other dominantly male customers.

When the waitress returned, I ordered the stroganoff by pointing to the entry on the menu to make sure my selection was clear. Shortly after she left the hostess returned followed by an attractive young woman. "Would you mind sharing your table," the hostess asked, leaving without waiting for an answer.

"What's a nice girl like you doing in a place like this?" I asked, smiling at my new dinner partner.

"Not too original" she replied, "but probably appropriate. My name is Jennifer Wilson, and I work at the American Embassy."

"Do many of the Embassy people stay here?"

"A lot of them do. There aren't many private apartments in Kiev, and most of them are either too small or too expensive to be acceptable. Hotel space is also scarce, so most of the embassy people stay here. Besides, it is the only place we are reasonably sure hasn't been bugged. We have our technicians sweep it once a week."

I could sympathize with their concern. When I traveled in China during the early 1980's, it was widely assumed the Chinese government wired all foreigners' hotel rooms and offices. The typical greeting between Americans was, instead of a handshake, a finger raised to pursed lips followed by a gesture to the ceiling light fixture to remind the visitor the room was probably bugged.

"What brings you to Kiev" Jennifer asked? "Are you a businessman?"

"Not anymore, I was, but now I am retired. I am going to be in Ukraine for two months with the IESC. Have you heard of the organization?" I asked Jennifer.

I was not surprised when she had not, so I explained it was similar to a free-market Peace Corps using senior citizens. "They sometimes refer to us as the paunch corps, which in my case is unfortunately more accurate than I would care to admit."

"Are all of the volunteers retired executives like yourself?"

"Many are, but others have a special type of skill that an organization in a developing country might need. The IESC has thousands of people on file that can fill a special requirement. They send them all over the world, but right now the organization is concentrating on the countries in transition from the Soviet system."

"Are there many woman volunteers?"

I thought for a moment then answered Jennifer's question. "Not many, but their number is beginning to increase as more women take up professions needed by developing countries. In my generation, most women were either homemakers, teachers, or nurses and they usually accompany their husbands on their assignments. Many of them find a way of contributing while they are in the host country with their husbands. A few are beginning to volunteer independently, and I am sure there will be many more in the future."

Now it was her turn. "So what are you doing here?" I asked Jennifer.

The waitress brought our orders. Both of us had ordered stroganoff and it looked good. Gazing around the room I noticed a couple of the men watching Jennifer and me talk. She was a good-looking young woman, and I imagine they were wondering what she was doing with me. I repeated my question.

"Well" she replied, "I studied Russian in college. When I graduated, I applied to the State Department. After I passed their exam and got my security clearance, I was assigned here. I am supposed to stay in Kiev during the summer to fill in for vacations and health leaves, and then move to Moscow."

I was curious, "do you have many people going on sick leave?"

"Not a lot but there is Chernobyl. The nuclear power station is just 60 miles north of here. Our medical people believe there is no danger for short-term visitors or tourists, but the residual radiation could be a possible problem for longer stays. The water in the Dnipro is also suspect, and some believe the silt bottom remains radioactive. Even then, most studies have concluded that after being in Kiev for five months, a person would have only absorbed a level of radiation similar to what they would get from a single x-ray. Still many at the embassy like to take R&R out of the area for fear they may begin to glow in the dark."

While she talked, I was becoming increasingly curious about the number of attractive women sitting together at several tables in the now filled dining room. When Jennifer finished telling about Chernobyl, I asked who they were.

"They're hookers" she replied matter-of-factly. "The economy here is bad and getting worse. The girls are paid in dollars, which are like gold in Ukraine. They make more money than doctors, and can earn more in one night than other women make in a month. I have heard some of them work through the floor ladies."

It was embarrassing being so naive. I would have much preferred to project the image of a man of the world; perhaps Cary Grant instead of Barney Fife.

Nevertheless, I enjoyed talking with Jennifer. For someone at the end of a career it is often hard to watch those at the beginning of theirs without a feeling of resentment. Her career was just beginning while mine was at its end. However, I envied her future without regretting my past and felt only admiration for my young dinner partner. She seemed to have her life together, and seemed to know exactly what she wanted to accomplish.

I would have liked to stay longer but jet lag was starting to take its toll.

We each paid our checks. Before coming to dinner I had stopped at the desk and exchanged $10 for 32,000 Ukrainian coupons. Shortly after becoming independent, the government left the ruble zone and instituted Ukrainian coupons as its legal currency. The new bills were printed in France, were very small, and resembled Monopoly money. My meal had included soup, bread, a salad of tomatoes and cucumbers as well as the main course and coffee. The check came to 6400 coupons or about two dollars. According to Jennifer, the hotel dining room was one of the most expensive restaurants in Kiev.

I wished Jennifer good luck, and headed back to my room. It had been a long day, beginning in Frankfurt and ending in Kiev. In between, I had met interesting people and visited a city I had never seen. Not bad for openers.

Chapter 3

Senior's Service

The sun crept cautiously through the hotel window, then quickly filled the dusty corners of the small room. It was still early, but a good night's sleep had swept away the jet lag of the day before. I was eager to begin the new day, and looked forward to meeting the Country Director and catching the flight to Ivano Frankivsk.

The Levines were going to stay over and tour Kiev. I thought about doing the same thing, but decided it would be better to get on my way and meet the people with whom I would be working.

I had come to recognize that during my lifetime, I had accumulated an ample supply of character flaws and the lack of patience was one of them. If patience is a virtue, is its lack a vice? I am not sure, but I do know, as I grow older my failings become more transparent and difficult to conceal. Even to myself. At the same time, things take longer to finish and paradoxically, since there is no consequence to leaving things undone, it becomes more important to complete what I start, as quickly as possible.

I vaguely understood that this was the same needless level of impatience which, in the past, had forced my youthful family to repress their bodily demands while our crowded station wagon wound its way, with minimum stops, from one corporate assignment to another. On arriving at our new home, I would eventually recognize my relentless haste had produced little substantial benefit, but that realization would fade to only a foggy recollection by the time it was necessary to begin a new journey to a new town.

Recognizing a fault is not the same as dealing with it, and this realization didn't diminish the desire to get on with the job. Anyway, I rationalized, I could always linger in Kiev on the way home.

The hotel dining room was already beginning to fill. The hostess who was working the night before led me to a table, while the same waitresses who served dinner were now attending to their new hungry customers. They apparently put in very long hours but they seemed cheerful and efficient in their freshly pressed black uniforms as they served breakfast.

The air was heavy with first-of-the-day cigarette smoke. A large Japanese tour group, seated at a long table by the window, energetically added to the enveloping haze as they discussed the day's sightseeing program. They looked out of place among the early rising Ukrainian businessmen; the *Novye Businessmeny* as the Russians refer to their new class of entrepreneurs and black marketeers.

There was no breakfast menu. As soon as the guest sat down, the waitress brought the first servings of Hotel Dnipro's complimentary breakfast. It consisted of a large plate of Ukrainian brown bread, two very hard rolls, juice in a cardboard box, and a plate with two perfectly centered pale frankfurters, which I soon discovered had the consistency and taste of a highly seasoned liver pate'. I washed the frankfurters down with the unrecognizable juice, and some very black coffee, hoping to remember to avoid them in the future.

As I was leaving the dining room, two of the "working girls" from the evening before entered hand in hand. They stopped to chat with the hostess like old friends at a college reunion.

On the way to my room, I passed the desk of the floor lady who was engrossed in her morning paper. Responding to my timid "good morning," she glowered briefly in my direction and immediately returned to the news of the day.

It was still early, and I had some extra time before leaving for the meeting with the Country Director. This gave me a chance to look through the package of material the IESC had sent to my home. While I read, it was interesting to see the difference between the "senior service" and the Peace Corps. Both organizations want to provide assistance to developing countries, and both rely on volunteers. However, their approach and the type of volunteers they use are markedly different.

The obvious difference between the two organizations is the age of the typical volunteer. The Peace Corps concentrates their recruiting effort on young people who have recently graduated from college. For the IESC volunteer, college is only a pleasant but rapidly fading memory.

The Peace Corps volunteers often view their assignment as a stepping stone to a career, while the Senior Service Corps staffs its organization with people who are willing to make use of a profession they have spent a lifetime developing. The young volunteer brings vigor and enthusiasm to his assignment. The VE also brings enthusiasm to his project, but somewhat less energy. While there may be less vitality on the part of the senior advisor, it is compensated for by their reserve of real-life experiences, which are not yet available to the younger recruit.

Women staff the majority of the Peace Corps ranks, while most of the VEs are men. The IESC member functions more as an adviser to a commercial organization or company, while a large number of the Peace Corps volunteers become involved with teaching, or some aspect of the environment.

Because of the nature of their assignments, and the average age of the volunteers, there is a considerable difference between the two organizations in the length of the required overseas commitment. The Peace Corps usually requires their people to stay for two years, compared with two to three months for the typical IESC assignment.

It occurred to me that the difference in the length of assignments was possibly a reflection of the way the two age groups view the passage of time. I know from personal experience, when you are young it is easy to believe each day will never end and you are destined to live forever. As you grow older you see your life passing at an ever-increasing rate, and you come to recognize the fallacy of your original assumption. As a result, the older volunteer is less likely to accept a longer commitment away from home than his more youthful counterpart.

While there are many differences between the two service organizations, and their volunteers, there are two overriding similarities. Both want to "do good", and both posses a considerable appetite for adventure.

The phone rang. It was the front desk. I thought I understood the word "auto" hidden in a rapid stream of Russian. I had apparently lost track of the time and the driver was waiting. I was embarrassed. I am an irritatingly punctual person who also hates being kept waiting. Having traveled a good deal in South America, I had learned there that time can often be a four-letter word. I managed to adapt to "Latin American Time", but I tried to avoid this characteristic in my own life.

I hurried to the lobby and was not surprised it still appeared as cold and uninviting as it had the day before. I spotted my driver idly gazing through the window of the dimly lighted lobby store. Joining him, I could recognize only a few items displayed on the nearly vacant shelves. There were a dozen bottles of Russian vodka (Stolichnaya), sitting alongside several large bottles of Ukrainian champagne. A small army of hand-painted wooden matryoshka dolls silently guarded the store's liquor stock. Some bearing the stern features of Michael Gorbachev, scarlet birthmark and all.

Another counter displayed individual bottles of beer from the Czech Republic, English cigarettes, and the ubiquitous Snicker candy bar that had become available throughout the former Soviet countries.

I knew from experience in other countries that foreign consumer goods entered the Ukraine through the efforts of a new class of entrepreneurs, widely referred to as "suitcase salesmen." These resourceful people would travel to adjoining countries with more liberal trade policies and a greater supply of available goods. Once there, they would confine their purchases to low-cost, easily transportable items such as confectionery, liquor, and tobacco products. They would then return with their luggage crammed with contraband goods that were not available through normal channels in their own country.

The driver recognized me standing beside him and led me to his car. It immediately became obvious the Lada's performance had not improved overnight. I held on, tightly clutching my briefcase to my chest, as we lurched from the curb spewing clouds of black smoke in our wake.

There were already a large number of people on the sidewalks. Unlike the early morning hustle typifying American streets, the Ukrainians seemed much less purposeful as they leisurely drifted from one store window to another, then occasionally pausing to study the poster montage plastered on each street corner kiosk.

As we drove, it occurred to me that the Ukraine was rapidly becoming Argentina. Inflation was running at the astronomical rate of 10,000 percent, making the worker's wages and savings almost worthless. Also like Argentina, the Ukrainian people were well educated, and their country had considerable natural resources. Both governments, however, were apparently unable to capitalize, or coordinate their considerable potential.

There was at least one significant difference between the two countries. Argentina has the highest number of psychoanalysts' per-capita of any place in the world. In Buenos Aires, " well, my analyst says ---" is a frequent conversational gambit. Judging from the men and women

I saw on the street that morning in Kiev, it was unlikely any of them could afford a psychoanalyst, regardless of how badly their services might be required.

A blistering torrent of Russian profanity suddenly interrupted my thoughts as we were cut off by another car. My driver furiously honked his horn while giving the offender the universal one-fingered salute.

The driver was more sociable than the day before, and kept up a steady flow of conversation as we continued our ride. I understood none of it, but he didn't seem to care. Occasionally he would point out a particularly attractive building, or an exceptionally well built young woman, and I would nod in exaggerated appreciation. This seemed to satisfy him, and entertain me.

As we passed a small park, the driver jabbed his elbow into my ribs. Pointing, he said what I understood to be "Tara Shenko." I nodded in unknowing agreement, thinking this was a strange name for a park. Later I learned the park was the location of a monument to the 19th century Ukrainian poet by the name of Taras Shevchenko, whose patriotic lyrics inspired the Ukrainian independence movement of 1989-1991. The monument has since become a shrine for Ukrainian nationalists, and a rallying point for demonstrations.

I was enjoying our ride, but we soon arrived at our destination. The IESC office was in an old tree-lined section of the city. It looked as if all of the buildings on the block were built at the same time, and all bore the unmistakable evidence of years of neglect. Their stone fronts were dingy and many had wide cracks running diagonally through the mortar. I walked up the well-worn stone steps and entered through a heavy wooden door.

Inside, was a large outer office where the young English speaking woman from the day before sat behind a green metal desk. It looked like thousands of others that for decades furnished U.S. military and government offices around the world. I had one like it myself, fifty years before, when I was stationed in Honolulu with the Naval Air Transport Service.

The other woman in the office was busily typing on an old manual Smith Corona and was far too busy to look up, even for a stranger. A middle aged man lounged on a sofa, reading a Russian paper and smoking a cigarette. He was also too absorbed with what he was doing to pay any attention to a newcomer.

The woman behind the desk smiled as she motioned for me to go through another door leading to an even smaller adjoining office. Ken Malden, the Country Director sat behind a large mahogany desk talking with another man who, I found after a round of introductions, was with the U.S. Agency for International Development in Kiev. I was aware USAID is something like a parent organization to the IESC and I wondered if he was, in effect, Ken's boss in Ukraine.

I was soon forgotten, as the two became engrossed in their own conversation. It was obvious they were both dissatisfied with the progress the new government was making in moving toward an open economy. The man from USAID was telling Ken "the problem is most of the same people who were in charge during the old Soviet regime are still heading up most of the important agencies in the new government. The country is still under the control of former communist officials, and they are showing little interest in the way things are run. Even if they had the will to change, I don't think they would know the way."

This was much the same opinion Trevor Gunn expressed on the flight to Kiev. I began to wonder why the hell I was here if the situation was as grim the two seemed to think.

Their conversation didn't get any more cheerful as Ken voiced his opinion of the role the western development agencies were playing. "Our government agencies never fully grasped the deep hold the Soviet Union had over all aspects of the lives of the people here. They don't understand how deeply the ideology of the old system continues to effect all levels of the society, even after the breakup."

This seemed to be a veiled criticism of USAID as well, but their representative did not seem bothered by the observation.

Actually, he seemed to agree. "All of the new states were left with a power structure reflecting 70 years of socialism and authoritarianism. Then we expected them to immediately rid themselves of the old beliefs and take on new ones, just like taking off an old coat. This was obviously unrealistic."

Listening to them talk, it was apparent the problem in the Ukraine was greater than they previously believed. I know from my marketing experience, changing people's attitude toward anything is very difficult, particularly when those opinions are deeply ingrained. In some cases, it can take generations and sometimes it is never successful.

Their conversation was not encouraging. My mind began to wander as I looked around the office. It was very drab, and had a musty odor that clings to many old houses. There was an ancient light fixture dangling over Ken's disk. Even my nearsighted gaze could identify a bulge where the wires were spliced together with black electrical tape. The dim florescent tube provided only meager light on the desk below, and cast a feeble shadow on the faces of the two men.

The light tended to mask Ken's ruddy features while it accentuated the AID man's pallid complexion. Earlier, a girl from the outer office brought coffee for the three of us and I now noticed how the government man's hand trembled each time he raised his cup. I wondered if this was the result of being in-country too long, or being out too late the night before.

Their conversation ended on a somber tone. When Ken and I were alone I asked, " if the situation in the Ukraine is as gloomy as the two of you think why are you bringing in people like me to help. It seems like it's a lost cause.

"In the first place Russ you don't say *the* Ukraine. It's just Ukraine. You can say *the* United States, but you don't say *the* Ecuador, or *the* France and you don't say *the* Ukraine. That's your first lesson."

"OK noted, but let me repeat the age-old philosophical question, why the hell am I here."

"Let me tell you. Next to the United States and Russia, Ukraine has one of the largest ICBM arsenals in the world. The country also has the second largest army in Europe, and currently has control over Russia's entire Black Sea Fleet. Because of its size, military power, and industrial potential, its critical to the West that Ukraine remains independent. Right now, after Israel and Egypt, this country is the third largest recipient of U.S. foreign aid. Do you get the picture?"

I admitted I did, quite clearly, but as Ken was "painting his pictures" I was growing increasingly embarrassed. Not with what he was saying, but with my stomach, which was loudly protesting the unwanted intrusion of two very pale and spicy Ukrainian frankfurters.

Fortunately, Ken seemed to be unaware of my discomfort and continued, "I have to admit your assignment is a little less clear than when we first drew it up. At that time, we thought you could help Karpaty move towards the private sector. We know now the Ukrainian government is very reluctant to let go of any of its military companies for fear they will come under foreign control. Karpaty falls into this classification."

"Where does the company get its revenue if the government can't pay for what they buy?"

"Damned if I know" Ken replied. "The bureaucrats want companies like Karpaty to continue developing their military systems but can't pay for them. It's pretty much of a Hobson's choice. They are trying to develop consumer products they can sell, and they are hoping to find someone to provide the company with investment capital to stay alive.

"The company is still involved in some sensitive research and development work, and I am sure there will be parts of the plant you will not be allowed to see. They want you to give them advice on becoming more commercial, but once you are there, you will just have to try to figure out what you can do for them. But you are going to have to be very careful what you do and say while--."

"Can I interrupt a minute." I turned to see Ken's wife Betty enter the room. "I have to do some shopping and wanted to let you know I will be gone for a couple of hours."

Betty was a wiry athletic looking woman, with the fading remnants of a tan, who clearly had spent more time on the tennis courts than at the bridge table.

After introductions, she apologized. "Sorry to intrude, but I have to come through the office to get out. Our living quarters include a little bedroom and bath just off the office, so I have to go through here whenever I leave."

Ken added, "After the staff goes home, the outer office serves as our living room. We have a small refrigerator there that we share with the girls, and a hotplate where we do our cooking."

"It's not exactly like home," Betty observed. "I guess it is really pretty rustic, but living space in Kiev is scarce and this is the best we can do."

"Don't you get tired of being so cramped? How long are you going to be here?" I asked.

Betty thought a minute. "About a year more, but the job has its compensation. We get to meet all of you interesting people. Ken and I really enjoy seeing you geriatric commandos coming through, ready to descend on your clients with all the missionary zeal of a medieval crusader. You come to Ukraine, wearing your sensible shoes, with your bifocals firmly in place, fully prepared to do what you can to save the world.

"We know how you feel because we are here for the same reasons. After he was discharged from the service, Ken had a satisfying career. We raised three wonderful children. Now we would like to do what we can to pay back a little."

Stuffing a large stack of Ukrainian bills in an already bulging purse, Betty wished me good luck and left for the market.

Ken watched her leave through the office door, then asked "how long have you been retired?"

"Almost a year."

"Are you having any problems adjusting to a life of leisure."

"Yes some" I admitted, "life without work is harder than it seems. At first I would envy the people passing our house going to the train in the morning, and wished I had some place to go. They had a purpose, and a structure to their day. After 40 years, suddenly I did not.

"I think a man goes through three major changes in his life. The first is when he gets married. The second is becoming a father, and the third is retirement. I am not sure which is the hardest adjustment to make, but right now I think it may be retirement. At the same time, it makes you realistically confront your own mortality. I know I no longer wait around for end of season sales."

"You could be right" Ken agreed. I know I had a hard time adjusting when I left the company. At first, I couldn't figure out what to do with my time. Before, I didn't have enough to do all I wanted. Now there was nothing I wanted to do with all the time I had. At first, I puttered around the house, but I am not very good at repairing things. Betty quickly decided to either fix things herself or hire a professional.

"After that, I turned my hand to gardening. Then I discovered that instead of a green thumb God had made mine black. Everything I planted died, and the only green things that grew well in my garden were weeds. All of the flowers died and the weeds grew tall—very, very, tall.

"I also found I was beginning to get on the nerves of my wife. After being alone in the house for all those years, Betty decided she could do without all of my "valuable" advice. She told me I should find a hobby. First, I tried photography, then woodcarving, then fly-fishing, then nothing at all."

"The problem is," I offered, "most of the men in our generation were very ambitious and worked hard to build a career. We were raised on the value of the work ethic. An honest days work for an honest day's dollar, and all that stuff.

"That work may have been hard but it provided an identity. They used to say you are what you eat. I don't know about that, but I do know we are what we do. When we stop doing it we either become someone different or no one at all."

"You're right Russ. You know, I think the academics may have it right, in one thing at least. After they retire, they refer to themselves as a professor emeritus. This gives them some identity. Even in the military, when an officer retires he will often continue to refer to himself as Colonel or Captain so and so, or whatever the hell he was. In business when you retire your just plain retired."

I laughed and told Ken about a fellow I knew who, when he retired, got around it by having cards printed with his name, followed by "Vice President of Marketing retired" and his former company affiliation. This pleased him, but he quickly became the joke of his country club.

As Ken and I continued to compare notes there was knock on the door, which was immediately followed by the entrance of one of Ken's assistants. "The man from Karpaty is here to take Mr. Miller to Ivano Frankivsk" she announced and turning abruptly left the room.

Standing alone in her wake was a tall angular young man. "Hello, I am Vasylenko Oleksander. They call me Sasha." He looked uncomfortable as he waited to be told what to do. Ken motioned him in and we introduced ourselves.

I studied Sasha with considerable interest. This lanky young man was to be my voice in Ukraine for the next two months. He was very slender with a large nose and ears, topped by a thick crop of dark brown hair. A long sleeved floral print shirt with the word *jungle* boldly interspersed among the brightly colored blossoms accentuated the initial impression of an awkward young man in unfamiliar circumstances.

The three of us discussed the project, my accommodations in Ivano Frankivsk, and our schedule for the remainder of the day. As we talked, Sasha's deep set eyes darted around the room and frequently returned to the English language dictionary that was his constant source of reference.

I had become very used to talking through interpreters. In my experience, most of those I encountered were very good. Some, on the other hand, were less competent. I learned through bitter experience it is important for the principal to speak slowly and clearly and avoid words with ambiguous meanings or words not commonly used. I also found any anecdotes relying on different interpretations of words or colloquialisms are better left untold. Telling a person "time wounds all heels" may not seem amusing if he is incapable of transposing the words back to the original "time heals all wounds", or he is unfamiliar with the double meaning of the word heal.

Ken apparently had not yet learned this lesson. His cadence was rapid, with a slight midwestern twang, spoken while peering over his glasses with the kind of wrinkled frown older men reserve for their subordinates. Sasha, on the other hand, was becoming increasingly dependent on his dictionary. The more Sasha struggled the more I worried. Two months of this could be longer than I expected, and my success depended heavily on this young man's halting command of English. I also realized if he was having trouble speaking with me, it would be even more difficult for him to translate my statements into Russian.

The rays of the Ukrainian summer sun began to pour through the grimy window at my side, brightening the otherwise dark office interior. As Sasha continued to struggle with the language, I could feel myself begin to sweat, partly from the warmth of the sun and partially from the difficulty my interpreter was having.

I was also becoming concerned about the time, and asked when our plane was to leave. Sasha understood this question and answered without hesitation. "There is no plane. We go by train. This is the middle of the month and the Ukraine airline can't get enough fuel to operate only during the first week."

This change in plans came as a surprise but it was not entirely unwelcome. I had flown enough third world airlines to last a lifetime. Airline ownership around the world is a matter of national pride. No county, regardless of size or finances, believes itself complete without its own flag carrier. Airlines are one of the few remaining manifestations of sovereign machismo available to developing countries. Consequently, there are the Air Surinam's, Aeroflots, and Lloyd Air Boliviana's of the world. All flying protected routes in and out of their countries, with only limited funds for equipment and maintenance.

These struggling airlines also lack adequate regulation and operating standards. I once flew from Miami to Paramaribo on Air Suriname. As I took my seat in the front row of the passenger cabin I could look through a passageway between myself and the cockpit to see huge crates of heavy equipment lashed to the cabin walls and deck. As the antiquated aircraft rumbled and roared down the runway, the Captain came on the intercom to advise us he was carrying an especially heavy load that day. He then asked all of the passengers in the front rows to occupy seats in the rear of the plane. He confidently assured us this would counter balance the increased weight.

We quickly did as he directed. Who would not? I had visions of the nose of the plane slowly rising while the heavy equipment careened down the aisle. Fortunately, however, we became airborne without incident and the passengers resumed their original seating assignments. Because of many experiences on third world airlines, I was not sorry to avoid a local carrier that could not buy fuel on a regular basis. I also wondered, if an airline can't buy gas how can it afford to maintain its planes?

Finally, the meeting ended to all our relief. Our discussion had become more difficult as it progressed, and I frequently had to restate and retry my original points. I often found myself acting as an intermediary between my interpreter and the Country Director. At times, the conversation had become so convoluted everyone lost track of the starting point.

Ken had a meeting scheduled with the Levines, and Sasha and I planned to return to the hotel for lunch and checkout on the way to the train station. We were to be met at the hotel by the IESC car and my luggage.

Before leaving the office, I asked one of the young ladies to send a hastily written fax to my wife letting her know I had arrived safely. This turned out to be a good move as it was a long time before she heard from me again.

During lunch, Sasha told me he was 28, single and a graduate of Lviv Polytechnic Institute in mechanical engineering. He had also attended art school. His specialty was in machine building technology and he had worked on electrical, mechanical and diesel equipment in the Russian Army.

Soviet companies love heavy machine tools with the same ardent passion they assign to large buildings. They rely on heavy equipment for their military production and even electronic companies such as Karpaty usually build their own tools and manufacturing equipment. Sasha, however, had somehow gravitated to the foreign economic section of the marketing department, presumably because of his extensive foreign language skills.

Casual conversation came more easily to Sasha, but it was still a struggle. I had hoped we could establish a better rhythm as we talked, but this wasn't happening. Most sentences had to be repeated, words replaced, and thoughts clarified. Sasha was becoming increasingly aware of his limitations. He explained he studied English for several years but this was the first time he had spoken to a native English speaker. Because of the isolation of Ivano Frankivsk, none of the language teachers had ever been outside of their limited boundaries.

In the past, all of his conversations were exclusively with Russian instructors. Among these, it was not politically advantageous to be expert in English. It was the Soviet's theory Russian was the most globally accepted language and other languages were educationally irrelevant. The more competent and ambitious instructors, therefore, concentrated on languages used in other Soviet satellite countries. In this environment, Sasha was considered fluent. Now he was finding he was not.

In spite of his linguistic limitations, Sasha was turning out to be a pleasant young man. He had a genuine interest in me, and our project. He also had a good knowledge of Ukraine, which he was eager to share.

Sasha also seemed to be unaware of our difference in age and spoke to me as he would a contemporary. Many people of his age are overly deferential to seniors, or avoid them in case their advancing age may prove to be contagious. Which of course it is. Little do these young people realize that deep within the wrinkled frames of their elder acquaintances dwell the souls of their youth, waiting to burst forth at the slightest provocation.

The only evidence of our generational difference was Sasha's insistence on referring to me as Mr. Miller. Shortly after we met, I told him Russ would be a more appropriate reference, but my suggestion was ignored.

I was not surprised at this formality. It is almost entirely a U. S. practice to use first names regardless of age, status, or length of acquaintance. Many foreign businessmen on their first trip to the United States are astonished to be immediately addressed by their first names.

I once had a manager visiting from Spain who told me "he enjoyed the friendliness and openness of his new associates in the U.S. and marveled at their ability to work hard and reach quick decisions." He was shocked, however, at how rapidly people referred to him by his first name. "In Spain" he told me " you don't do that until you know someone for 10 years—and never if you are at a lower rank."

I was always careful to refer to my foreign associates as formally as possible, at least in the early stages of our relationship. Because of this, I was not surprised at Sasha's formality and I remained "Mr. Miller" during my entire stay in Ukraine.

As we continued to talk, I found I was frequently raising the level of my voice. The more vacant his stare, the louder my voice became, more in frustration than anger.

There is a common tendency among people having trouble in communicating with someone of another language to attempt to increase understanding by amplifying the volume of their speech. The more difficult comprehension becomes the louder people talk. Though I was aware of the futility of my approach, it was still necessary to remind myself frequently to lower my voice.

My increasing frustration did not seem to be apparent to Sasha. He ate his lunch with unconstrained gusto. My appetite was less robust. That morning I had found my assignment was less clear than I had originally thought, and my interpreter was considerably less skilled than I had expected. I knew this could be a devastating combination in my future dealings with Karpaty management.

When we finished our lunch, Sasha insisted on paying the check, saying this was part of Karpaty's obligation. While he was paying the waitress, I could see the amount. It was 12,000 Ukrainian coupons. The lunch consisted of soup, meat, potatoes, bread, mineral water and coffee. It was nothing fancy, but certainly filling. Converting the 12,000 coupons to dollars, our bill would have amounted to $3.43.

Weeks later, Sasha told me that the cost of our hotel lunch, in the days of the ruble, would have been sufficient to pay for the purchase of a new automobile. After telling me that, he paused for a moment and wistfully said, "first we had communism, now we have chaos."

Chapter 4

Russia's Breadbasket

As the Lada deposited us outside the terminal, the clock in the tower above the Kiev train station struck two - when it was actually three. The driver wrestled my bags from his trunk and, with a farewell wave of a hand, he and his ancient automobile disappeared in their signature shroud of blue fumes.

Entering the depot, Sasha and I found it difficult to make our way through the throng of people waiting for their trains. Many of the tired travelers appeared to have been there for days, commandeering personal sections of the terminal by spreading blankets on the worn tiled floor. An assortment of satchels, bags, sleeping children, and wilting vegetables anchored their blankets in place.

We cautiously threaded our way through the complex puzzle pattern of Ukrainian humanity, taking care not to step on a small child or a prized cucumber as we attempted to avoid each family's territorial claim. Sasha led the way, bent almost double by the weight of my bulging B1 Bag strapped over his shoulder. Trailing timidly behind, I was equally weighted down by my swollen canvas carry-on, and over-stuffed briefcase.

Although my bags were faded and unfashionable, they had served me well for more years than I cared to remember. The Boyt Luggage Company is located in the town where I grew up, and has been making their style of luggage since the Second World War. Their luggage is constructed out of parachute weight canvases, held together with industrial strength stitching, and heavy weight zippers. The bag allowed an increase or decrease in its size in proportion to the contents I desired.

Such flexibility can be a blessing or a curse. Contrary to logic, the more I traveled the more I carried. I found myself irrationally insuring against the repetition of past emergencies though an increasing accumulation of travel items. On this trip, they included an alarm clock, flashlights, a short-wave radio, extra batteries, and a variety of medications I once sorely missed and afterwards always included.

My pack rat tendencies become even worse when I traveled to developing countries lacking things self-indulgent Americans, like me, have come to consider necessary. In post-Soviet countries some of the normally unobtainable items are toilet paper, toothpaste, hand soap, laundry soap, ballpoint pens and writing pads, rulers and templates, cartons of Marlboros and ladies pantyhose to be used as gifts, and a variety of other items I believed important for a comfortable and productive trip.

My advancing age also assigns a greater priority to personal comfort than I usually required for earlier excursions. This personal indulgence resulted in the addition of even more "indispensable" incidentals. Some of those I considered to be vital included miniature candy bars, cheese and cracker snacks, several paper back books, an audio cassette player and tapes, a flask containing Bombay Sapphire martinis, and of course an obligatory plastic bottle of stuffed olives. Each seemingly essential item contributed its own measure of extra weight to an already bloated bag.

The consequence of the essential, non-essential articles, combined with a two-month collection of casual and business clothing, resulted in luggage so ponderous normal movement through the train terminal was virtually impossible.

The structural design of the Kiev railroad station further hindered the process of locating our designated track.

Airport planners postulate their claim to architectural acclaim on achieving the maximum distance between the check-in counter and departure gates.

Having to concentrate their work in the central city, train station designers are more restricted by available space. They apparently believe their professional reputation will depend on the greatest number of stairs they can squeeze into the most limited amount of space. These devious designers have little regard for the poor American or foreign traveler, loaded with luggage, who must successfully navigate innumerable stairs before reaching their desired destination.

Sasha and I wound our way through the waiting crowds, up then down another series of tiled steps, until finally giving in to the weight of both our burdens, we paused to regain our breath and restore our strength.

At the beginning of our trek through the station, I had seen an uncommon sight in a communist country. There were several porters in the main lobby apparently eager to assist passengers with their bags. I had urgently called to Sasha who seemed to ignore me as he kept his pace through the crowd.

Irritated I asked, "didn't you hear me shout when we passed the men who could help with our bags?" I thought he was probably unfamiliar with the term porter.

"Yes "he replied "but we do not need to depend on others to do our work."

It was too late to argue but, unlike Sasha, I would have been delighted to hire others to do my work. I was also certain the poor porters would have been equally pleased to receive money for their services, even if it conflicted with their Marxist anti-capitalist philosophy. Sasha's dogmatic attitude provided an additional insight into my new friend.

Finally we reached our destination. A uniformed guard closely examined our tickets, then directed us to our assigned car and compartment. We squeezed through the narrow brown-carpeted train corridor, past a group of too-young soldiers fortifying themselves against their journey by sharing a bottle of too strong vodka. Eventually we reached the middle of the carriage and our compartment.

Sasha tugged open the sliding wooden door to our overnight home. The compartment was in "soft class," which bought two dusty crimson banquettes across from each other. The seats were partially separated by a foldup table that supported a dusty, small green-shaded lamp.

Our next test of strength was storing my luggage above the bank of seats. It took both of us to heave my B1 Bag into the small overhead compartment. Sasha's luggage, stored between his feet, consisted of a single blue plastic gym-bag, identical to hundreds of others carried by people all over the former Soviet countries.

I was thrown to my seat as the train abruptly pulled away from the station. The clicking of the rails quickly fit into a pattern as we crossed the iron bridge spanning the Dnipro River.

Trains always travel through the least desirable and rundown sections of a city, and our train was no exception. We slowly passed abandoned factories and warehouses, and then sped past never-ending blocks of dreary government housing. Soon, the larger buildings were replaced by small communities surrounding the city, then forests, and eventually open country.

I have always enjoyed rail travel. Having grown-up in a town that trains regularly pass through, few houses escape the plaintive sound of a lonesome whistle riding on the cruel wind of a frigid winter's night. This forlorn wail evoked nocturnal visions of future journeys to distant places, leaving an indelible mark on many young men in these small communities throughout the Midwest.

There is a romance of the rails that is undeniably lost as you hurtle across the country at 30,000 feet. In a train, you are able to pass the farms and through the villages while watching the people that provide the social fabric of a region. Looking from your train window it is easy to fall under the illusion you are the one standing still while the world is quickly moving past like scenes in an old movie.

I have taken many train trips in foreign countries, often accompanied by my wife. Some of those journeys were wonderful, while others were less enjoyable. One of the better trips was traveling overnight from Mombassa to Nairobi, Kenya. While Elsie and I sat in an immaculate dining car, we could watch through the window as an occasional flickering campfire pierced the ebony darkness of an African night.

Another less enjoyable journey may have been the real cause of my wife's decision to remain home while I traveled to Ukraine. This was a ride from Mandalay to Rangoon, (renamed Yangon) through one of the world's few remaining Communist countries.

I know now I pressed the envelope of adventure too far when I scheduled a trip to Burma. At the time, it seemed like a great idea. The country has been renamed Myanmar, and it is one of the most exotic and seldom traveled areas in the world. In spite of terrible repression, the Burmese people remain gentle and outgoing to their visitors and to each other.

The Shwedagon Pagoda encompasses several blocks in the center of Rangoon and its glittering gilded spires are an extraordinary sight. Throughout Burma, other imposing temples date back to antiquity. The country, however, has been in an advancing stage of physical decay since the British left and the communists took over.

Before then, Burma was one of the richest countries in Asia with one of the best health care systems and highest literacy rates in the region. It is now one of the poorest. Government spending is diverted from schools, buildings, roads, and health care to sustaining the military junta that has ruled the country since 1962. Now most people live on less than a dollar a day and drug smuggling and AIDS have grown explosively.

The Communist government has isolated the country from the outside world, and tourism is discouraged. Entry visas were limited to 10 days, which proved to be more than long enough.

Once inside the country we found the tourist facilities were incredibly poor, and internal travel tightly restricted. The country's airline operated only four small planes. Reservations could be canceled on a moment's notice, depending on the travel desires of government officials who take precedence over the lowly tourist. Elsie and I flew from Rangoon to Pagan and later to Mandalay. Once there, we were unable to arrange for a flight back to Rangoon before our visas were to expire.

This left only the train. The trip lasted 19 hours. It began before daylight in a cool Burmese morning, through a hot dusty afternoon, and into the late evening. It had no diner and we had no food, but we did have two bottles of water. The carriage in which we rode had only open windows, and the toilets were so filthy neither of us would dare hazard a visit.

The train stopped often, and each station was like a photograph from an old National Geographic. The water sellers visited each train window with a large ceramic pot on their head and a single tin-drinking cup, which was shared by all the thirsty customers.

Food vendors would also come on board and stay from one station to the next where they would leave and new vendors would arrive. The view through the window was extraordinary as the train followed the Irawaddy River, which was Kipling's real "Road to Mandalay."

While the views were magnificent, the dirt and grime were not. At one point Elsie turned and asked, " why do you think the people on the train keep looking at us and grinning?"

"I don't think they have ever seen a white man turn into a native before their very eyes", I replied.

That train ride combined with peeling paint on hotel walls, salamanders in the bath, taxis made from pickup trucks with benches, and overly officious public servants, dramatically reduced Elsie's desire for further travel in the developing world. The experience in Burma weighed heavily in her later decision to forgo the opportunity to spend two months in Ivano Frankivsk. I could appreciate her decision, but still wished she was traveling with me.

As the train swayed through the countryside, Sasha and I worked on our ability to communicate. He spoke of his family, his stay in the Army and assignment to Siberia, which he hated. It was Sasha's opinion most of the men from Ukraine and other satellite countries were billeted there to reserve the better duty assignments for the Russian soldiers. Sasha was also shocked by the heavy drug use by the troops from the Central Asian Republics where growing poppies is an important crop.

The flow of our conversation was erratic. At times, we could speak to each other for several sentences without the need for clarification. Unpredictably then, the conversation would spiral completely out of control.

Looking out the window I could see electrical power lines stretched between huge steel stanchions that seemed to march across the Ukrainian plains like gigantic Cossacks.

"Are there still Cossacks in Ukraine" I asked Sasha. He smiled broadly and answered, "I don't smoke, my father doesn't smoke and his father never smoked."

I was willing to go with that. "I don't smoke either" I replied.

"How old is your father?"

"He works for the oil and gas company." "He is an inspector."

"Are you married" I asked Sasha?

"Married—married" he replied, "No I am a young man, just 28."

He did have, as I was to learn later, "an intended."

Soon, the swaying motion of the train caused Sasha to doze. I was relieved. The strain of attempting to help my companion struggle with English was tiring for us both. I also believed we both shared a concern for the weeks ahead.

My ability to communicate with the management of Karpaty was critical, and my chance of success was growing slimmer with each of Sasha's troubled sentences. I had learned to expect problems on any project, but I had not expected this type of difficulty. I was very worried, and the specter of failure was sleeping benignly in the seat across from me.

I gazed through the train window as the Ukrainian countryside rolled past. Soon the view absorbed my thoughts and the future problems were consigned to a far corner of my mind.

The train passed large fields filled with workers laboring on their cooperative farms. The view was similar to one a traveler might find crossing America's heartland. This was the steppes of Ukraine that have long been known as "Russia's breadbasket", since this area formerly supplied 20 percent of the Soviet Union's total grain production.

Agricultural is critical to Ukraine's economy and contributes 30 percent of the country's total economic output, while employing 20 percent of its entire labor force. This high level of agricultural productivity is possible because of the area's *chernozem,* or black earth. Many agronomists believe the land we were so quickly passing through is some of the most fertile in the world.

As important as farming is to Ukraine it was obvious that the laborers working the fields were terribly inefficient. The field hands, both men and women, wielded antiquated long-handled wooden scythes and rakes. Other workers driving teams of horses accompanied them. Engine driven farm equipment was seen occasionally, but only on the larger cooperatives. Even then, the machines appeared to be of a pre-1940 design.

Slightly distorting my view of the outside world was the condition of the train window. Glass in communist countries never achieves the same level of transparency found in other parts of the world. Our rail car was no exception. In addition, a grimy coating on the window made everything in the distance seem to be enveloped in a pale brown mist. This gave the perception I was viewing a vast agricultural history diorama portraying farming methods plucked from the past.

The country is rich in natural resources as well, with iron ore in the east central Kryvyy Rih area, large coal deposits in the southeastern Donets Basin, along with some of the world's largest manganese deposits in south central Ukraine at Nikopol. The country also has considerable deposits of oil and natural gas in the Carpathian foothills, the Donets Basin, and along the Crimean coast.

Ukraine's fertile soil, along with its abundant natural resources, have been both a benefit and a bane to the country's continued sovereignty, often leading to its historical downfall. These natural riches have been the targets of invading armies dating back to the 13th century Mongol hordes. As generations passed, at least a portion of Ukraine's territory at any one time was under the control, of Lithuania, Poland, Austria, Hungary, Romania, Checkoslovakia, Germany, and frequent invasions by Russian forces.

Invading armies were never noted for their reluctance in dispensing their genes among the vanquished population. Evidence of generations of their generosity can be seen on the varying faces of the people of Ukraine.

Its changeable past has left the country's population of 52 million widely diversified. Ethnic Ukrainians comprise 73 percent of the total population. Russians represent the largest minority group at 22 percent and, although they are a minority, it is their language that is generally spoken throughout the country. Jews (who are considered an ethnic group as well as a religion) and Belarusians each account for about 1 percent of the total. Other important groups include Bulgarian's, Poles, Hungarian, and Romanians.

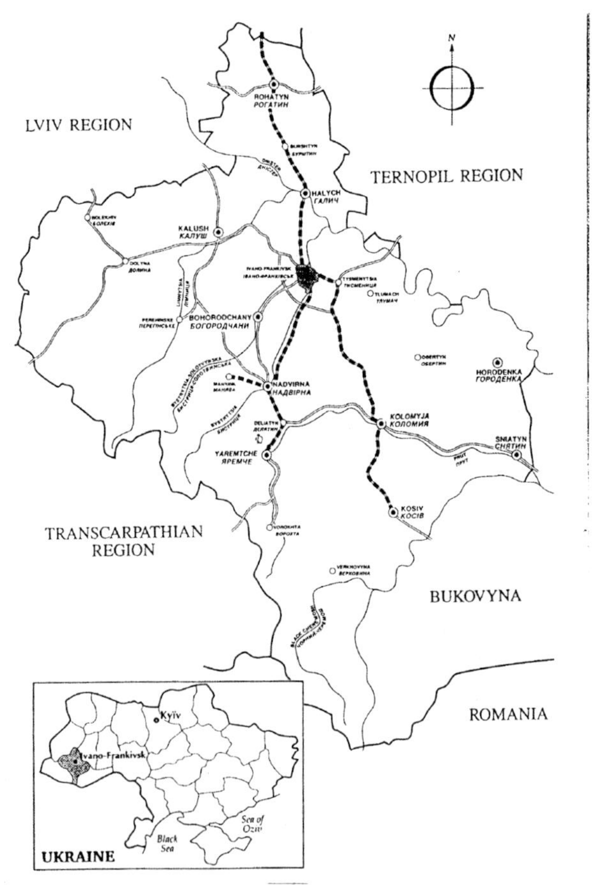

Ukraine covers approximately 230,000 square miles, and geographically could be the second largest country in

Europe. However, it has only a meager history of independence. Before declaring its autonomy from the Soviet Union in 1991, the country had been a sovereign entity only once before in its entire history, and this was for less than a year, at the end of World War I.

Before independence, the lines of ultimate authority within the Ukrainian Government led directly to Moscow where all the major decisions were made. After independence, the new government faced the future with a good deal of trepidation having little experience in establishing either a political or economic policy and a proclivity for, and an affinity with, the communist system. When you fear the future you are unable to abandon the past. The former communist officials in control of the new Ukrainian government have clung to the known and avoided the unknown, which places considerable reliance on maintaining the status quo. As a result, gradualism has prevailed and the economic ramifications have been disastrous.

Not all the Ukrainian people are eager for independence and their politics tend to be divided on an east/west axis. The people in the eastern regions of Ukraine, where close to 25 percent of the population live, are more inclined toward their Russian neighbors.

In the more agrarian western Ukraine the Nationalists dominate. This group wants little to do with Russia. They believe it was the Soviets that ultimately ruined their country. These people prefer to integrate, at least economically, with the European countries. Many in this area are fluent in Polish and feel a greater bond with that country than with Russia.

Because of the conflicting currents flowing through the country, Ukraine's continued independence rests on a very fragile foundation.

The sound of a sliding door banging against its frame abruptly interrupted my thoughts. Sasha sat upright, as a young man approximately his age entered our compartment. Looking at us both, the newcomer focused his gaze on Sasha and spoke to him in Russian. Sasha replied by nodding his head and gesturing to the seat beside him.

The two men conversed in Russian with frequent glances, and an occasional smile in my direction. I am sure it was a welcome relief for Sasha to speak without having to first weigh each word.

The newcomer was wearing a denim jacket, plaid shirt, jeans and Adidas running shoes. He carried a plastic workout bag similar to one at Sasha's feet.

Reaching across the aisle, he extended his hand toward me. "Arkady Ostrovsky" he said. He had a youthful face but old man's hands-gnarled and callused.

"Russ Miller" I replied.

They continued their conversation. Occasionally Sasha would interrupt to include me in the discussion. I appreciated his effort. It would have been very easy to ignore me, particularly when translation was as difficult as it was.

Arkady worked in a factory many miles from his home and family. He had originally worked for several years in a plant in his hometown, but it had closed and he had to find work in another town. He shared an apartment with three other men, then took the train once a month to spend a weekend with his wife and children. When he returned home, his friends had still not found work and spent their time drinking vodka and talking about the past.

Now Arkady worried he would lose his new job as there were already many layoffs where he worked and he feared he might be next.

Sasha explained it was very difficult to find work in Ukraine because the government failed to base their economic policies on logic and their regulations were constantly changing.

"Our system is like a peculiar sort of *Solianka"* Sasha said. "This is a Russian soup made of sausage and vegetables that varies with each cook. Each new group changes the recipe and none of it is good for the people. Many of the factories still open are close to shutting down, and many of the people that do go to work have no work to do. No one knows from day to day what change will be next so they can't make any plans. I have a fiancé and we have postponed our marriage several times because of the economic uncertainty."

I had nothing to say. Both Sasha and Arkady were young men with considerable concern about their future. It was sad to see a country so rich in resources and so poor in spirit. It was especially troubling for them since neither had encountered such uncertainty before independence.

The communist system had taken care of the people from their cradle to their grave. This type of life required very little initiative. When the system failed, the people were poorly prepared for taking care of themselves.

"Are you hungry" Sasha asked? I assured him I was. I had been looking forward to going to the dining car for some time. Rising I said, "let's go."

"No, no, we eat here. Much better than dining car, much more interesting" Sasha replied, digging into his bag. I reluctantly returned to my seat as he and Arkady began to assemble our co-operative dinner. Sasha's contribution was a sausage, rolls, a can of sardines, a bottle of water made from bread (terrible), and a flask of vodka.

Arkady's offering consisted of hard-boiled eggs and two of the largest pickles I had ever seen.

Sasha was right, it was more interesting.

The conversation turned to fishing. Arkady was an avid angler and I mentioned my wife and I had a second home on a lake in Wisconsin, and I liked to fish as well. We then told about the types of fish we would catch. Even with good translators, comparing species of fish from one language to another is an almost impossible task. With Sasha doing the interpretation, it became an amusing exercise among the three of us.

I noticed Sasha would often respond with the word "tuk" during any pause in the conversation. I was to learn that tuk is one of the multi-purpose words all languages have. The Ukrainians use it as a positive response to note agreement or as filler, similar to the way an American might say, "you know" or a Colombian might say "claro" or clear.

I found Sasha also used "tuk" when he did not understand what I was trying to tell him and he was unsure of how else to respond. As we became better acquainted I formed a conversational criterion that after three "tuks" I had struck out.

If I asked a question and received a blank look in response accompanied by a tuk; tried again restating the question in a different way, then tried once more with a similar response I would then give-up, or move to a different subject. On days I was tired, I would concede defeat at the two-tuk level.

As night began to fall the sky turned from cobalt to gray. The workers had long ago left the fields, and their last cow returned to the barn.

The sliding door of our compartment banged open again and a heavy-set unsmiling female attendant, her arms loaded with blankets and sheets, squeezed through the wide opening. On Ukrainian trains you pay the *provodnik* or attendant extra for your bedding. Sasha gave the uniform clad woman several coins for ours, while Arkady gestured he would forgo this "luxury".

I left the compartment to go to the toilet. The long train rocked from side to side as I attempted to navigate the narrow aisle. At the end of the compartment, the young soldiers were now sound asleep, their vodka bottles empty. I stepped over them and entered the toilet.

Inside there was only a basin and a hole in the steel plated floor of the car. Peering through the opening you could see the graveled track-bed rapidly passing by. On each side of the hole was an indenture for your feet. A steel bar was fastened to the wall to steady any unlucky passenger that required a squatting position. There was no toilet paper or paper towels. Only a single well-used linen hand towel hooked to the wash basin.

I returned to our compartment. Sasha was in one of the upper berths, leaving the lower bunk for me. Arkady lay in the lower berth across the aisle.

Unlike traveling by plane, I usually sleep well on a train. Not only can you stretch out but there is also something about the gentle swaying of the carriage that induces sleep. I fell into a troubled slumber thinking of my wife, and wondering what I would find in Ivano Frankivsk.

The stops were infrequent. When they did occur I could glimpse the lighted station platform from the window. At each stop, there was a distant, tinny sound of a woman's voice over an ancient loudspeaker. Her announcement would be followed by ghost-like shuffling of departing passengers moving with their baggage down the narrow, dimly lighted corridor.

Once during the night, a shaft of light coming through the gently sliding compartment door awakened me. As I watched in the shadows made by the pale blue night light above our door, I saw a young woman's' denim-clad behind furtively disappearing into the upper bunk across from me. When I awoke the next morning, she was gone.

I hoped, like the practice on Chinese trains, an attendant would soon come to our compartment with steaming pots of strong tea. No such luck. The night before there was a tarnished brass samovar at the end of the corridor, standing guard over the tiny cubicle that served as the office for our lady *provodnik.* This morning she had disappeared, departing like a thief in the night at one of the remote stations, leaving the samovar unmanned. Also temporarily abandoned was the small mirror she had rigged to keep an eye on passengers entering and leaving their compartments.

There was also no hope of shaving or washing away the grime from a night on an old Russian train. The washroom, by now, was far too foul for that.

With a weak smile and a strong handshake Arkady left at the next station. I hoped his luck would be better than I expected it might be.

The outskirts of Ivano Frankivsk eventually came rolling into view. Sasha rose hurriedly from his seat motioning to start gathering our belongings. Reaching for the large bag my palms were noticeably sweaty against the handle and I was briefly overcome by apprehension as I began to fully realize how truly alone I was in this very troubled land.

Chapter 5

Karpaty

The train came to a jolting stop. Sasha and I struggled with my bags, and joined the line of departing passengers inching down the narrow compartment way. Nearing the carriage door we were buffeted by the boarding passengers anxious to find their seats before the train left for it's next destination. Once outside, Sasha motioned for me to stay with the bags as a sharp blast of the train's whistle signaled its departure.

While the train was pulling away from the station, Sasha ran along the platform looking for someone who was to meet us, but who was obviously not there. He looked like a Ukrainian Ichabod Crane as he ran in one direction then another. Finally, he found his tardy colleague. I learned it was Bogdan Goodzak, Manager of the Marketing and Foreign Economic Relations Department, and Sasha's chief.

Bogdan was an amiable looking man in his late thirties. He was even shorter than I, and sported a small continental mustache. He was the first person I had seen in a communist country with that type. At one time, a burly Stalin style mustache was in favor among the Soviets, but it went out of fashion with Stalin's passing. Bogdan's mustache, on the other hand, gave him the appearance of a Latin dandy in a grainy old movie.

The marketing manager's superior position apparently enabled him to dress in a style befitting his organizational status. He wore a neat brown suit with a dark shirt and flowered tie, which immediately separated him from the rest of people standing on the platform who were dressed more modestly.

Sasha shouldered the larger bag while Bogdan reached for the smaller one resting at my feet. A look of surprise came over his face as his knees buckled underneath him. With an embarrassed smile, Bogdan made another attempt-this time successfully-to lift the bulging bag. Listing mightily to his left as he walked, Bogdan led us from the platform to a parked car and waiting driver. After squeezing the bags into the trunk of the black company-owned Volga, we began the trip to my apartment.

Bogdan provided a running commentary, through Sasha, about the history of Ivano Frankivsk. While they talked, I looked out of the car window at my new surroundings. The city of 300,000 looked smaller than I expected. I was to learn later, the majority of the people lived in apartment complexes clustered around each of the several large factories the Russians had placed in the town. In addition to their living quarters, each company provided their employees with most of their basic needs so they rarely visited the downtown area

It was a cloudy day with a clay-colored sky that made the buildings look more drab than they probably were. Even without the sun, it was warm and we rode with our windows down. The glass in the window next to me did not fit tightly in its housing, and rattled as we rode.

Bogdan lighted his second cigarette, and I was relieved our windows were open. It was very warm in the unairconditioned Russian car, and I began to perspire. The decision to wear a sport shirt instead of a suit was paying off and I felt sorry for Bogdan who looked very uncomfortable in his probably unaccustomed shirt and tie.

Most of the buildings we were passing were gray stucco, but we would occasionally pass blocks where all the structures were pink, then another block where each was decorated in a faded yellow, or pale green. When I asked the reason for the contrasting color arrangement I was told the central paint factory could produce only one shade at a time. When the municipal government decided a block might need to be repainted, they took whatever color was available.

Trees lined most of the side streets and we occasionally passed small parks. The green foliage and occasional pastel buildings were a pleasant contrast to the drab appearance of the rest of the town, giving the immediate area a mildly Mediterranean look oddly out of place in a Carpathian setting.

As we rode, Bogdan provided background on the city. Speaking in a tutorial cadence that Sasha emulated, Bogdan lectured "Ivano Frankivsk was founded in 1661 and is situated between two rivers and close to the Carpathian Mountains. Because of its location and history, it is the cultural heart of the Precarpathian Region. Before 1962, the town was known as Stanislaviv in honor of a Polish nobleman. It was renamed Ivano Frankivsk after a renown Ukrainian writer and poet Ivan Franko."

Sasha, who had been translating, began talking on his own, while Bogdan puffed on a cigarette. "Ivan Franko was a Ukrainian writer in the 19th century. He wrote dramas, poetry and plays. In 1875, he entered the university in Lviv where he became a socialist and wrote for literary journals and newspapers."

Sasha added in a lowered voice, "In his later years he was critical of Marxist socialism and supported Ukrainian nationalism." Using a softer voice when criticizing communism had apparently become instinctive for Sasha, as I was reasonably sure he and I were the only ones in the car that understood English.

In spite of the political references, I was impressed with the element of romanticism that seemed to underlie much of Ukrainian culture. This was evident by the monument in Kiev dedicated to the poet Taras Shevchenko, and here another poet served as the town's namesake. The only other place I had seen this sense of reverence paid to writers and poets was in Ireland and I wondered, driving through the narrow streets of Ivano Frankivsk, if tragedy might be a fundamental element of poetry.

Bogdan resumed his history lesson as Sasha translated. "Before the reunion with Soviet Ukraine the territory of the present Ivano Frankivsk region was part of bourgeois Poland. The ruling circles deliberately hindered the economic development of Precarpathia and squandered the tremendous natural resources of the region. Not only did the Polish and Ukrainian landowners and capitalists lord over the land, but also the German, American, French, and English imperialists. They robbed Precarpathia of its riches and forced the cruel yoke of economic and national oppression upon the wide masses of people."

Bogdan spoke as if he was reciting lines from a lesson memorized long ago.

"This was a time when the landowners, the wealthy peasants, the church and the state owned 70% of the best land, woods, and pastures. The people of Precarpathia lived under terrible conditions and backwardness."

I was startled by the intensity of his words. He paused to light another cigarette and continued. "When the USSR liberated Ivano Frankivsk and instituted their five-year plans all of this changed. Now there is no more sorrow, no more misery in the Ukraine. There are no more people in baggy, home spun trousers, patched skirts, and primitive homemade footwear. The people are all well dressed and live in comfort. Soviet power, free labor, and working heroism on free land have raised the workers to the heights of national fame and honor. The people had become cultured and enlightened. Now all of that is threatened."

Sasha looked at me and rolled his eyes.

Perhaps Bogdan was right in a sense. Many people in Ukraine were possibly worse off presently than they were under Russian rule. Many of those nurtured in the old system lost everything with its collapse, and nostalgia can cloud the memory of previous hardships while focusing on only the advantages. On the other hand, many people were now better off. They had their independence and greater future opportunity, but I could understand how that might not be a completely comforting thought for someone facing the loss of their livelihood.

I was surprised, however, that Bogdan was so forceful in extolling the virtues of communism this early in our association. Conflict doesn't usually come like this. Not so early and not right between the eyes. It is common business protocol to postpone the discussion of potentially contrasting positions until some level of rapport is established between the parties yet, immediately after we met, Bogdan was lecturing me on a system that his country had already abandoned.

I wondered why he was doing this, and why he was being so forceful so early. Did he assume everyone felt this way? Did all of them at Karpaty feel the same and believe the same things? Or was it an early warning to me that this was the way it was and the way it was going to stay.

I could only interpret Bogdan's comments as an accurate reflection of the depth of his ideological convictions. I had hoped that he and the other managers I would be working with were, if not eager for change, at least willing to accept it. Now I didn't think this was going to be the case. I understood how difficult it would be to change the beliefs of men like him, and I wondered how long it would take them to adapt to a new philosophy. I was upset by our conversation and viewed it as a warning of problems that could lie ahead.

Bogdan's statements also factually contradicted what I was told by Sasha during our long train ride from Kiev to Ivano Frankivsk. As I had watched the workers in the field, Sasha described how Stalin once had forcibly collectivized the peasant landholdings and confiscated their crops to support a new plan for Ukrainian industrialization. The result of his actions was a terrible famine in 1932 and 1933 that caused an estimated 5 to 7 million Ukrainians to die of starvation.

The famine didn't have to happen. After the farms were collectivized, Stalin ordered the production of unrealistic quotas of grain to support his industrialization plan. The peasants could use no crops from a collective farm until all quotas had been met. Party workers made house to house searches and confiscated all the farmer's grain. Anyone-adults or children-caught stealing from a government warehouse could be executed. Internal passports were issued to prevent the desperate peasants from traveling elsewhere in search of food. Many people starved to death under the control of gun-wielding Communist Party activists, while storehouses overflowed with grain. Misguided government policies had managed to create famine in one of the world's most productive granaries.

Not long afterwards, Stalin also initiated mass arrests and executions of his opponents and potential opponents, which resulted in the devastation of the country's intelligentsia. Those intellectuals that were not killed were summarily exiled to Siberia. At the same time there was an enforced "Russification" that required the Ukrainian schools to use only the language of Moscow. I often heard during my stay, from native Ukrainians that the loss of intellectual leadership was a major reason the country was experiencing so much difficulty adjusting to its new independence.

Sasha went on to tell me he, and many other Ukrainians, believed it was this harsh treatment by the Russians that led to the growth of nationalism, and later to the independence movement. This longing for independence was also the basis for the country's national anthem *Ukraine Has Not Yet Died* that summarizes the national psyche dominated by the desire for national sovereignty, and an intrinsic will to survive.

However, this was certainly not the time to get into any argument about the past, or for that matter, the future of Ukraine.

We pulled into the apartment complex where I was to live for the next two months. Bogdan dropped Sasha and me in front of one of the buildings while he and the driver went on to the factory.

As Sasha and I gathered my bags, I looked around the area. It was a quadrangle composed of a half dozen identical white concrete buildings clustered together. Each building was 12 stories high and housed almost 300 units.

My building was five years old and looked as if it was going on fifty. The paint was peeling and windows were broken out. Laundry hung from many of the open windows although there was an area alongside that accommodated several clotheslines. Tethered to one of the clotheslines was a large cow grazing contentedly on the grass underneath.

Inside, Sasha spoke to a middle-aged woman standing behind a counter. She looked closely at me and pointed down a hallway. My room was halfway down the dark corridor. Entering my apartment, I quickly looked around and decided this was going to be fine. The rooms seemed well furnished, and the apartment looked as if it would be a comfortable place to stay for the next two months.

Sasha attempted to tune in the television set while I went into the bedroom to change my clothes. I took a quick shower and an even faster shave.

The bathroom was tiny but it contained a stool and a European type shower with a hand held nozzle detached from the central fixture. I am sure its designers thought such a configuration provided the bather with greater bathing flexibility. For an unfamiliar American it meant I was more apt to spray water on the floor and walls than on the part of my body I was trying to bathe.

After showering, I considered what I would wear to my meeting with the company director. The decision came quickly. It was a suit and tie. I wasn't sure what the dress code was in a Ukrainian factory. In the Russian companies I had visited before, the men's clothing varied considerably from one location to another. But I was reasonably sure they would be expecting their new adviser to be formerly dressed, and it would be poor form to show up in a sport shirt and chinos.

Anyway, I was part of the generation for whom "casual Fridays" meant wearing a blue, rather than a white, shirt with your suit and tie. For us, the suit had replaced the uniform as a mark of our profession, and the shirt and tie became a designation of rank. As I finished creasing the knot in the new rep tie Elsie had bought for my trip, I heard Sasha call from the living room to hurry. Grabbing my briefcase, we rushed out the door.

We walked up the path between the apartment complexes and then passed a building with empty schoolrooms. Sasha explained this was where Karpaty held training classes for its employees. We continued past a small church, then more apartments, and finally to a main sidewalk adjoining a busy road. The day was warm, and I began to perspire as I tried to keep pace with Sasha's longer stride. I noticed I was breathing more deeply as our walk continued up a hill with a steep grade.

Later, I was to see cars frequently stall and trucks shift into low gear as they fought their way up the steep incline. Our walk continued for two more blocks. When the sidewalk ended the steps began. There were twenty-five of them before we reached a level area the length of a football field. At the end, was another series of twenty-five more steps leading to the entrance of the administration building.

Before starting up the second flight, I motioned to Sasha I needed to stop. As I caught my breath, I looked around. To my left was a landscaped lawn. Almost hidden among a stand of trees was an old lady holding a rope tied to another grazing cow. IBM this was not.

I turned and looked behind me. In one direction was the Carpathian Mountains that gave the Karpaty Amalgamation its name. Looking the other way, in the distance, was the town of Ivano Frankivsk.

There was a security guard stationed behind a tall desk as we entered the lobby. He was apparently expecting us and handed Sasha a badge, which he then gave to me. As we walked toward the elevators three stray cats scurried away and down a labyrinth of darkened halls.

There were only two elevators. On one was a sign I assumed to be the Russian equivalent of "out of order." Sasha pushed the button on the other, and we waited. And waited. Finally Sasha motioned to the stairs "we walk." The Director's office was on the sixth floor. When we reached the fourth, I thought that my heart would pound through my chest. By now the perspiration starting as a trickle down my back had turned into a torrent. My laundered white shirt had become a moist linen handkerchief.

I recalled Dr. Smyth telling me it would be a good idea for a man my age to have a stress test. I usually followed his advice, but in this case I postponed making the appointment and finally forgot it entirely. My first thought was to regret my procrastination. Then it occurred to me if I reached the top without a coronary I didn't need the stress test in the first place.

Breathing with considerable difficulty, I followed Sasha through a doorway leading to a poorly lighted hallway with several closed-door offices. Halfway down the hall Sasha turned into a large open area with a single desk and several chairs lined across one of the walls. Behind the desk was a plump, pleasant looking woman commanding a bank of telephones (one red), and an intercom box.

The phones produced a serpentine mass of brown cables cascading from her desk and entangling its legs before terminating in multiple black boxes on the floor. Behind her desk was a doorway, and across the large waiting room were three other offices. The secretary smiled at me and spoke briefly to Sasha.

"We will wait" he told me, motioning to one of the chairs lined against the wall. "The Director is having a meeting with his wise directors."

I thought this was an odd reference, but I was delighted to wait. My breath was coming in suppressed gasps and I welcomed any opportunity to recover my composure before meeting the Director. After awhile, I rose and wandered to a large window that provided light to the waiting room and overlooked the rest of the amalgamation.

Below the office tower was an enormous complex of buildings. Soon, Sasha joined me and proudly pointed out the production facilities, machine shops, clean rooms and a myriad of other facilities once required for Karpaty's military products. The company was much larger than I expected and, in addition to its manufacturing facilities, was an almost completely self-contained societal unit.

Between the tower and the main production area was a large enclosed hothouse where vegetables were grown for use in the two plant cafeterias. The plant's facilities contained its own bakery and butcher shop. Karpaty also operated a small vegetable farm and a pig farm located on the outskirts of the city. In addition, according to Sasha, Karpaty operated a series of shops in other nearby buildings selling food at reduced prices to employees, as well housing its own clinic, kindergarten, and fire department.

As I continued to gaze out the window, it occurred to me this huge industrial complex was only one of several massive military production operations located in this small Ukrainian community. I knew this location was not unique and there were thousands of similar installations spread throughout the Soviet Republics, from Kazakhstan to Kaliningrad.

I always believed in the seriousness of the Cold War, but never more than the day I looked out over Karpaty's immense manufacturing facilities. The struggle that took place between the United States and the Soviet Union for most of my adult life was more than a conflict of arms in Korea and Vietnam. It was also a competition of ideals and economic systems that played out in the countries I visited in Africa and Latin America.

Even with this exposure, I had little idea how powerful and pervasive the Soviet machine had become. Winston Churchill once described Russia "as a riddle wrapped in a mystery inside an enigma." It wasn't until the Communist Party lost control over the Soviet Union that the mystery began to unravel.

The more I traveled in the former Soviet countries the more I came to realize how fortunate the Western world was that such great military might was never put to use. It was the largest armed force ever mobilized in the history of the world, and it must have been extremely frustrating for the Russian generals to have a Ferrari sitting in their garage and never having the opportunity of running it on the road.

As I gazed at Karpaty's facilities, I wondered if I was doing the right thing trying to help a former enemy. Would I regret my activity at some point in the future if the Soviet countries were to regroup and emerge as a power to again threaten the world? I knew my actions were too insignificant to have any lasting impact on the world order, but they could affect how I would view myself in years to come.

A loud ringing on the secretary's desk interrupted my thoughts. After putting down the phone, she motioned us to go into the Director's office.

I led the way. As I opened one door I immediately encountered another door identical to the first, but without a handle. I stood perplexed until the second door slowly opened from the inside. As I entered the room the Director stood and motioned me to take one of the two vacant chairs. Two members of his staff occupied the others.

As I shook the Director's outstretched hand, Sasha made the introductions. "This is General Director, Anatoly Kuvika, this is Vladimir Skulsky Chief Engineer, and Igor Tachinsky Director of Economics. They are Karpaty's wise directors."

By now, I had decided Sasha was pronouncing his v's as w's. Once I grasped his pronunciation, Karpaty's wise directors were linguistically relegated from wise to merely vice directors.

The general director welcomed me to Karpaty, and inquired if my living arrangements were satisfactory. I assured him they were.

As he began to tell me about his company, I noticed from the corner of my eye that the members of his staff were closely watching me. I focused my attention on the Director, and trying to understand Sasha's troubled translation.

At the same time, I noticed there seemed something different about the Director's office from those I had become accustomed to in the United States. It finally occurred to me there was nothing personal about it. There were no family portraits on the desk, or pictures on the wall. There was no executive bric-a-brac on the desk, no letter openers, paperweights, clocks-nothing. There was nothing at all in the entire office personally associated with Anatoly Kuvika. It was if the general director could move out at a moment's notice, leaving nothing of himself behind.

According to him "Karpaty was established in 1976 by the Russian Ministry of Radio for the design, development, and production of hi-tech, highly sensitive, military acoustic sensing and measuring devices. In 1985, we reached our peak employment level of 5,000 people. At that time, almost 70% of our activities involved defense production, while 30% was devoted to the production of loudspeakers and some civilian audio products. To-day almost all of the military activity has disappeared but the employment level is still 5,000 people."

Recalling the plant facilities I had seen from the office window, it seemed there was a good chance there were many more people working at Karpaty than I was being led to believe.

I interrupted, "why haven't you reduced your manpower if you don't need them all any longer?"

Director Kuvika paused to clear his throat and light a cigarette. As he talked I had been watching his actions as he made his points. The Director was a large man with a square Slavic jaw. His hands were the size of small Christmas hams and he had the neck of a NFL linebacker. He sat behind his large desk with a stubborn rigidity across his shoulders. His appearance gave the impression of a self-confident truck driver. He also gave the impression of a man attempting to be cordial, with very little practice.

He dragged deeply on his cigarette, exhaling his words in clouds of smoke. "You don't understand the communist system. We have an obligation to these people. They have no place else to go. But now we have to think about lay-offs for the first time.

"The Ukrainian government is still buying some of our military products for its armed forces and because of the sensitive nature of some of the company's development work we can't privatize. We are trying to broaden our efforts into new products and, at the same time, trying to attract foreign investment. But we don't know how to do it.

"The reason we contacted the IESC for an advisor was to help us broaden our product base and find new investment."

"Have you made any attempts to contact foreign companies on your own?" I asked. He looked at his associates and shook his head no.

Then it was my turn. I provided a quick summary of my experience and a description of the companies I had been associated with before retiring. This seemed to satisfy him.

Pointing a beefy finger at me he said through Sasha, "Miller I want you to start by talking to the Vice Directors to find out what we do here and then let me know what you think you can do for us. Do you want to work at the plant or in your apartment?"

I quickly chose the plant.

Director Kuvika spoke to Sasha ending the meeting. The Director and his staff impressed me. From what I had seen they looked like upper management people you would find in any large western company.

None of the assistant directors had interrupted while Kuvika spoke, but they would occasionally say something to one another in a lowered voice while stealing a sidelong glance at me. I was probably the first person they had seen from a non-communist country.

They seemed to be paying particular attention to my wingtips, the shoes with a thousand eyes that many American businessmen wear. They were considerably different from the bulky Bulgarian style shoes common throughout the Soviet countries. In addition, my shoes were black, while all the Russian shoes I had ever seen were brown. I had often heard you can easily identify an American in a foreign country by his shoes, and mine seemed to be the subject of considerable scrutiny.

The meeting had been difficult for Sasha, and I was certain he was relieved when it was over. I tried to help him as much as possible without embarrassing him in front of the director. It was obvious communicating with the personnel at Karpaty was going to be a problem, and I was worried. The meeting took twice as long as it should, and I was not confident I was fully understood.

I trailed behind Sasha as he led us out the door, down the hallway, and into an office directly behind the Director's. This was apparently the office assigned to me.

Inside the doorway was a small inner office with an empty desk and several chairs for visitors, and a doorway leading to a larger inner office. A large wooden desk and a straight back chair with an orange seat cover dominated the room. The desk was almost as large as the Director's. There was a small conference table at a right angle to the main desk, with two chairs on each side.

As I sat down, I noticed a small table with three telephones beside the desk. Sasha explained one phone was for in-plant calls, a yellow one for calls outside the plant, and the third for a special private line to the general director's office. Also on the table was a faded bouquet of strawflowers in a cracked vase, along with three empty glasses and a carafe of water, which I was afraid to drink. The room was poorly lighted by two sets of flickering fluorescent bulbs.

I found in later visits to the vice-directors' offices that my layout was the standard configuration, except the furniture was larger. My quarters apparently were meant for an assistant general director, or a super vice director's facility, and I wondered if he may have been an early casualty of the impending cutbacks.

The office had two large windows that looked out on the town and the Carpathian Mountains. One of the windows was cracked, and the other was so out of plumb it was impossible to close. They were partially hidden behind orange curtains with brown horizontal stripes that were filled with small rips in several places where the material seemed to be slowly separating from itself. They looked as if they had been hanging limply there for many years.

The most unusual thing about my quarters was the leather padding covering the wall behind me. I had never seen an office wall so heavily cushioned. Turning to Sasha I asked, "why is the wall so heavily padded?"

"What does padded mean?"

I pointed to the wall behind me and Sasha smiled and shrugged his shoulders. It was a gesture I was to see many times afterwards.

Changing the subject I asked, "Am I able to send a fax to my wife from here?"

"No problem." I had learned from my earlier travels that when I was told "no problem" by someone, it was frequently the forerunner of impending disaster.

I hastily wrote out the message, giving the number of a service in La Grange I had used before. The people there were familiar with my travels and knew how to contact my wife.

Sasha took it with him while I put away some of the office supplies I had brought in my briefcase. While I was alone I thought about the meeting. I had expected a warmer greeting. I had traveled a long way and was, after all, giving up my time to help them. The vice directors seemed suspicious of me, while the general director was formal and aloof. I had the distinct feeling of someone who was invited to a party then finds his host is not pleased he could come.

"The communications people can't send faxes to America. They don't have the necessary lines." Sasha returned my unsent message.

This could be another problem. I had never been where I was completely out of contact with my wife. Some of the places such as Lima and Shanghai were difficult, but with patience I was always able to get through. A fax was the easiest method, and if that didn't work I didn't have a great deal of confidence in getting a phone line, but I decided to try that later.

Sasha wasn't aware of my concern. "Let's go to dinner" he said "come with me." As we entered the dark hallway, I noticed the office doorway across from mine was closed and secured with a heavy padlock.

The elevator was now working but not working well. The cables made an ominous sound as we descended, as if the strain was more than they could bear. In the lobby, a group of workers looked curiously at me as they left for the day.

The grounds surrounding the plant were laid out in neat flower gardens maintained by a group of older babushkas. The sidewalk was lined with tall lampposts each supporting nine glass globes at their top. Four of the globes were dark blue, four others were dark green, and one white globe crowned the top of each lamppost.

I had seen similar layouts of sidewalks, flowerbeds and lampposts around many Russian plants. Somewhere in a small office deep within the cavernous Kremlin, a planner, long ago, must have decided this was the most effective layout for industrial plants. Unfortunately, he failed to include in his descriptions that the lamppost globes should be replaced when they become broken.

"Where are we going?" I asked Sasha.

"To the disco."

"We are going to eat in a disco?"

"It's in the cultural center" Sasha said as we approached a large two-story building. "We used to have concerts, folk dances, exhibits, and Communist Party meetings here, but we haven't used it for those things for quite awhile."

As Sasha talked we walked through a patio with tables topped with faded umbrellas. "They used to serve refreshments here but we don't use it since we stopped having the cultural events," Sasha wistfully explained.

We entered a massive marble lobby. There was a lone security guard seated behind a counter reading a newspaper. He nodded at Sasha, and stared at me, as we started up a wide decorative staircase. On the second floor was a series of offices that, according to Sasha, were occupied by people who plan the activities they don't have any more.

We entered a large unlit room at the end of the long corridor. Past the entranceway I could make out a dance floor, an empty bar, and a bandstand. A single table was set on the edge of the dance floor. On the table was a faded linen tablecloth, a small vase of flowers, and service for two. Sasha and I took our first of many meals in the abandoned, dimly lighted, Ukrainian discotheque.

Chapter 6

The Wise Directors

I leaped from my bed and fell sprawling on a strange floor; my legs hopelessly entangled in the pita pocket-like comforter that serves as bedclothes on many Russian beds. As I tried to untangle myself, the loud sound that had awakened me with such alarm reverberated again through the bedroom wall. It sounded as if the Queen Mary had become entrapped during the night in a dense fog while cruising through the adjoining apartment. I later discovered the source of the violent convulsion was a flatulent-like passage of air through constricted water pipes, as my unseen neighbors began their early morning bath.

This loud disturbance was to serve as my unwanted six o'clock wake up call each weekday morning during my two-month stay.

I had time to survey my apartment before Sasha was to arrive. I had been too tired to pay much attention to my new surroundings the night before. My unit was composed of a bedroom, living room, kitchen, and a small washroom housing a sink and a mirror, which was adjacent to another room with a western toilet and a separate tiny room with the shower I had used the day before.

In case I might become confused which room to use, the toilet room entrance had a red emblem with a small pig-tailed girl, outlined in white, sitting on a chamber pot. The shower room had a similar designation with a blue background and the same little girl immodestly standing underneath a shower with her bare bottom displayed to any ill-mannered onlooker.

My bedroom was decorated in "early orange", each shade more shocking than the one before. There was a bright orange silk cover on the bed, a similarly colored cover on the sofa, orange chairs, and a tapestry covering an entire wall was a kaleidoscope of orange, red, pale green, and cream colored yarn. The room also contained a small desk with a green chair and a lamp, with a burned out bulb, apparently left over from the 1920's.

My bed was difficult to become accustomed to. It had a small cotton mattress over bunk-like springs, then a large eiderdown quilt, a sheet, a gigantic pillow, and a blanket in a duvet cover that had so effectively bound my legs earlier that morning.

The living room was large and comfortable and contained a 25" table model color TV which, of course, broadcast only Russian and Ukrainian stations. The room also had two chairs and an end table. Both chairs had a similar design but only one was a rocking chair. It was not meant to be, but I found that if I leaned too far forward it would easily tip and rock me onto the floor.

Against one wall were three large wood cabinets that contained shelves and a glass enclosure serving as either a bookcase or china cabinet. In one of the cabinet drawers was a pamphlet inexplicably written in English which proclaimed "on the 50th anniversary of the establishment of the USSR, the Vihoda order of the Red Banner of Labor was awarded to the Precarpathian Ivano Frankivsk furniture factory for its high quality production made for home and foreign consumption." It was an elegant looking piece of walnut cabinetry, with a highly polished finish, but none of the drawers fit, the doors overlapped and were difficult to close, and there were margins of unpainted wood where the poorly fitting joints came together.

There was newly laid wall to wall carpeting in the living room. It was loudly appealing in shades of blue, lavender, and light green. But there was more carpeting than floor. Rather than having been trimmed to size, it crept up the wall and buckled in the center.

The kitchen had an oil cloth covered table and two chairs, a small 1950s style refrigerator, and electric stove which, when turned on, would make a loud grinding noise as if somewhere deep in its mechanism it was required to digest something before it could provide heat. The noise would have been annoying if I had required the stove for anything other than boiling water. The kitchen floor had been recently covered with new linoleum, which, after a week of wear, began coming apart and curled at the seams. The raised edges could easily trip the unwary walker, and I had it resealed several times during my stay.

The apartment was bright and cheerful, and was without the strong odors that frequently accompanies many of the Soviet style housing blocks I had been in before. It was obvious Karpaty management had tried to make my stay as comfortable as possible, and I was grateful for their effort. The flaws in workmanship were more a source of interest than irritation. They were, however, indicative of the lack of attention to detail endemic throughout the system, and was something I too frequently saw repeated at the factory.

My next project was to find an acceptable hiding place for the $600 I brought with me. The amount of money I had to carry was a problem. There were no facilities in Ivano Frankivsk for credit cards, or traveler's checks, and I believed it was necessary to have enough funds to carry me through an emergency. Or to pay my way out of the country if it would be necessary. Cash was the only solution.

I planned to carry part of the money in my wallet. I also put some inside my folded umbrella, more in two of the books I brought, and the rest in an envelope I taped to the back of a drawer in the bedroom desk. If I was to be visited by a burglar who liked to read English books on a rainy day I would be in trouble.

I had just finished disposing of my limited riches when there was a knock on the door. The knock was immediately followed by the entrance of the woman I had seen in the lobby the day before. I had thought the door was locked but I learned she had a key to all of the apartments and was not hesitant about their use. I found that if I was to have any semblance of privacy it was necessary to rely on the sliding bolt and ignore the lock.

My intruder was a reasonably attractive middle aged woman named Valentina, who was carrying a pail of water. Even with her burden, she managed her years with an easy grace many mature women seem to acquire. She examined me closely and, apparently satisfied, proceeded to the kitchen, talking in rapid Russian as she went.

Pointing to the sink, she made a choking motion at her throat, then made a pumping motion while pointing outside. I had no problem getting that message. I had already noticed the water from the tap had a decidedly brownish tint. There must have been a cistern outside producing cleaner water. She left as abruptly as she came.

Sasha soon appeared for our trip to the culture center. He told me more about our building as we walked. It was a standard socialist housing project and similar to thousands of others built throughout the USSR. It reminded me of the Cabrini-Green housing complex in Chicago. Individual living units came in three standard sizes, one, two, and three rooms plus a kitchen and bath. Some of units were forced to share cooking and bathing facilities.

Sasha lived with two other single engineers in a one-room apartment that was part of a four-unit cluster. The four units shared a kitchen with three other similarly sized apartment units. The kitchen cupboards were divided into separate compartments where each residential group had their own dishes, staples, spices, and whatever else was individually needed. Each kitchen was equipped with two stoves, and a narrow counter space to fix meals, which were eaten in the resident's rooms. The engineers also shared communal bathing facilities, much like a barracks or college dorm.

The stated theory behind such communal flats, aside from the obvious reality they were cheap and expedient to construct, was they would show that people could share quarters, live equally, and in the process get along so well the neighbors would become like second families to one another. They were, in a sense, the epitome of a collective society. Like many social theories, however, such shared living conditions did not lend itself well to practical application.

Sasha's fiancé also worked at Karpaty and lived with her parents. Sasha and she had postponed getting married until the fall, when they hoped to be able to get their own apartment. They had put their names on a waiting list over a year ago and were hopeful one would become available by then.

There was no note of reproach in Sasha's voice as he described his living conditions. It was more a matter of information than complaint. I did understand, however, he was also informing me how well off I was with my large apartment, and I knew he was right.

The hill approaching Karpaty was as steep as it had been the day before. I wondered if I would ever become accustomed to the climb. I noticed Sasha was able to keep up a steady flow of conversation while I found myself puffing and perspiring.

Eating at the disco I soon learned that, like in the rural Midwest, there was very little caloric difference in the content of Ukrainian meals. Breakfast was typically sliced tomatoes and cucumbers covered with sour cream, along with meat, potatoes, brown bread and coffee. Lunch was the main meal and was the same as breakfast with the addition of a pastry dessert. Dinner resembled lunch, with slightly smaller portions. Occasionally brown rice, mashed lima beans, or a heavy pancake might be substituted for potatoes.

Misha managed the disco and would often sit with us while we ate. His responsibilities were not demanding and he welcomed his two new customers, making every effort to see what he served was acceptable. In fact, it was too acceptable and I quickly concluded I was eating too much.

During my stay, I studiously avoided making many requests of my hosts. I was grateful for the care they took in providing comfortable accommodations. I also soon learned that any request that was made would often result in something quite different from what was originally intended.

After a few days, I tried to convey to Sasha that just a bowl of soup and bread would be enough for my lunch, while he could continue to get the full meal. After that, each noon, I got a bowl of soup (usually borsht or vegetable) along with the usual serving of salad, meat, potatoes, and bread.

My next attempt to limit my diet proved more successful. Instead of taking the time for breakfast at the disco, I managed to convince Misha it would be more convenient if I could get some kind of juice, rolls, and a can of coffee and eat breakfast in my apartment. After some objections, this was accepted and at the end of dinner Misha would supply fresh rolls or bread along with cheese, sausage, a pound of butter, a tin of coffee and whatever else he felt might be appropriate. Later, a two-gallon bottle of brown liquid made from a mixture of strawberries and lime juice eventually appeared in my refrigerator.

During our meals I learned that Misha had grown up in Siberia where his family had been sent, along with many Ukrainian families, as part of a massive Soviet resettlement effort. Living conditions were very hard, and he had little affection for the Russians. He showed me scars on his arms he received while attempting to cut wood in frozen Siberian forests.

Misha knew some English words and was pleased to have an opportunity to use them. He was also extremely curious about American life. Through Sasha, he would ask about the price of American cars, cigarettes, houses, TV sets, and hundreds of other items.

His questions were typical of the people I met in Ukraine who seemed to be interested, above everything else, in the cost of living in the United States. I don't recall ever being asked about freedom of the press, opportunities for advancement, freedom of religion, or the American political system; but I was often asked about the price of a loaf of bread.

Unfortunately, I was unable to answer this question, since my wife had done all the shopping. When I would say I didn't know I had the feeling they believed I was avoiding their question. Eventually, I made up the price of $2.50 a loaf. This answer would usually be met with pursed lips and a furrowed brow, but I was never certain if this meant my imaginary price was very high or very low.

My first task at the factory was to meet individually with Karpaty management so I began to organize my work and prepare for my meetings. It was good sitting behind a desk again even if it was only a temporary accommodation. I had heard people often miss their office when they retire, but that had not been a problem for me. I think I missed most the people I worked with, and the challenges. Nevertheless, it felt good to have a project to complete and a desk to sit behind.

"Mr. Miller?" Startled I looked up and saw a woman standing tentatively in my office doorway. "My name is Tanya. I am the librarian and I speak English. Sasha said we should meet. He believes I can help."

Sasha had become increasingly aware of his language limitations. The meeting with the general director was very difficult for him. For all of us in fact.

Tanya was a timid, slightly plump, little woman. As we talked she became less nervous but continued to twist a small handkerchief she carried in her hand. She had a ready smile that often contrasted with her dark sad eyes. Tanya had studied German along with English but, like Sasha, had never met anyone who actually spoke the language.

She loved to practice her English and asked if I would like to learn some Ukrainian words. I unenthusiastically agreed. The next day she provided me with a vocabulary to study. The list was fortunately very brief.

Good morning	Dobrogo ranku
How are you	Yak pozhyvajeta
How are things	Yak sprava
Goodbye	Do pobachennya
Sure	Bezumovno

I got through dobrogo ranku reasonably well but failed miserably on yak pozhyvajeta. There was no chance I could manipulate my midwestern tongue around such difficult words, and my attempts succeeded in only producing giggles from Tanya. I consoled myself by recalling that, anyway, everyone spoke Russian. Of course, I couldn't speak that either.

As we became better acquainted, I learned Tanya had been married and was now divorced. She told me divorce was not unusual under the old system, or *ranshe,* as she elliptically referred to the former communist era. "Now it is even more common. I think it's because of the bad economy and the pressure it creates, as well as our cramped living conditions," she added sadly.

Tanya joined Sasha as part of my interpreting team. She had a better command of general vocabulary words, while

Sasha was better on technical terms. Neither of them, however, was entirely proficient, and they would often argue between themselves over the meaning of a particular word or phrase.

Before I began my discussions with the wise-directors, as Sasha called them, I told him and Tanya what I planned to cover during the meetings so they would have less difficulty with the translation.

My first meeting was with Vladimir Skulsky who was the chief engineer, and had been in our meeting with the general director. I had spent most of my own career in industries involved with technology, which were in a sense similar to Karpaty. During this time, I had spent many hours discussing business with chief engineers, and Vladimir appeared to have come from the same mold.

Vladimir was very intelligent and dedicated to his job, and to Karpaty. He was the consummate technocrat embracing his technology with a passion others might reserve for women or wine. Had there been plastic pocket liners available in Ukraine I am sure Vladimir's would have been filled with the assortment of pens he carried in his frayed brown shirt pocket.

We spent the morning reviewing the company's history, its products, and organization. It wasn't apparent from the orgchart, but Vladimir's comments left little doubt he considered himself as second in command, and the other vice director's positions far less important than his. For all I knew this may have been true.

Karpaty was involved in an impressive array of technologies, and Vladimir seemed to have a firm grasp on all of them. He could talk in considerable detail about the wood laminating process for loudspeakers, thick film production, signal capture processing, transmitting devices, test equipment for nuclear atmospheric radiation, and a myriad of other techniques that tried the abilities of my interpreters, and the limits of my attention span.

In the afternoon, we toured the plant's technical and manufacturing facilities. A dying factory is a sad thing to observe. They are filled with ghosts of worker's hopes and manager's dreams haunting the hallways and swirling between the empty aisles once filled with the deafening clamor of heavy equipment. This factory was filled with an almost palpable air of depression as sullen workers performed their choreographed movements for the strange looking visitor from a foreign land.

Departing an area, I would furtively glance behind and often see workers putting away the things they were ostensibly involved with as we entered. I soon realized we were participating in a Potemkin pretense of activity. I was reminded of the traditional Russian worker's lament. "Everything is pretended. They pretend to pay me and I pretend to work."

As we passed one large building with windows painted over in black, I asked Vladimir what it contained. He told me it was vacant. Later I watched from my office window as people entered and left the building on a regular basis. I was sure there was much I did not see, and much that I saw was not real, but it was of no particular consequence to me. I had a better understanding of Karpaty's capabilities than I had before the tour, and that was my principle objective.

In the evening, when I returned to my apartment, I was very tired, but not as tired as my interpreters who had a very difficult day. I was also becoming increasingly concerned about my inability to contact my wife. That morning, at the office, the general director's secretary had tried to place a call for me but was unable to get a line out of the country. She had said the only call she was ever able to place outside Ukraine was through the red phone on her desk that had a direct line to Moscow. She shook her head sadly and said "that phone hasn't been working lately either."

Sasha tried to place a call from a phone on the wall in the living room. This proved unsuccessful as well. I had given the apartment phone number to my wife before I left for Ukraine and told her I could be reached there if needed. Now I worried something might happen to her and no one could contact me.

The next morning, Tanya asked the general director's secretary if she would try and call the IESC office in Kiev for me. I thought perhaps Elsie and I could communicate through them. The secretary tried most of the morning but was unable to get a line through to Kiev. This made me feel even more isolated than before.

The next meeting was with Igor Tachinsky, Vice Director of Economics. Igor was responsible for all of the company's financial activities. The accounting records in communist companies are one of the major obstacles to foreign investors. In the past, these companies were not concerned with making a profit, only to provide employment and produce product. Because of this, there was little reason to maintain accurate records of production costs and no reason to examine levels of profitability. This lack of financial transparency has caused many potential investors to throw up their hands in disgust and despair.

Igor was aware of this problem and was trying to convert his records to a more western style system. As he explained his actions, I watched the vice director as he hunched over his desk, leafing through a yellowed stack of financial reports. He was a tall man with a relatively small head perched on narrow shoulders. It gave him a rather bird like appearance as he looked up, then down, and then repeated the ritual like a feeding fledgling. Speaking in a hushed voice, Igor appeared to be as dry as the stack of old ledgers lying on his cluttered desk.

We discussed relative wage levels in the U.S. and Ukraine. Factory workers at Karpaty were earning the U.S. equivalent of $10-$12 a month, while office workers were earning $11, and engineers $14 a month. Their monthly wages were roughly comparable to an American's hourly rate.

The workers also receive fringe benefits in addition to their salary. An engineer with good performance can earn a bonus of up to 50% of his base salary. Lower level employees, including engineers, are given free housing in the factory units, and the cost of a nursery for their children.

Medical expenses are free of charge, and the company pays the government 36% of their salary into a pension fund. Women typically retire at age 55 and men at 60. If the workers are involved in occupations that are physically harmful or hazardous, they may retire at an earlier age.

Even at these low levels of compensation, the company was unable to pay their employees on a regular basis and they were often required to go several months without pay. The pensioner's financial position was also deteriorating as their payments were frequently missed and their savings were being continuously eroded by hyperinflation. Even more devastating to workers and pensioners alike was the lack of hope that things would eventually improve.

Before our meeting, I thought an upper level manager such as Igor, with his financial background, would view the communist system unfavorably. I was mistaken.

It became very apparent from our discussion Igor was a staunch believer who attributed all of Ukraine's problems to the collapse of the old system. He believed communism failed because of poorly educated administrators in Moscow and Kiev. Quoting Karl Marx, Igor pointedly told me "from each according to his abilities, to each according to his needs." That's the way it should be, but it is not the way it is any longer. The fault was not in the system but in its administration."

I listened but did not respond. He was wrong. Dead wrong. I had seen the effects of the communist system in most of the other former Soviet states and they all had the same problems. The countries such as Poland, the Czech Republic, and Hungary that were under the communist system for the shortest period of time were the ones recovering the quickest. I had also seen the effects of communism in China and Burma where it was a disaster. But, this was not the time to argue.

No one likes a wise guy. Particularly, if he is from somewhere else. People who are involved in a failed organization are sensitive to advice from outside "experts," and I did not want to make that mistake. I needed the future cooperation of the vice directors to complete my assignment, and I wanted to avoid antagonizing them at this point.

I also tried to reverse the situation and put myself in their position. As I thought about it, I decided I would be equally resistant to change as these managers were, if I was sitting across the desk from a Russian commissar telling me I should now do everything differently than I had done before. I know change is a difficult thing to accept, and the older a person becomes the harder it gets.

I learned there was a dual track to upper management. One course ran through the Communist Party while the other led through the company's organizational structure. A person's rise in a company's organization depended largely on his position in the Party. As a result, you could have people in management whose only qualification was their political contacts, rather than their knowledge of the job or management capability. All of Karpaty's management had risen through the party's political process. In spite of this, the people I met, like Igor, appeared to be knowledgeable and generally competent managers, but rigidly devoted to the old system.

When we finished our discussions, Igor took us on a tour of his accounting department. One large room was filled with a rhythmic click-clack-clicking noise as Karpaty's bookkeepers slid wooden beads, with lightening speed, across the thin wire strands of their individual abacus. I was astonished to see such ancient equipment being used in a seemingly high-tech industrial environment.

After I returned to my office, the general director's secretary came in with my afternoon cup of tea. She had apparently decided I was also part of her responsibilities and made sure my pencils were sharpened and I had an adequate supply of writing paper and erasers. She would carry on long single sided conversations with me, smiling and gesturing as if I could easily understand exactly what she was saying.

I was beginning to understand many of the people I met were intellectually unable to accept the fact that there were actually people in the world who did not speak Russian. They apparently believed if they talked long enough, and loud enough, I would eventually admit I knew exactly what they were saying.

The next meeting was with Bogdan Goodzak, Karpaty's marketing manager, and Sasha's boss. Since I had spent most of my life in one marketing function or another I looked forward to talking with Bogdan. I learned his department had been formed only six months before and reported to the vice director of purchasing. The placement of both buying and selling in the same organizational structure was a novel organizational concept. Prior to his new appointment, Bogdan had been head of the plant's trade union, and before that had been foreman of the electrical maintenance department.

As we talked, I had the feeling Bogdan was trying to take my measure. This is usual among businessmen. There is always an initial attempt to judge one another to determine how tough an adversary the other might be. In this case, however, I began to believe Bogdan saw me as a distinct threat to his new organization.

The marketing group included an advertising department, and Bogdan proudly showed me the photographs being used in a new brochure for their audio products. The ads were well done and included photographs featuring beaming Karpaty employees dressed in attractive precarpathian costumes prominently displaying the company's products. The ads strategically implied that the company's mountain setting endowed their products with an enviable element of old world craftsmanship.

In addition to preparing advertising, the department's role was to receive orders from a central bureaucracy in Kiev. The central government would then handle the distribution of Karpaty's audio products to a network of state-owned stores within Ukraine. The bureaucracy would also barter Karpaty's products with other post communist countries for whatever goods or commodity they might produce that would be of value to Ukraine. Telling factories what to produce was one of the basic government functions under a communist command economy, and the practice apparently remained unchanged under a newly independent government.

The marketing department's principal function was to track the completion of these orders in the factory and then arrange for shipment to wherever it was told by Kiev. The idea of the factory independently identifying customer needs without relying on a central organization in Kiev was a completely foreign concept. Bogdan believed his principal problem was computerizing his organization to improve the flow of paper work.

Because of Ukraine's large population, and high level of education, the country could potentially provide a sizable market for Karpaty's products. The company's geographic position would be a significant incentive if the economy did improve enough to attract foreign investment. Before this could occur, it would be necessary to establish an independent distributing organization that could capitalize on this potential, but Bogdan's only interest was in improving his record keeping process, and he seemed very resistant to change.

In technology companies, individual managers can be usually divided into two distinctly different types-the producers and the seducers. The first category will devote their energies to achieve tangible and measurable results. The second group, on the other hand, will spend their time attempting to convince others they are the ones who actually are the most effective. It is sometimes difficult to distinguish one type from the other. This, however, was not a problem with the managers at Karpaty. Bogdan Goodzak obviously depended more on words than deeds to achieve his career objectives, and was extremely reluctant to consider any action that would jeopardize his present position.

Throughout the interview, the addition of Tanya to the team was proving to be of value, but the flow of conversation was still tortured, requiring considerable consultation between the two interpreters and their omnipresent dictionaries. I tried to be especially careful to not embarrass Sasha in front of his boss and, consequently, left many references unclear and much left unsaid as we finished our meeting and prepared for the next.

Years ago, in American companies, the term "bull of the woods" was often applied to the blustering head of many manufacturing departments. In Karpaty, the vice director of manufacturing was known as Medvid, the bear, Tichonovick. Sasha explained to me that Medvid means "bear" in the Ukrainian language. As is often the case, the name fit the man. Medvid was a small man with a barrel chest and powerful arms; he was also painfully and purposefully brusque, and appeared to be the type of man who would be dangerous to have as an enemy.

Sasha told me Medvid was the plant's political boss and the communist party leader for the area before becoming head of manufacturing. In his former role, Medvid reported to the First Secretary of the city's Central Committee. It was his responsibility to provide the required slogans and banners for the frequent worker demonstrations, as well as maintaining close watch on the political correctness of the individual factory workers.

"I am like my name" Medvid said with noticeable pride. I am a bear, and bears always survive. When I accepted my position as head of manufacturing in 1989 it was over the objections and advice of all my political colleagues at the Central Committee. Now all of them tell me, Medvid, how could you have been so farsighted? With the change of the political system in Ukraine, they are all out a job, and I am a vice director of manufacturing."

I asked Medvid how his role interfaced with the new head of the plant's workers union. Medvid grinned, and with a sly conspiratorial wink offered "authority is not what you are given, but what you can take."

It was obvious from our conversation his next objective was to take away the marketing department from purchasing. He believed that because he made the products, he should also have the responsibility of selling them. I believe he was also afraid if he did not move quickly, engineering would beat him to it. Apparently, all of the managers except Bogdan realized how important the marketing function could become.

Back in my office, as we went over our meeting with Medvid, Sasha told me "on the outside Medvid is part of the new system, but inside-in his soul-he is still a communist. When the vodka speaks, Medvid will often wish for the old days."

My final meeting with the vice directors was with Mr. Salitara who was head of purchasing and the marketing department Medvid wanted to acquire. Salitara looked like an executive in his suit, white shirt, and tie. He was a balding, middle aged man who seldom smiled, but when he did, displayed a dazzling array of gold teeth. From what I had seen, the people in Ukraine were very fond of their gold dental work, and it seemed to serve as a mark of distinction, rather than an indication of deficient dental hygiene.

"In the old regime" Salitara began, thumbing the flywheel of an old Zippo lighter as he spoke, "Karpaty reported directly to the Defense Minister of the USSR. It was much easier to work then because the Ministry provided us with the funds to purchase whatever we wanted. We were high priority, and we got whatever we asked for. Now we have to deal directly with the suppliers and either pay them immediately or barter our products for theirs." The overpowering aroma of his Russian cigarette floated across the desk and slowly filled the room.

"It is very difficult", he continued. "Our currency is not convertible so we can't do business outside of Ukraine, and we wouldn't know where to start if we could. The old vertical structure is gone, and there is nothing to replace it. There used to be rules and procedures, and now there are none. Today's Ukraine is like a jungle with no one in control. Powers that rule in one area do not rule in another. There are no more loyalties to the state, to the company, or one another."

Igor's lament seemed to sum up my conversations with all the vice directors.

In real life-back when I was working, I came to realize companies eventually take on an identity, or a character, of their own, in much the same manner as individuals. An experienced person can spend a short time walking through the offices of an organization and, with a fair degree of accuracy, determine the type of company he is visiting. Some companies are conservative, while others tend to be more flamboyant. There are companies that are paternalistic and others that are indifferent to the needs of their employees. Some organizations are dynamic while still others exude defeat and desperation.

Karpaty was a company living in the past, with little thought about adapting to the future. Its vice directors were a group of disparate personalities that fit together like a crazy cat's cradle with strands irrevocably intertwined, but never interconnected. The engineering manager wanted to acquire as much responsibility as possible, while the head of manufacturing believed his production problems were caused by poorly engineered products and wanted to absorb the marketing department to solidify his position. The manager of marketing was preparing for yesterday's business, and his boss had no interest in the future.

Each of these "wise directors", in their own way, was longing for a return to the past, with little interest in finding a path to the future. Yet, the Karpaty they had known was gone, packed away with the furled communist banners they used to fly at the workers rallies. It would never return, but they were not yet convinced.

In the meantime, the atmosphere at Karpaty was one of fear and apprehension. It felt like a company whose time was passing and no one knew how much time was left. I found myself feeling sorry for these men, and especially for the workers who were involuntarily conscripted in a conflict not of their making. I wished, more than before, that I could find a way to help them. Initially the assignment had been more of a personal challenge, but it was rapidly becoming a desire to help these people adapt to their new conditions.

The problem was, I did not have the feeling the directors had any interest in changing.

Chapter 7

The Mysterious Man From AARP

The rain fell diagonally, driven by a brisk wind out of the Carpathians. The downpour began in the night and grew stronger with daylight. The weather in western Ukraine was much the same as the Midwest and in both places it was turning out to be a cold, wet summer. It was too windy for an umbrella, but my hooded jacket provided some measure of warmth as I bent forward against the biting gusts.

While I trudged up the hill to Karpaty a large truck carrying a heavy load of equipment passed. As the grade grew steeper its tires began to spin on the wet pavement, forcing the driver to pass me in reverse as he slowly backed down to a place where he could acquire greater traction. The driver glared through the window as he passed, raising his palms to the heavens as if to say "what is a man to do in an old truck on a day like this." By the time I reached the top, the truck was again attempting to make the climb, this time more slowly, and in a lower gear.

My office was cold. The wind whistled through a crevice between the window frame and wall, like a left over sound effect from Dr. Zhivago. A rivulet of rain entered through a breach between the windows and, cascading over the sill and down the wall, ended in a growing pool of water on the hardwood floor. It was apparent from the well-defined stains this path had been taken many times before.

I searched for Kapitolena, the general director's secretary. When she was finally found, I led her to my office to show her the problem. To dramatize my discomfort I clutched the collar of my coat and pretended to shiver. She nodded in sympathy and left, returning shortly with a steaming cup of tea. It was welcome, but I had hoped she could provide a more lasting solution.

As it turned out, she could. I should have had more confidence in the powers of an executive secretary. Later that morning, a workman arrived with a large wooden tool chest slung over his shoulder with a worn leather strap. Looking at the leaking windows, he shook his head in dismay. Within an hour, the cracks were sealed and the windows could again be tightly closed.

I appreciated his effort but had to wonder why this problem had not been taken care of long before. This was obviously one of the executive offices, and the problem was not new. At the same time, there were more people than work in the factory, and it seemed some of them could easily have been assigned to maintaining the facilities.

After returning to my work, I was distracted by a soft shuffling sound that caused me to look up. Standing in my office doorway was a tall Teutonic-looking young man with a severe crewcut and pale blue eyes. I have no idea how long he had been standing there, but when he saw me looking at him he announced in flawless English "I am Valerie and I would like to work with you." I did not fully realize it at the time, but the answer to all of my interpreting problems had just walked through the door.

"Young man, you seem to have a badger on your chest" I offered. And indeed he did, in the center of his bright red sweatshirt strode a leering, brazen, badger.

"That's right, it is Bucky Badger, the mascot of the University of Wisconsin. I studied there for two semesters as an exchange student from the University of Moscow."

"Hey, we were neighbors" I offered. "I have a lake home near Fond du Lac. Do you attend the University of Moscow now?"

"Yes I do. I will be going back in the fall."

"What's your major?"

"Inorganic Material Science."

"That's a pretty heavy major," I told him, wondering what a person did with that type of specialty. In the Soviet sphere, the best and the brightest were channeled into the deep sciences, and the better the students were, the more sophisticated their disciplines became. It was widely known the Russians favored such exotic degrees, but it was surprising their universities continued to accept applicants from former Soviet countries, and even more astonishing that they were permitting some of these students to travel to American institutions.

Sensing my surprise, Valerie volunteered that the number of foreign students had been reduced since the breakup of the USSR, but there were still scholarships available in the more specialized curriculums. He believed it was a way for the Russians to maintain their old influence in the newly independent countries.

One thing was certain, Valerie was not randomly selected to attend the University of Wisconsin. It was not like winning the lottery. Not only would he have to be exceptionally bright, but he and his family would also have been thoroughly checked out for ideological purity. It was curious that such a person was now in my office volunteering his services. I was mildly suspicious, but then what is it they say about looking gift horses in the mouth?

"Can you get a job in today's Russia with such a specialized major?"

His brow wrinkled slightly, "I really hadn't given it much thought," Valerie replied. "But you have a good point. I should start to think about what I want to do when I graduate."

The young man spoke very thoughtfully and his English was excellent, almost without accent. Unless you listened carefully, it would be difficult to know he was not a homegrown American. He did, however, speak in a clipped monotone, pronouncing each word very distinctly. It was like talking with an automaton. At times, I had the impression I was carrying on a conversation with HAL, the computer in *A Space Odyssey*.

He also spoke very softly. I often had to ask him to repeat what he said, which is something I am reluctant to do. There is always the impression that an older person's inability to hear is a function of their age, rather than a reflection of the person who is speaking. Having to frequently ask him to repeat, however, didn't seem to bother Valerie, and I eventually grew more accustomed to his quiet voice.

"Was there much difference going to school at the University of Wisconsin and studying in Moscow?" I asked Valerie who seemed to enjoy using his English.

He thought for a minute before replying. "No, I was actually surprised they were so much the same. The biggest difference was that in the states people studied so they could get the knowledge they were paying for, and then find a good job. In Russia, they study so they can stay in school. If you get expelled you can never return, and school is easier than work. Without a degree you will never get a good job, so I guess it comes out the same in the end."

As we spoke, I came to recognize Valerie's facial expression rarely changed. Occasionally there would be a slight upward movement in the corners of his mouth, which I learned later served as a hearty laugh.

With the addition of Valerie, it now seemed I had a staff. Sasha the interpreter, Tanya the librarian, and Valerie the college student. All three had their regular jobs at Karpaty but they all seemed eager to spend as much time with me as I required.

My life began to take on a distinct pattern as I concentrated on preparing my work plan to present to the general director. I was also becoming more familiar with my surroundings. Directly across from my office was the sealed and padlocked door I had noticed on my arrival at Karpaty. I once asked Sasha what it contained and he gave me his familiar "who knows" shrug. When I would get that response, I was never certain if Sasha really didn't know, or if he felt I shouldn't know.

Next to the sealed door was the "executive washroom". It contained two sinks, two mirrors, and two stalls. The stalls were unlike any I had seen before. Inside each was a raised marble deck, about three feet off the floor, with a circular hole in the center. Each stall resembled a marbleized outhouse but, because of the height of the deck, I was never able to decide if it was meant for sitting on, or squatting over. Fortunately, there was never the necessity to experiment. The washroom was also unencumbered by the normal sanitary accoutrements such as soap, paper towels, or toilet paper.

Adjoining my office, at the end of the dark hallway, was a large conference room with approximately 20 rows of theater seats, facing a raised stage with a standing podium. This was where the general director held his weekly staff meetings. At times, the shouting grew so raucous it penetrated the thick walls of my office. It was obvious from the elevated sound level that there was considerable conflict among the upper management at Karpaty. Valerie once told me, at some of these meetings, the discussions were fueled by copious amounts of Russian vodka.

The company began its day at eight, and I arrived at nine. I would begin by meeting with Sasha then ask him to get Valerie and Tanya if they were needed. I first had to have my presentation translated into Russian from my penciled English so I would slowly read it to them to see if they understood.

Sasha would do the first translation and then review it with the other two before it went into final typing. Once it was typed in Russian, I had it read back to me in English to see if it still was making the points I wanted to make. It was a difficult and time-consuming process.

Tanya had the only English typewriter at Karpaty. All of the others were based on the Cyrillic alphabet. There were no copy machines similar to those that occupy any unused space on every floor of a typical American Company. The only machine at Karpaty that could make copies was in the Engineering Department, and it was designed for reproducing blueprints.

The gigantic copying equipment had an operating staff of twelve technicians. Their sole job was to run the three-foot wide sheets, then cut them into the desired dimensions, and finally to staple them together as required.

The staff was also responsible for making the necessary repairs frequently required by the ancient equipment. The machine's downtime exceeded operating time by a 5:1 ratio because the staff was having difficulty finding replacement parts for the antiquated machinery. With luck, it usually required a week to get the necessary copies. Since the information being prepared was for the general director, my requirement was handled with more urgency.

As we worked, I asked Sasha and the others to avoid discussing the information we were preparing with their associates at Karpaty. It was not intended to be a secret, but I preferred to have the general director and his staff learn of my recommendations all at the same time.

Our work routine would break at noon, and in the evening Sasha and I would have our meals at the disco. His English was slowly improving but his understanding remained unpredictable, sometimes with startling results.

At dinner one evening, I recalled that I was running out of butter in my apartment refrigerator. Before I forgot it, I turned to Sasha and said very slowly, "Sasha I need more butter for my apartment." As I spoke, an attractive young woman who was our waitress arrived with the soup.

"Apartment-apartment? You want this girl for your apartment?" Sasha asked. I had to admit his idea was better than mine, but I stuck to my story of the butter.

Another evening I asked Sasha if he would ask our waitress for a sausage to take back to the apartment. She soon appeared with an article wrapped in brown butcher paper. The next morning, as I was preparing breakfast, I unwrapped the paper to find a giant green cucumber.

At first, I was merely amused by these mistakes. Later I began to wonder what other linguistic blunders might have occurred that I was not aware of, and which could have been more serious.

After dinner I would usually return to my apartment to read, listen to music on my audio tape player, or try and locate the world news on my small Sony short-wave radio that, over the years, had become an essential part of every overseas trip. It was not only a source of entertainment in lonely hotel rooms, but provided the only understandable method of receiving current news as well.

At one time, I did business with a firm in Argentina during that country's Dirty War (1976-1983). This was a period when American businessmen in the country were often being kidnapped and held for ransom. Even many of the Argentineans were disappearing, and there was considerable conflict between the military government and some segments of Argentinean society. The conflict became so intense and divisive it eventually separated many old friends and families.

A bomb hidden underneath his bed while he slept assassinated the Police Chief of Buenos Aires. An investigation later uncovered the device was placed there by his daughter.

This was not the type of environment I cared to explore, and to avoid it I attempted to conduct all of my business with Telesud by phone. Except once when it was necessary to have an urgent personal discussion with the two partners who owned the company. We agreed to meet in Montevideo, Uruguay to avoid my traveling to Buenos Aires.

I flew all-night and stopped over in Rio de Janeiro. During my stay I listened to my short wave and learned there was a revolution expected the next day in Uruguay. I called the Argentineans who agreed to fly to Rio instead. The revolution took place as scheduled, but without me.

The problem with listening to a short-wave radio is that it is not as simple to use as a standard AM/FM radio. Stations will broadcast the same program simultaneously on different frequencies and then, at different times of the day, broadcast on a completely different set of frequencies making them difficult to locate with any degree of consistency. The stations are also more subject to atmospherics as their signals go careening through the ionosphere hundreds of miles above the earth. Once you do find the station you want, it may quickly disappear in a burst of static. The intensity of the atmospherics is highly variable depending on the season, and the current phase of the sunspot cycle.

While I was in Ukraine, I would regularly search for the strains of *Yankee Doodle*, which was the identification for the Voice of America. Once it was located, I would listen for news of the floods ravaging the Midwest. The chimes of London's Big Ben would announce the BBC that dwelled on the negotiations between the Western countries and Ukraine regarding the planned disposal of their large arsenal of ICBMs. Later I could change the dial and hear the Kremlin bells proclaim their English language news broadcast that would often focus on negotiations with Ukraine regarding the seizure of the Russian Black Sea Fleet.

As the days went by, I also began to watch the Ukrainian news on television. I could not understand what was being said, but I could occasionally identify what was happening.

A typical scene, shown almost every night, was a large cooperative farm with government officials talking to smiling field workers as they harvested grain. Another frequent news story would involve the visit of a foreign dignitary being greeted by happy Ukrainians in colorful costumes offering a loaf of bread and salt, which is an essential part of the country's traditional welcoming ceremony.

Often, in the evening, Sasha would visit the apartment, and occasionally bring books he once used in his English classes. Many of them were Ukrainian fairy tales that told of valiant princes' and beautiful princesses, as well as the little people that live in the woods, in much the same manner as American stories. According to Sasha, Ukrainian fairy tales were often used as an aid in foreign language classes, and it was said this was the way Gorbachev learned to speak excellent Ukrainian from his grandmother.

One evening Sasha proudly brought a copy of the English words to the Ukrainian National Anthem.

Ukraine is Not Yet Dead

Ukraine is not yet dead, nor its glory and freedom,
Luck will still smile on us, brother-Ukrainians.
Our enemies will die, as the dew does in the sunshine,
And we, too, brothers, we'll live happily in our land.
We'll not spare either our souls or bodies to get freedom
And we'll prove that we are brothers of Kozak Kin.
We'll rise up, brothers, all of us, from the Sain to the Don.
We won't let anyone govern in our motherland.
The Black Sea will smile, yet, grandfather Dnipro will rejoice.
Yet in our Ukraine luck will be high.
Our persistence, our sincere toil will prove its rightness,
Still our freedom's loud song will spread throughout Ukraine.
It will reflect upon the Carpathians, will sound through the steppes,
And Ukraine's glory will arise among the people.

The anthem was very sad, but I believe it accurately reflected the resilient character of the Ukrainian people.

In spite of our language problems, Sasha and I worked well together. He was amiable and cooperative and I used him to coordinate our work with Tanya and Valerie. After a few days the proposed work plan was completed and translated into Russian. Additional copies were prepared for all of the expected attendees at the meeting. I believed I knew by then what would be most helpful to Karpaty and planned to propose an analysis of their product line, new marketing techniques, and recommend the preparation of a document that would describe the advantages Karpaty could offer to a prospective investor. Before I began work I wanted to make sure there was general agreement on the direction the effort should take during the remainder of my stay.

I met with the general director to establish a date for our meeting. It was agreed that it would be in two days. Leaving the office that evening Sasha and I rode in the elevator with Kapitolena. She asked Sasha if I was a millionaire. If I was, perhaps I could buy Karpaty and get them out of their trouble. After her question was translated, I told her, unfortunately, I was not a millionaire, not even in Ukrainian coupons.

I learned at dinner she had also told Sasha our meeting would probably be postponed. It was. Secretaries always know, even in Ukraine.

The day of the meeting finally came. Sasha arrived that morning better dressed than he normally was. He wore a neatly pressed suit with a brown shirt and tie. Even his hair was more carefully combed than usual.

Valerie seemed unimpressed. He wore the same black short sleeved shirt he had worn all week, along with a clean pair of jeans. My three translators had decided Valerie would handle the translation, while Sasha took notes, and Tanya stayed in the office if we should need any additional information.

It was a good decision. Three would have been too many in the meeting. I needed Valerie, and it would have been humiliating for Sasha if he was not involved. Tanya had been very helpful, and I was afraid I would hurt her feelings if I asked her to stay away after working so hard typing the translations. As it turned out, the three of them reached the same decision by themselves.

The vice directors were already seated, and the room was rapidly filling with smoke. They had been reasonably cordial during our previous meetings, but seated around the long table in the general director's office they did not look cordial now. They had their "meeting faces" on that morning, and those faces were gulag grim. I had the feeling I was facing the Politburo, and wondered what had caused the change.

I began the meeting by summarizing what I planned to discuss. As I was finishing, there was a commotion at the door. All eyes turned to observe the dramatic entrance of Medvid "the bear" Tichonovick, followed closely by two assistants. They took their seats at the end of the table, with only a nod to the general director.

I discussed the problems I had observed at other companies that were attempting to convert their business from defense products to something that could be sold to commercial markets. It is not an easy thing to do. One of the major problems is management has no idea how to go about it, or how to determine the needs of the market.

As I spoke, it was obvious Valerie was keeping up a continuous pace of translation. This was a considerable improvement over the previous meeting where Sasha handled the primary responsibilities. Occasionally, I would motion to Valerie to raise his voice but, aside from that, he was doing a very competent job.

I continued my presentation, pointing out that another problem is the difference in culture between a military and consumer products company. In defense work, the emphasis is on extreme reliability in an hostile operating environment. In consumer products, great attention is paid to appearance and cost. The requirements of the two product categories are incompatible, and it is very difficult for a technical workforce to make a successful transition between the different product demands.

Marketing techniques are also vastly different between the two product categories. Military products are usually sold to a single customer-the government, while commercial products have to be marketed to a broad range of buyers. The two methods are considerably different, as are the type of people that do the selling.

In addition, the defense company wishing to convert its product line will usually require new tooling and fixtures.

Many companies are unable to afford this expense, and are unable to convert existing equipment to the production of other products.

Because of these factors, it was important for Karpaty to obtain assistance from an outside company, and I proposed steps for them to take that might attract foreign investors. I also proposed the preparation of a document that could be distributed to interested companies that would describe the advantages Karpaty could provide to prospective partners.

When I finished speaking, the general director rose and walked quickly to his desk. After reaching into a drawer, he returned to the table with his own program, written in English, which he asked Sasha to read. Fortunately, his program and mine were very similar. I learned later this was not a coincidence.

After agreeing to a few changes, I passed out an outline describing in Russian, the information I would need from the individual directors, and the dates the information was required.

I had the impression Karpaty's staff was not accustomed to the type of organization and meeting preparation they saw that day.

Sasha told me later that during the meeting Medvid whispered to his assistant that I must have been in many Russian companies to understand their problems so well. I was pleased by his comments, but wondered how much cooperation I would actually receive from him and his fellow vice directors.

After the meeting Valerie, Sasha, and I returned to my office to go over the details with Tanya. "Why had all of the directors seemed so grim at the beginning of the meeting?" I asked Sasha.

"They were disappointed with what you proposed. The general director wanted you to meet with the vice directors to learn about Karpaty. When the meetings were finished they expected you to call your business associates in the United States who would then immediately come over with much money to invest."

"That's not the way it works", I explained " foreign companies don't just shell out money without knowing every detail about the organization they are investing in."

"We know that now" Sasha said, "but they didn't know that then. They think American companies are very rich and will invest anywhere they want to. You have to understand these people have no experience in dealing with anything other than government owned communist companies that do exactly what they are told. The general director and his vice directors are disappointed because they thought you could immediately bring people to save the company. Now they understand they will have to work at finding outside investment."

"Had you prepared the general director's program for him Sasha?" The color began to rise slowly from Sasha's brown shirt collar to his forehead, as he nodded in embarrassment.

"For him to prepare his, you must have also given him a copy of my presentation. Is that correct? He knew several days ago what I was going to say?"

"Yes, that's how he already knew you weren't going to call your friends to come over and invest in Karpaty. That is also why he postponed the meeting, and had me prepare his own program so he would appear to be in control."

I was badly disappointed. I had asked Sasha not to do that, but it was expecting too much. He had to work with these people long after I was gone, and I should have understood this. It was a valuable lesson, however. I now realized that everything I might do or say while I was at Karpaty would be reported back to Sasha's management.

Valerie had been quiet during our discussion. When it was finished, he asked, "how was my translation?"

"Very good, it was sometimes hard to hear you in the crowded room but, otherwise, your translation was terrific."

"Do you think the general director would give me a raise? I really don't earn any money here. Both of my parents work for Karpaty, but it is just a place for me to work in the summer to get some experience while I go to college."

"I really don't know Valerie. Why don't you ask him. He can only turn you down, and even if he does you don't have anything to loose."

He looked at me, then rose from his chair and left the room. It wasn't long before he returned. "The general director agreed to give me a raise," he told me with the ghost of a smile. I believed that Valerie had the beginnings of a future capitalist.

That evening at dinner Misha sat at our table. He spoke to Sasha who then turned to me. "He wants to know if you heard about the big lay-off?"

"No, of course not. I don't hear anything unless you tell me." I was still a little upset by his earlier deception.

Sasha continued, "Misha says that after the meeting today each of the vice directors met with their staffs and told them there was going to be large layoffs. The news has gone through the factory like a forest fire."

Sasha and Misha resumed their conversation. There was a pause. "Misha thinks I should tell you that many workers think the lay-off is because of you. They believe you have been sent here by the CIA to cause problems for our plant."

"That's ridiculous." I snorted. "No one in the United States is interested in what happens at Karpaty, besides I am too damned old to be a spy."

"We know," Misha said in English. "The better educated people know that, but some of the ignorant workers don't believe it."

"You have to understand that all of their lives these people have heard they have to be careful about spies from the United States " Sasha added. "That's why no one could leave or visit here. We had many lectures about how we need to have tight security at the factory so the Americans don't come and steal our secrets. You are the only American any of us have ever seen, and now many of the workers are going to lose their jobs so they want to believe it is because of you."

"It also helps the vice directors if they can tell their workers this is what the American recommended," Misha added. "It shifts the responsibility from them to you."

Back at my apartment, I decided it would be a good time to finish the last of the martinis I had brought with me. It had not been one of my better days. I found that the work I intended to do was not what Karpaty management had expected, and what I planned to do was not really what they wanted. At the same time, many of the workers thought I had come to steal their secrets, and ruin their company. I was sure I could never convince them that their superannuated spy, instead of the man from UNCLE, was merely a mysterious man from AARP. The American Association for Retired Persons would be shocked to learn that one of their members was considered a secret agent operating undercover in far off Ukraine.

The next day was Friday. Sasha announced he had not been home for several weeks and if I didn't mind he would go home this weekend to see his parents. Of course, I had no objections.

As I walked alone from the administration building to the culture center, I noticed three men standing by the doorway. Drawing closer, I could see they were watching me intently, and it was obvious I was the topic of their conversation. Trevor Gunn was right when he said as we were leaving the airplane, "pay attention to the hair on the back of your neck, it's a good early warning system." I could feel mine begin to rise and, as I drew closer to the group, sweat started to trickle slowly down my back.

When I neared the door, the largest of the three very deliberately ground out his cigarette under his heel, crushing it with his shoe like a peasant squashes an offending bug. It was a menacing gesture, meant to intimidate me. And it did.

Grinning to the other two with a sly Slavic smile, he began to swagger toward me. He was head and shoulders taller than I was, with a black stubble and vodka-red eyes. Time remained suspended for me, like an ant in amber.

He spoke menacingly in rapid, agitated, Russian. I had no idea what he was saying, but I could tell from his expression it was not very complimentary. His two friends snickered at everything the big man said. I had seen the routine before. One of the thugs will get you into an argument that leads to a fight, and his lackeys join in. In this case they wouldn't have to. I was sure black-beard could handle me easily by himself. I was equally certain this would not deter his friends from piling on.

I wanted no part of this. Always believing that any action was better than no action, I began to talk very rapidly. At the same time, I started to gesture like a demented dervish attempting to give directions to someone who was too foolish to comprehend. I pointed left, then forward, then dramatically to the right toward the towering Carpathians. All the while looking him directly in his red-rimmed eyes, as though he was expected to completely understand everything I was saying.

He stared in bewilderment. His mouth dropped open in consternation, and he returned to his companions to get their opinion on how best to handle this crazed foreigner.

With his back turned toward me, I quickly entered the cultural center, walking breathlessly up the stairs. Misha was also off for the weekend, and I was served by one of the kitchen help. That evening at the disco, I ate my solitary dinner very slowly--very slowly indeed. When I left an hour and a half later, much to my relief, the men were nowhere to be seen.

Returning to my apartment, I was sorry I had drunk my last martini the night before. I watched that evening's television news portraying a group of smiling costumed Ukrainians, with their traditional loaf of bread and saucer of salt, graciously greeting a recent group of visitors from a foreign land.

Watching, I could not avoid comparing this idyllic scene with my reception, and wondering who might have organized my own welcoming committee. After years of being taught that Americans were the enemy, it would be easy to place the mantle of blame on a distinguishable foreigner, particularly if he was perceived to be responsible for the loss of a large number of precious jobs.

More importantly, I wondered if they would try again. Was this the beginning or the end of their attempted harassment? It was hard to tell if it had been a random act, or a calculated strategy to get me to leave Ukraine.

If this type of thuggery was to continue, I had no defense. I could discuss the problem with the general director, but he might be the very root of my predicament. Once he learned I was not bringing in immediate financial relief my stock had declined considerably. Perhaps it was better for him to tie the problem to the foreigner. If he was not directly involved, I was sure that his sympathies would lie with those that were.

I could also discuss my situation with Sasha. He was a well meaning young man, but he had been conspicuously absent this evening. In addition, I had just learned that whatever I confided in him was transmitted immediately to the general director.

Communicating with the IESC in Kiev for advice was also out of the question.

Watching the flickering television screen, I seriously thought about ending my project and returning home.

After considerable thought I finally decided to hell with it. I had made a commitment and would stay and finish the job, but I felt very alone and hoped I would not regret my decision.

Before going to bed that night, and every night thereafter, I made doubly sure my door was very securely locked.

Chapter 8

The Children of Chernobyl

I finally decided to avoid discussing my experience at the culture center with anyone. I really did not know what it would accomplish. It was obvious the encounter had not occurred by accident. Men never loitered there before, and it was clear they were waiting for me. It was planned, and I had no idea who was involved in the planning process or what their objective might be.

The next week Sasha came into my office to tell me the general director thought I would enjoy spending the following weekend at the company's resort in the mountains. While considering the offer I wondered if this was their way of getting me out of sight for a few days, or merely a gesture of Ukrainian hospitality.

I knew Karpaty, like most of the Soviet amalgamations, operated recreational facilities for their employees. Company Party officials primarily used these retreats for themselves, and occasionally to reward deserving workers. I had heard that Karpaty maintained one of these camps on the Black Sea near Odessa, and another in the mountains near the town of Yaremche.

Whatever their motivation was, I was curious about their facilities. I told Sasha I appreciated the offer and would look forward to the trip. Apparently, he was looking forward to our trip as well because he quickly asked if I would mind if his fiancé came with us. Of course, I did not.

As I prepared to leave, Valerie came into the office with a translation he had just completed. "Have you been able to contact your wife yet?" he asked.

"No" I replied brusquely. "It was very difficult for me to understand how a society with the technology to put a space station into orbit is still unable to provide simple telephone connection between two major countries."

"Have you tried sending a telex? I know we have telex connections to the United States."

Restraining my sarcasm, I replied "we don't have teletype equipment in our home." Then I recalled I had seen a telex address on my son Paul's business card. He was an executive with a large offshore insurance company in Bermuda. If I could send him a message, he could then telephone his mother. This was not the way I would have preferred to contact my wife, but it was certainly better than no communication at all.

I quickly wrote a note to let Elsie know I was doing fine, and apologized to Valerie for being abrupt. I gave him the message as I rushed out of the office, hoping this would prove more successful than previous attempts.

The company's Volga, and its driver, were waiting for me at the factory door. Sasha and Lydia, his "intended", were already holding hands in the back seat.

Lydia was a computer programmer who also worked at Karpaty, and lived with her parents in another housing block. She was as slender as Sasha was but was still a pleasantly attractive young woman with blond hair and dark brown eyes. She wore a T-shirt and jeans, which were gathered at the waist with a narrow belt. Her knowledge of English consisted of only one word. "OK." Such a positive and limited vocabulary can be an endearing trait in a woman. However, in this case, it meant that Sasha was forced to translate for her as well.

It was a bright sunny day. The rain that had been pounding the Carpathian region for several days had moved on into Central Asia, leaving behind milder summer temperatures. As we left the outskirts of Ivano Frankivsk, I turned to Sasha to ask if he had been to the camp before.

"Yes, once. I was there years ago when I was with the Komsomol. Do you know what that is Mr. Miller?"

"No I do not."

"Komsomol was a communist youth organization. It means unity of the young. Almost everyone became a member. First, you were a Young Pioneer, then when you reached 14 you joined Komsomol. You had to belong to the organization to get any place in the Party; and you had to be recognized by the Party to get into a good school, get a good job, or enter a military academy. It was like a game with formal rules. You attended a meeting every month. It was supposed to be an ideological preparation for your adult life."

Lydia chimed in through Sasha, "It wasn't all ideological training. Sometimes they would take a group to recreational camps, or on a holiday. We also sang patriotic songs like *Brave Comrades on the March, The Motherland*, or *The Long Road*," Lydia added giggling.

There were few cars on the road, but we would occasionally pass a farmer traveling to town in his horse-drawn wagon. The people in the area still relied on the type of Russian hitch they had used for centuries. It was composed of a single long wooden pole running from the wagon and strapped to the side of the horse. The wagons were approximately six to seven feet long, and shaped like an elongated V.

We passed by small farms and through tiny villages. Men and women were working in the fields with large two handled scythes and wooden rakes. It was a scene from an old Flemish painting as they cut and stacked their hay for the summer harvest.

We passed young girls herding geese along the roadway and saw old women sitting stoically in the ditch beside their tethered family cow. In almost every small town we passed through there were workers constructing or reconstructing churches that had been banned during the period of communist control.

The trip to Karpaty's camp took less than an hour, but it spanned several generations.

Eventually we drove down a dirt road that led to the campgrounds. Before the car could come to a complete stop the camp director rushed from a small administration building to greet us. He spoke briefly to Sasha and led us to a large two-story building where we were to stay.

Our rooms were on the second floor. Sasha and Lydia shared a single room while my quarters consisted of a room with a sofa, shelves, and a small refrigerator. This room led to a larger room with two beds, a large table and chairs, and a window looking over the campgrounds. The rooms were rustic and smelled slightly musty but seemed quite comfortable. I offered to trade accommodations with Sasha, but he indicated he was satisfied the way it was.

As I unpacked, I watched the activities through my window. It was soon apparent we were staying at a camp principally for children. I identified several other dormitory style buildings, a mess hall, and two buildings with separate toilet facilities and showers.

In my distant youth I spent three delightful summers as a swimming instructor at Foley Camp in northern Minnesota, and was very familiar with what a children's camp looked like. This place, however, was very different. These children seemed to wander about as they wished. At Foley Camp they moved seamlessly from one activity to another, much like classes at school. There was archery, rifle practice, handicrafts, sailing, swimming, canoeing, and other types of diversion that would appeal to young children. Here, the pace seemed far more leisurely and unstructured.

My reminisces were interrupted by Sasha and Lydia knocking on my door, to take me to lunch. The children were already waiting outside the mess hall, boisterously pushing and shoving like happy children the world over.

Inside the dining room, the air was saturated by years of boiled cabbage and sweating youngsters. We were quickly seated at a separate table and served before the others were allowed to enter. Shortly, after sitting down, the building was rocked by a tidal wave of hungry, noisy children whose principal purpose apparently was to locate their friends, and then grab as many slices of bread as possible before it was taken by others at their table.

Conversation was difficult, but above the constant din I was able to learn that Sasha and Lydia had been seeing each other for five months, and hoped to be married later in the year. Because of the conditions in Ukraine, and the continuing uncertainty at Karpaty, they were not sure this would be possible. The two were not eager to marry if they were going to lose their jobs, or if they would be unable to be assigned space in the controlled apartments enabling them to live together.

They spoke matter-of-factly about their problems, and without rancor, but with noticeable concern for their future. Their cares were in marked contrast to the noisy, seemingly carefree children frolicking at the other tables.

We ate quickly, as Sasha and Lydia wanted to begin their walk. We started out on a path through the woods, down a hill to a rapidly flowing mountain stream. We followed the streambed for some distance, then began to climb a steep embankment. The delicate scent of pine offered a pleasant relief from the heavy odors of the mess hall. Sasha and Lydia led the way wearing matching bright yellow tee shirts and, as we climbed, I developed the distinct feeling I was being led through the woods by a matched pair of number two pencils.

As the hill grew steeper, I became increasingly upset that someone my age would be put through such a strenuous climb. Pausing to wipe the perspiration from my forehead, I saw Sasha turn toward Lydia and make a fluttering motion with his hand over his heart. If Sasha's heart was fluttering, mine was beating like an ancient drum.

Pushing on, I recalled that the IESC had advised that if possible, Ukrainian doctors should be avoided. That would be no problem here, we were miles from even an incapable doctor or medical facility. I could die in this remote part of the world and my family would be unaware of my passing for weeks.

I knew a few associates who had met their maker traveling overseas. I believed that nothing could be worse than dying alone, in a strange hotel room, in a remote country. Not only for the deceased, but also for the unfortunate surviving family required to deal with an unfeeling foreign bureaucracy.

Sasha's shouting interrupted my morose thoughts,

"Do you want to turn back?"

Hell yes, I thought.

"Oh no", I said.

I would be damned if they would make me give up and cause them to miss their "walk." I clawed my way up the embankment, grasping onto any shrub or tree that would help propel my aging frame upwards. I have heard there comes a time in every man's life when he is forced to finally confront old age. For me, that day was this.

Gasping for breath, I finally joined my companions at the top of the hill. After a few minutes rest, we resumed our walk. It was easier keeping up on level ground.

The scenery was magnificent with rolling mountains, swiftly running rivers cascading through deep ravines sheltered by a variety of trees and shrubs. As we continued, I fully expected to encounter the von Trapp family gaily running down a hill, hand in hand with Julie Andrews, loudly caroling the "the hills are alive," etc. etc.

We would occasionally pass other people gathering the plentiful wild berries. I had seen workers and their families getting off the buses by our apartment block carrying tin buckets filled with the fruits of their excursion, and wondered where they had been.

The idyllic scene was partially spoiled by the realization that wherever we were going it would be only halfway, and there had to be an equally long trip back to camp. Hopefully, it had to be more down hill.

Finally we reached the village of Yaremche, which apparently had been our unstated destination all along. It was a peaceful little town set in a valley with steep mountain slopes on both sides. There was a post office, a train station, several souvenir shops, a coffee shop, and a restaurant. It also had enough people wandering through the streets carrying cheap Russian cameras to qualify as a tourist attraction.

As is so often the case in Ukraine, things are not always the way they appear on the surface. In this seemingly serene mountain setting, I was surprised to learn that during WWII Yaremche was the center of fierce and violent partisan activity. Their effort was first directed toward the Germans and then, for almost ten years after the war, redirected toward the Russians. Judging from the terrain we just covered I could easily see how these men could hide in the surrounding hills and remain there for years.

The same mountains that so effectively concealed the partisans, just a generation later provided the hiding place for massive missile emplacements aimed at unseen but imagined distant enemies in Europe and the United States.

These missiles were supposedly in the process of being dismantled under funding from the United States, This, and the departure of the Russion Army, were the reasons the Ivano Frankivsk area was no longer isolated from the rest of the world.

The mountain fighters were made up of Ukrainian nationals known as the Ukrainian Insurgent Army, or UPA. Their headquarters was in Ivano Frankivsk, but they fought throughout the Carpathian region. They were supplied by the Allies during the war with airdrops of food, arms, and advisors. At one time, they were believed to have 20,000 to 40,000 men under their command.

Their troops fought the Russians for almost ten years with weapons left behind by the German Army. Their goal was to separate Ukraine from the Soviet Union in much the same way as the Chechen guerrillas would fight with Russia half a century later.

Even before the partisans depended on the surrounding mountains for concealment, Oleska Dovbush, the legendary Ukrainian Robin, found shelter in the nearby caves and crevices.

Dovbush Rocks, as they are presently known, boast a peak of 800 meters above sea level and have become a limited source of much-needed tourist revenue.

In the center of Yaremche was an imposing monument dedicated to the partisan soldier. The bronze fighter stood,

in the town's square, with his gun forever raised fiercely over his head, dramatically framed between two towering concrete tree trunks.

Across from the massive monument was a small museum containing pictures of partisan leaders and their groups, exhibited beside parts of their uniforms, insignias, and some of the guns and grenades that they used. The most intriguing objects displayed, however, were two large white plaster statutes of a slender woman partisan leader. One pose showed her on horseback with a gun strapped over her back. In the other, she was standing with her Kalashkinov propped defiantly against her leg.

I asked Sasha and Lydia if they knew who she was, but they did not. Lydia added "there was a woman partisan leader by the name of Maria Savchyn who joined the underground movement when she was only 16. The statute may be of her. Do you see how she wears her hair? It is said the partisans would fold secret messages into slender cylinders and conceal them in the thick braids they wore

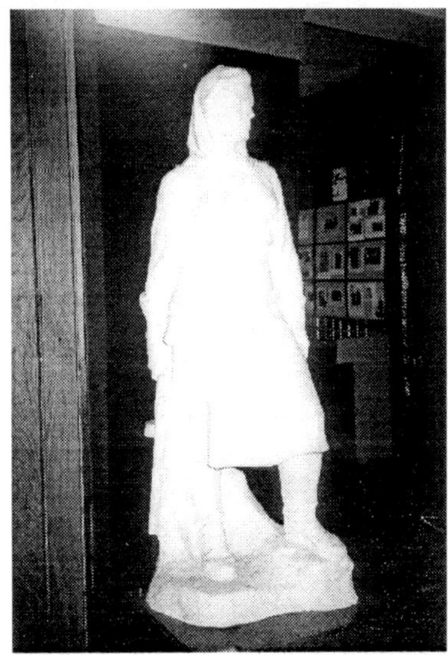

on top of their heads. This way, the messages were hidden from the enemy soldiers as the women traveled between their lines."

Studying the starkly outlined features of the alabaster figure, I was reminded of Hemingway's Pilar, another woman partisan fighter described by him in his classic story of the Spanish Civil War, *For Whom the Bell Tolls*. But Pilar was only a fabrication of the writer's imagination, fictionally fighting another enemy, in another place, in an almost forgotten other war. Whoever this Ukrainian woman was she was once very real, and must have been one hell of a warrior to be singled out by the men in one of the hardest fought fronts of a drawn-out war.

On the trip back to camp, we walked along a main road. We must have traveled at least five miles through the mountains to get to Yaremche, and I wasn't looking forward to the return trip. As we walked, I looked anxiously for a bus stop, but saw none. Sasha and Lydia, on the other hand, seemed as fresh as when we began. I was sure their children would be as slender as reeds and climb like mountain goats.

We eventually wound our hot, sweaty, footsore, and weary way back to camp. We must have covered ten miles since we left and I was very tired. After taking a much-needed shower, I lay down for a nap before dinner.

I was asleep, for what seemed to be only a short period of time when I sensed I was not alone in the room. I slowly opened my eyes to find a large woman in a white uniform and cap studiously gazing down at me. I don't know how long she had been watching. My first thought was someone had wisely sent for a nurse. On closer examination, I decided that my visitor was instead one of the kitchen help.

When she saw I was awake, she began telling me a long story, in Russian, on an unknown subject. When she finally paused for breath, I made my usual apology for not speaking her language. She continued undeterred, her two gold teeth shining brightly in the front of her mouth.

I had no idea what my culinary companion was telling me, but it was obviously a detailed explanation of a very serious subject. I was not being lectured and there was no sense of admonishment. Only the sense of a lonely woman who wanted to tell her tale to someone, anyone, rather he understood or not.

When she would pause, I would inject some inanity such as "I believe the rocket goes up at dawn", or "you say Liz Taylor is married again?" She would listen politely and then continue her lengthy narrative, not to be side-tracked by such a minor obstacle as an uncomprehending listener. Finally, her story apparently over, she stopped and signaled me to follow by waggling her crooked fore-finger in my direction. That was the first thing I had understood since she came into my room. She apparently had been sent to bring me to dinner.

The food at camp was simple but palatable, composed primarily of rice, potatoes or some kind of pasta shells, some meat, usually baloney, and the ever present Ukrainian staple of cucumbers and tomatoes. The meal was served on metal plates or in metal bowls. There were no knives, only forks and spoons. The children certainly, seemed to have no complaint about their meals, judging by their rate of consumption. The menu also appeared to please Sasha and Lydia who were both hearty eaters.

Dinner that night was a quiet affair. Even the children seemed tired from their day's activities. As we were finishing our coffee, Sasha smiled at Lydia and me. "Tomorrow we climb to the cliffs of Dovbush to see the caves" he told us with gleeful anticipation.

I didn't share Sasha's enthusiasm for cliff climbing. The next day I stayed behind to read and listen to my shortwave radio while Sasha and Lydia left, hand in hand, to scale the cliffs of Dovbush.

It was interesting to watch the camp activities. Most of the campers were twelve and younger. They would gather in the morning for a rather passive form of calisthenics then leave in groups, accompanied by a counselor, for hikes in the woods or a swim in one of the mountain streams.

In the afternoon, I took my book to an outside bench where I could relax in the sunlight, as befits a man of advancing age. After awhile I looked up to find myself encircled by a group of smiling, giggling little girls. I felt like Gulliver surrounded by the Lilliputians.

"Where from?" one asked timidly.

"Amerikanzie?" asked another.

" Yes Chicago," I replied forming my fingers in the shape of a gun, which was lost on my newly found friends.

"Have children?" another asked.

"Yes" I told them holding up three fingers. Then one for "girl" and two for "boys." This time they understood my pantomime.

The boldest of the group would try their grade school English, and were pleased when I would answer in acknowledgment. Others would point to themselves and pronounce their names and I would respond with mine.

Finally, the girls grew tired of their game, and wandered off in search of a new and more exciting past time than talking with an elderly stranger reading a book.

Later I learned most of the children in camp were from the Kiev area, close to Chernobyl. They had been sent to camp for a few weeks as a way of removing them, for awhile at least, from lingering radiation. These happy children were the sad legacy of Soviet mismanagement of the lives and safety of their citizens.

The explosion of the nuclear power station at Chernobyl triggered a large fireball that blew off the steel and concrete lid of the reactor. The radioactivity it created was several times greater than the amount that resulted from the atomic bombs dropped on Hiroshima and Nagasaki, and although it had occurred seven years before, much of the surrounding area remained contaminated.

The nuclear blast released large amounts of radioactive material into the atmosphere, where it was carried great distances by the swirling air currents. The poisonous air was spread by the wind over Belarus, Russia, and Ukraine and soon reached as far west as France and Italy. Millions of acres of forest and farmland were contaminated; and although many thousands of people were evacuated, hundreds of thousands more remain in polluted areas.

The full extent of the catastrophe was unknown for weeks in Ukraine as the USSR's leadership attempted to keep its secret from the rest of the world. "First of May" celebrations were held five days later, and millions of Ukrainians unknowingly gathered under blooming chestnut trees to watch parades as deadly radiation rained down upon them.

Even now, the land around Chernobyl remains barren and unlivable. Cancer rates are far higher than average in Ukraine and Belarus, particularly thyroid cancers among children. Experts believe each month a child spends outside of this environment prolongs their lives by two years. The time away from home allows the children's immune system a chance to rebuild, and that is why they were sent to this camp in the Carpathian Mountains.

As I returned to my cabin I thought about my daughter Cheron's children, my grandchildren, Tim and Melinda, who were approximately the same age as the young people with whom I had been talking. It seemed a long time ago that she had brought them to the airport to see Papa off on his Ukrainian adventure. How fortunate they all were to be growing up safely in the United States.

In my room, resting on my sofa, my thoughts drifted back many years to my lunches with General Groves. General Leslie R. Groves was the man in charge of the "Manhattan Project" that developed the world's first atomic bomb. He was later played by Paul Newman in the movie *Fat Man Little Boy*, which was the code name for the two bombs dropped on Japan.

The circumstances of our meeting were unusual. It was during my second tour working for Univac. My previous boss at General Electric had taken me with him when he became Director of Planning for the troubled computer company. We were temporarily housed in an old stone mansion in Connecticut, used as an executive retreat by the company, until office space was available at Univac's New York headquarters.

Local residents called the mansion Rock Ledge. It had been built by a local steel company magnate who had seen the original castle while vacationing in Scotland. He was so taken by its appearance, he decided he wanted it for his home in Connecticut. He had plans drawn up, and the castle torn down stone by stone, then shipped by sea to the United States. During this lengthy process the steel executive belatedly discovered there was more attractive local stone that could be he used to build his estate. When the dismantled Scottish castle arrived, the ship's captain was ordered to dump his cargo in the nearby bay.

Occasionally some of Univac's senior executives would spend time at Rock Ledge when they wanted to work away from the distractions of New York. One of them was General Groves, who had been brought to Univac as vice president of facilities by General Douglas MacArthur who was, by then, a member of the company's board of directors.

All of those who were present at the mansion, on any given day, would assemble for lunch in the dining room at a long mahogany table set with fine china and silver, along with freshly cut flowers from one of the estate's many well tended gardens.

Houseboys wearing stiffly starched white linen jackets ubiquitously and silently served us our multi-course meal. While I was considerably lower in the organization than most of those at the table, it was still a remarkable experience for someone from small town Iowa.

General Groves was portly and aging, with a thick mane of white hair. Apparently, his previous responsibilities had taken their toll. While the rest of us ate our finely prepared lunch, the General found it necessary to be content with a form of liquefied cereal, which I believed to be Pabulum. But I never asked.

The conversation would often turn to his experiences during the war. The General had managed one of history's most complex projects, with highly classified facilities spread throughout the United States. He was also responsible for the productivity of men like J. Robert Oppenheimer, Enrico Fermi, and Harold Urey. Rather than talk about those experiences, the General's most frequent topic was his problems relying on the vague and variable opinions of his weather advisors when he was preparing to explode the test device at Trinity Site. The weather was extremely critical since a miscalculation could have not only wiped out the nearby technical advisors, but very possibly a large part of the population of New Mexico.

I am certain General Grove's only objective in successfully completing the Manhattan Project was to save lives by ending the war as quickly as possible. Yet, under the theory of unintended consequences, the misuse of the developed technology was still being felt fifty years later in the lives of the smiling Ukrainian children that I had met.

The conflicting images of these children and General Groves filled my thoughts, and I must have dozed. The next thing I knew there was a hand on my shoulder gently urging me to wakefulness. I looked up at Lydia who motioned me to follow her. Sasha was standing impatiently at the foot of the stairs.

"Come see the place we have found, you will like it."

"How far is it?" I asked.

"Not far."

"That means close, yes?"

"Yes."

"Close?" I asked turning to Lydia for confirmation.

"OK", she said.

With that kind of reassurance, how could I refuse? I also must admit I found their eagerness to share their find with me pleasing, and I was glad to join them on their adventure. As long as it did not include climbing the cliffs of Dovbush.

We walked along a paved, but narrow, mountain road enjoying the view of the deep gorge, and the mountain stream rushing over the rocks many feet below. Across the ravine, the cloud shrouded mountain peaks rose to considerable heights against an otherwise clear blue sky. Occasionally a farmer, on his way into Yaremche, would nod and smile as he and his family passed in a wagon drawn by their plodding family horse.

Suddenly a motorcycle and sidecar careening past broke the mountain serenity, forcing the three of us to leap to the side of road. As the ancient vehicle pulled away, we could see the leather helmeted driver raise one hand in salute, while his passenger clung tenaciously to the sides of his precarious perch. They looked like ghosts from the past escaping from the old WWI movie *What Price Glory* where Jimmy Cagney and Dan Dailey careen drunkenly across the French countryside, returning to the war torn front lines after spending a night in Paris with the lovely Charmaigne.

It had been many years since I had seen a motorcycle and sidecar of that vintage. Turning to Sasha, I asked "how old?' At the same time making motions, which I thought accurately simulated a motorcycle driver.

"Tuk?" was the puzzled response.

I tried once more. Then finally took my third tuk, high and inside, and dropped my motorcycle pantomime.

Eventually, we soon came to Sasha and Lydia's discovery. They were right, it was a remarkable find. Secluded in a valley, along side of a cascading mountain stream, was a newly constructed, luxurious vacation resort. The facility was composed of broad sidewalks lined with flower gardens accompanied with flowing fountains and alabaster statues. There were half a dozen four-story hotel type

buildings. One was larger than the rest, with dining rooms and recreational facilities. The buildings were made of sand colored stucco with red Mediterranean tiled roofs.

The most unusual aspect of all was, while everything was well cared for, there was no one around. All of the buildings were unoccupied. It was also notable they were all unusually well constructed. Most Soviet buildings begin to deteriorate well before they are completed. This builder had obviously used quality construction materials and paid careful attention to detail.

Sasha and Lydia were delighted with their find and we peered into the windows and rattled the doors as we explored the grounds. It was as if my friends had discovered a modern Brigadoon, except that mystical village was rooted in the past while this ghost resort was planned for the future.

The resort had to have been started by the Soviets, since it would have taken several years to complete. Particularly in view of its location, and the logistical problems associated with bringing in material as well as the extensive work force that would have been necessary. It was equally obvious the resort facilities were intended, not for ordinary workers, but for the *nomenklatura* with its many privileges, that controlled the upper echelons of the communist party.

The tremendous disparity between the recreational facilities for the Party leaders, and those available to the average Ukrainian worker in the land of enforced equality, seemed to go unnoticed by Sasha and Lydia as we made our way back to camp.

The afternoon sojourn with my two young friends was enjoyable. The scenery was magnificent, and their discovery was intriguing. The vacation retreat they had found could prove to be a valuable asset to the Ukrainian government if marketed properly. The country was badly in need of foreign exchange and the new resort could provide a desirable attraction for foreign tourists. There was no way of knowing if the new government was even aware of their secluded asset, and if they were, if they would want to do anything with it other than providing another benefit for their own political faithful.

Making conversation as we walked, I mentioned I was impressed by the low price of a bottle of Stolichnaya at the liquor store across from the apartment complex. A bottle that would cost around $12 in Chicago sold for 2500 coupons or around 75 cents at the store.

"Do you know the meaning of the word Stolichnaya?" Sasha asked.

"No" I admitted.

"It means capitol, like in the capitol of Russia." The picture on the bottle's label is the Moskva Hotel in Moscow," he added smugly, pleased with the opportunity to display the depth of his worldly knowledge in the presence of his lovely Lydia.

He continued to describe a highly codified government system for providing inexpensive vodka to Ukrainian citizens. "I get to buy two bottles a month for 1700 coupons each. Each Ukrainian man is issued a card, which he can then take to specified stores. The clerk looks for his name in a registry of qualified males, and then punches his card so he can buy no more than two bottles during a thirty-day period at the low price.

If he wishes, the Ukrainian can buy as many bottles as he wants at "list price", but only two bottles can be purchased at the reduced price. There is a similar system for other commodities such as bread, flour, butter, and other staples."

From what I had seen, two bottles of vodka a month would not go very far in many households. The bottles did not even have a replaceable cap; strongly implying that once a bottle was opened it is expected it to be finished.

Watching Sasha and Lydia walking hand in hand beside me, I was struck by how much in love they were. There were not the physical signs of affection young couples often display, but it was obvious they enjoyed the same things, and appeared very comfortable with one another.

As we entered the campgrounds, the children were already waiting for their dinner outside the closed mess hall. The campers seemed to be always hungry and lined up for meals long in advance of the designated times. Entering the door to the dining room behind Lydia and Sasha, I heard a familiar little voice-"Amerikanzie"-"Amerikanize." I looked back to see my little lady friends from earlier in the day, waving happily to me. I gave them the thumbs up signal and went in to eat.

Chapter 9

The Night Director

When Sasha first mentioned going to camp, I thought we would be returning Sunday evening. This was later changed to early Monday morning by a call from the driver to the camp director. The battered old Volga finally pulled into the campgrounds around noon. The trip took more time than I planned. While I enjoyed the weekend, I wanted to make sure that any future excursions were less time consuming.

I was certain no one at Karpaty cared what my working hours were, particularly after they found I would not immediately be hosting groups of rich American investors with pockets filled with money. I thought, however, as an unpaid volunteer it was important to maintain a good working schedule. Without some level of discipline, and no career consequences, it would be easy to give less than a full day's work for no day's pay. I intended to make sure Karpaty received as much as I could provide in the time available-rather they wanted it or not.

Returning to Ivano Frankivsk, we drove past small hillside farms and through tiny villages with cottages surrounded by tall stalks of hollyhocks, and bushes covered with vibrantly colored roses. The women were at their assigned roles of guarding their family cows grazing in roadside ditches, while the goose-girls busily herded their wards to wherever geese need to go.

As we passed through another village, the driver pulled abruptly into a parking lot in front of a large apartment complex. After turning off the engine, he darted furtively into one of the look-alike buildings, only to reappear thirty minutes later, with an attractive young woman clinging to his arm. She joined the driver in the front seat while I was relegated to the back, squeezing in with Sasha and Lydia. I now had a better idea why our return to Ivano Frankivsk was delayed.

When I returned to the office, there was a message on my desk from my son in Bermuda. He had received my telex and dutifully phoned his mother. Paul wanted me to know his mother was fine and everything was in good shape at home. It was encouraging to finally have at least some method of communications with my wife, even if it did resemble an international version of the childhood game "pass it on."

Later in the week, I asked Sasha if I could get into the plant if I wanted to work on Saturday. His answer was that it was locked up beginning Friday afternoon.

"Besides the plan is, you spend your weekends at Yaremche. This weekend you are to go with Tanya and Regina from marketing."

"That's very thoughtful Sasha, but it takes too much time. Tanya and Regina are very nice and I would like to spend the weekend with them but I wanted to make sure I get everything done before I leave."

"But Mr. Miller-you can't even boil. How will you eat?"

"Wrong Sasha, I am a very good boiler it's the cooking I have a problem with."

Instead of spending my weekends eating in the camp mess hall with the children, I arranged to eat in my apartment or at a restaurant in town and turning in the receipts.

I also explained to Tanya that I would enjoy going to camp with her and Regina, but I needed the time at Karpaty. She understood. I am not sure she was particularly eager to spend her weekends in Yaremche either. I knew she lived with a friend who was a doctor.

One day, she had told me how poor medical treatment was in Ukraine. The only qualification for getting into medical school was being proposed by the Communist Party, and the Party had no criterion other than organizational loyalty. Because of this, many unqualified people got into medical school, and once you were in school you eventually became a doctor.

Because of the general level of medical mediocrity, the better doctors were able to charge for their services, but only the communist elite could afford them. Her mother, who was very sick, could only afford competent treatment through the services of Tanya's "friend."

When I returned to my apartment after the trip to Yaremche, I was glad to see my laundry was returned during my absence. Earlier in my stay, I wondered how I could get my laundry done in Ivano Frankivsk, and asked Sasha. He found that Valentina would be happy to take care of it for me. She seemed to run the apartment complex, and was the woman who warned me about using the water when I first arrived.

During the week, I would collect my soiled clothes in a pillowcase and, when it was full, place the bag in the middle of the room. When Valentina came to clean the apartment she would remove it, and several days later return the clothes nicely folded or pressed.

Sometimes, things that seem to be a good idea when you first think of them become questionable when you put the thought into action. When Elsie and I had traveled in Russia and Eastern Europe, we found one of the things that Soviet woman really coveted were pantyhose. They were almost as valuable to them as Levi jeans. As a result, we would carry packages of them with us for gifts and special tips. Before I left for Ukraine, Elsie bought a dozen packages for me to carry.

The first time I paid Valentina for my laundry, I doubled what she asked, and reached into my desk drawer to get a package of pantyhose as a gift for her. As I withdrew my hand it suddenly occurred to me that what was suitable for my wife was not necessarily appropriate for a man to offer to a middle aged woman in his apartment. I hesitated handing the package to her and blushed with embarrassment. My chagrin was short lived as Valentina quickly grasped the package from my partially outstretched and sweaty hand.

Afterwards, I had no trouble getting laundry done. I did have some difficulty, however, limiting it to a once a week. Unless I hid my soiled clothes, Valentina would take them after just a few days, and I worried I would not have enough packages for the remainder of my stay.

I would have also liked to have given Tanya several pairs of pantyhose, and I am sure she would have appreciated them. I was too cowardly, however, to repeat the embarrassment I initially experienced by my gift to Valentina.

The next week I concentrated on an analysis of Karpaty's commercial product line. When I suggested at the meeting with the Directors it might be helpful if I reviewed the potential marketability of their individual product offerings the offer was met with resounding apathy. I intended to do it anyway.

Their product development programs seemed to be based on the "if we build it they will come" theory instead of first trying to determine what the market needed, then attempting to figure out how the need could be filled. Consequently, their product line lacked cohesiveness and continuity, and they were spending as much time on unmarketable products as they were on those with greater sales potential.

In addition, the information I needed for the preparation of a document that would help them attract foreign investment was alarmingly slow in arriving from the operating departments. Until this data began to arrive, the analysis of Karpaty's product line gave me something productive to do while I waited.

Fortunately, I had brought a stack of advertisements for comparable American consumer products to use as illustrations. They would show, for example, that the appearance of international audio products had changed from the traditional wood veneer and square corners to the more high-tech look of black and silver with rounded contours. I believed it would be easier to make that point through visual examples of contemporary products.

I cut out the product illustrations from the advertisements and began to scotch tape them to sheets that could later be replicated. I had brought several rolls of scotch tape with me, along with some magic markers that I used for underlining and numbering. I soon realized I had not developed any more talent for cutting and pasting than I displayed in grade school. After inadvertently taping my tie to the desk, I urgently called Tanya for help.

She had never seen transparent tape or magic markers, but immediately took charge. After working for awhile Tanya looked at me pensively and said, "You know Mr. Miller, I have a cousin that moved to the United States several years ago. She is married and would like me to come and live with her and take care of her children while she is away at work."

"Why don't you go Tanya?" I asked.

Tears welled up in her eyes and she told me with some hesitation, "I would really like to, but my boy friend tells me it would be demeaning to work for someone else taking care of their children. He believes I should not spend my life waiting on other people. He believes I am better off here, where I can maintain my pride. What do you think Mr. Miller?"

"I don't think there is much pride in not getting paid. Moving somewhere else, particularly to another country, is difficult, but it should be easier if you have a relative to help. The idea of it being demeaning to serve others is communist dogma. I think it would be great if taking care of someone's children can help you get started. You don't have to do it forever. People who came to the country from somewhere else built the United States. They learned to speak the language, found a job, and moved up as they acquired more experience. You already know the language so you are a step ahead of them."

Tanya was an intelligent woman and a good worker, and I am sure she would be successful wherever she went. It is difficult, however, to accept change when you have lived in a society where all decisions have been made for you. It is even more difficult when someone close to you is very much opposed to it.

After we finished the cutting and pasting process I had to have the English words translated into Russian, then pasted into the text, and finally copies made for distribution. In order to get the necessary copies I then had to get on the schedule of the group that operated the massive blueprint copying equipment.

Not only did everything connected with work require an extraordinarily long time to complete, but also all facets of day to day life in Ukraine were equally complex and tedious. It is generally very difficult for a normally efficient American to adjust to a culture where everything takes three times more time to complete than it should, and frustration becomes a way of life.

The Ukrainians, on the other hand, seemed to accept every problem with a good deal of stoicism, while they docilely waited in long lines for most of the things they needed. Their reluctance to complain was sometimes surprising. The water in our apartment building was shut off for several days while the pipes were repaired. During this time, Valentina would bring in buckets of water I could use to bathe and flush the toilet. While it was a minor inconvenience for me, it was a considerable problem for families living on the upper floors.

After five days, I mentioned to Sasha that I was surprised the problem with the water had not been taken care of by now. He told the head of department at Karpaty who was in charge of building maintenance, and the problem was fixed the next day. Later Sasha told me the director had not known the water was shut off since no one had mentioned it.

On another occasion, I wanted to exchange some additional dollars into Ukrainian currency. I had been exchanging money at the Ukraine Hotel where the rate was 3,000 coupons (cps) to $1. When I mentioned this to Sasha, he advised that I should go to the National Bank of Ukraine where I could get 3,700 cps for a $1. The Bank's hours were 9:30-12:30, a working day that would make even American bankers envious. I planned to be there when they opened and back in my office by at least 10:30.

I had become an experienced trolley rider, and jumped on Trolley #4 at the stop by the plant for my trip into town. Ivano Frankivsk operated their streetcars by the standard Soviet honor system. There are no conductors to collect or punch tickets.

A ticket cost 50 cps or approximately a penny. The riders would purchase their tickets from a seller at their stop (if he was there), board the bus, and then punch their tickets at a small mechanical device at the front and back of the bus. Inserting the small ticket into the even smaller opening of the machine in a crowded bouncing bus is not a simple task.

Once the passenger successfully inserts their ticket, the handle is pulled, and a pattern is impressed on the ticket representing the particular vehicle the passenger is riding. All of this is done out of the view of the driver, or anyone other than your fellow riders. Inspectors supposedly will occasionally appear to check passenger's tickets to make sure they have paid, but I never saw one in two months of trolley riding.

The majority of the people avoid the process, and ride without going through the trouble of paying. While this majority is understandable, I often speculated on the admirable character of those who paid without having to. I thought it must take an exceptionally high level of integrity, or adherence to regulations, to pay your way when most people do not.

Since no one in Ukraine can any longer afford cars, the public transportation system provides the only means of getting around in the city. Passengers board with children in carriages, dogs on a leash, baby chickens in cardboard boxes, or anything else that might require cheap transportation from one location to another.

I purchased a ticket before squeezing aboard the jammed vehicle. The local people, with their cramped living quarters, lack ready access to adequate bathing facilities. On that hot July morning, the atmosphere aboard the bus was even more pungent than usual.

The trolley was filled with a large group of jostling school children, their frayed books securely held together with faded leather straps. The carefree young people were being critically scrutinized by the usual assortment of elderly countrywomen whose gnarled hands clung protectively to the precious produce they were carrying to market. A few tardy office workers were also scattered throughout the bus. Each clutching their worn plastic briefcases, furtively glancing at their watches, and futilely attempting to hold their breath as they rode.

Gradually making my way from the back to the front of the bus my attention was diverted to a tall young woman sitting near the exit door. Her exceptionally short skirt displayed a shocking expanse of slender thighs. Continuing through the tightly packed crowd I—*wait, wait, what is she doing? No, oh no she can't be. She is. Good Lord, she is getting up to give me her seat. What would James Bond do in this situation*? I never decided. I could only try to hide my embarrassment by offering a feeble smile and an artificial thank you, while taking her place.

I always preferred to picture myself as a somewhat portly, but aging Sean Connery. The young woman's courtesy destroyed that treasured illusion. How ironic? Many people at Karpaty thought I was a secret agent. Now, this kind girl saw me as a doddering old man. If only the situation could have been reversed.

Gathering the tattered remnants of my shattered pride, I quickly exited the bus at the town's giant rynok. This time of year the large open-air market was filled with village women who had come to sell their fruit and vegetables. They offered an abundant supply of raspberries, blueberries, gooseberries, turnips, gigantic cabbages, tomatoes and that staple of all Ukrainian diets, cucumbers. The conflicting colors of produce made a crazy mixed market salad, monitored closely by the ladies strategically positioned behind their baskets and scales. Carefully weighing and measuring each purchase, the women exhibited the latest fashion in headscarves and sweaters. Many of the older vendors continually shifted their cotton swathed legs to ease the discomfort of varicose veins.

There were also heavyset men in soiled white coats behind dripping counters stacked with recently butchered sections of pork and beef. There was no refrigeration in sight, and the fortunate flies were making a feast of the bloody scraps of meat.

Sasha had told me that in the past there were shortages of all kinds of food in Ukraine. Now, he had said, food is plentiful but there is no money to buy it. This did not seem a problem that sunny summer morning in the busy rynok. I was curious, however, what the market would look like in the winter when the fresh vegetables and fruit were no longer available.

Walking through town, it suddenly occurred to me that I might be followed. This was the first time I had been in Ivano Frankivsk since the incident at the cultural center. Since then, I had been unable to entirely shake the fear I experienced when I was confronted by the three thugs.

Occasionally I would pause, and attempt to casually peer in an unwashed store window to see if I could recognize anyone from the factory, or an ominously recurring face. Staring intently at the soiled glass, the only familiar countenance I saw was that of an aging American volunteer.

A "wilderness of mirrors" is a phrase used to describe a state of extreme paranoia experienced by people who no longer are able to distinguish reality from unreality. Laughing at my own reflection, I decided to refrain from dwelling on the problems associated with my assignment, and give up these amateurish attempts at identifying illusory threats.

The route to the bank passed an imposing church with a blue façade trimmed in brilliant white. A large golden Madonna, with arms outstretched toward a cloudless azure sky, nestled between its tall spires.

The place of worship had only recently been reopened. Earlier, the communist regime had turned the ancient church into a Museum of Atheism, in order to taunt the religious Ukrainians. I often wondered what they displayed in such a exhibition. Perhaps a large expanse of nothingness.

Continuing toward the bank, the street was lined with vendors selling their wares from the tops of wobbly peach crates. Each sidewalk salesman's goods were almost indistinguishable from those of his neighbors, and included candy bars, chewing gum, shoe laces, cheap little plastic toys from China, haphazardly arrayed beside numerous brands of European cigarettes. The number of customers this merchandise attracted was considerably less than number of entrepreneurs willing to spend their time, seated behind peach crates, selling identical low margin items.

At last the National Bank of Ukraine appeared. My timing was perfect. A uniformed guard was straining to open the heavy ornate doors. I demonstrated my mission by holding a Yankee dollar and a Ukrainian 100 coupon note. Standing aside, the guard pointed to the stairs.

Reaching the top of the worn marble steps, I noticed a young man seated behind a dilapidated old desk. His frail form was handsomely bookended by two blond woman seated at each side. Their sole responsibility apparently was to watch me, which they performed with considerable concentration.

Attempting to explain the purpose of my visit, I was informed the current exchange rate was 3600 cps to the $1.00. I demonstrated my acceptance by signing his extended form, and was ushered hurriedly to another office by one his two assistants.

A dozen women were seated behind old wooden desks, each with their own PA (personal abacus). Two of the younger women appeared to be dozing with their heads resting sedately on folded arms.

As I approached the counter, an unsmiling older woman rose to greet me, carrying with her a large stack of yellowed forms. Her demeanor displayed a Russian-bred bureaucratic disdain for an irrelevant public. Adding my request to the stack, she frenetically stamped each with the uninhibited enthusiasm of a displaced customs agent. Only an occasional movement of the worn black beads on her ancient calculating device interrupted her furious activity.

I looked more closely at the office as I waited for her to finish whatever it was she was so intent on completing. The paint was peeling from the wall, and there were large holes in the plaster. On the window side, there were half a dozen unoccupied desks covered with thick layers of dust, each holding a dormant electronic computer. Since there were no chairs at any of the desks either the equipment was not working, or no one in the office knew how they operated.

There was also a six-inch trough roughly gouged in border-like fashion completely around the concrete wall. All of the bare wiring was exposed, as well as the bricks behind them. I could only speculate that the electrical system was so antiquated, and so frequently in need of repair it was easier to leave it exposed than to constantly replaster.

Behind me, were six large vaults or safes, each about five feet high with thick metal doors that required a key to open. The era of the combination lock was yet to come to Ukraine.

After I finally completed my forms, I was ushered to still another office. This one had a smoked glass enclosure protecting employees from the view of the customers. As I approached the counter, a hand reached through a sliding glass panel, grasped my forms, and disappeared. Leaving the counter I noticed a calendar hanging on a nearby wall. It was three years old.

I sat on a bench along with three other people who were there when I came in. "Out of money" one of them said, holding up a $100 bill. Since he was waiting, I assumed this was a temporary condition.

After waiting for fifteen minutes, the Ukrainian version of Brinks appeared in the form of a middle-aged woman with a plastic shopping bag. The bag was common to everyone in Ukraine. None of the stores wrap their articles, or provide sacks for their customers, so shoppers are required to carry their own bag to the store. Mine lay neatly folded in my briefcase.

The courier knocked on the glass window as three large stacks of bills were taken from the bag and given to the hidden hand that once again appeared, and then quickly disappeared, through the small window. No receipt was given to the woman who had brought the money, and who was now disappearing down the dark stairwell of the National Bank of Ukraine.

I could see people through the clouded glass partition as they huddled around a desk counting and recounting the money they had just received. Thirty minutes later. I was finally able to exchange $50 into Ukrainian currency.

I returned to the plant in time for lunch. My planned quick trip had taken an entire morning.

The next Saturday, I decided to see if Sasha was correct when he said I would be unable to get into my office on the weekend. I had held meetings with some of the engineering people during the week and wanted to write up my notes while the information was still fresh in my mind. I had long ago given up depending, for very long, on my flagging memory.

I felt very continental preparing my breakfast of juice, sliced sausage, cheese, bread, and tea. I also tuned in my short wave to the Voice of America, which every Saturday morning had a program of big band music. As I sat in the kitchen of my Ukrainian apartment, with my Japanese radio, preparing to go to work in a former Russian defense factory, I listened nostalgically to the familiar strains of *Opus One*, *Song of India,* and *Take the A Train,* while thinking about days and nights gone by.

In particular I recalled the dances at the Surf Ballroom in Clear Lake, Iowa where the big bands infrequently played when I was in high school. Generations later, the Surf became famous for *the place where the music died*, when rock and roll icon Buddy Holly's airplane nose-dived into a nearby cornfield, on a frigid winter's night, after playing to a crowded ballroom. For my generation, however, it was a place to listen to the orchestras of Benny Goodman, Tommy Dorsey, Woody Herman, and Glenn Miller when they stopped on their way to bigger ballrooms in larger cities.

Listening to the VOA that morning also brought back distant recollections of USO parties on sunny, San Diego, Sunday afternoons at the Hotel Del Coronado. The local young ladies were kind enough to entertain lonesome sailors on liberty, while matronly chaperons looked on, and a small band played the latest musical hits of the 1940's.

Finishing breakfast, I wondered if every generation had their musical tastes frozen in the nostalgic melodies of their youth. I was definitely part of the generation that recognized *In the Mood* as a musical standard rather than an amorous attitude.

Perhaps others acquired musical preferences that became more sophisticated with maturity, but I am certain almost every one of my contemporaries could still identify a 40's tune by hearing only the first few notes. These old melodies are always there, running through the mind, and cascading through the veins, sometimes unnamed but never forgotten. Such memories are the food that nourish older men, and mine were being rekindled in the troubled transitionary times of Ukraine.

As *Yankee Doodle* signaled the Voice was signing off for another Saturday morning, I put the dishes in the sink until I returned that evening. Saturday was my usual day for doing the week's dishes so I stacked today's plates along with the others, and rinsed out my juice glass. I believe my wife used a different approach to her dishwashing duties, but she probably was not as familiar with the benefits of "batching theory" as I was.

As I suspected, the door to the plant was unlocked and there was a guard stationed in the lobby. I showed my pass, and pointed upstairs, but he signaled me to stop. Picking up the phone he called someone somewhere, then waved me past. I don't recall ever seeing this particular guard but it was obvious he knew who I was. This didn't surprise me. I believed by now everyone at Karpaty could quickly pick the American out of a crowd.

Leaving the elevator, I immediately noticed all of the hall lights were out and the empty corridors were even more dark than usual. As I passed the General Director's dimly lit outer office, I saw the Night Director sitting at Kapitolena's desk. He gave me a casual salute of recognition, and I was sure it was he who had told the lobby guard to let me in.

The Night Director was a waspish little man with a large balding head. I never knew what his responsibilities were, but I had seen him come to work at the end of the day as other people in the office were leaving. As far as I could tell, his sole function was to monitor the red telephone connected to the General Director's office in case the Kremlin should once again decide to call.

Sharing the Night Director's gloomy surroundings was his assistant Mr. Kim, who sat beside him now. Mr. Kim was a Korean who was even more diminutive in stature than the Night Director. The two seemed inseparable, and I wondered what trick of fate had brought this Asian gentleman to such an unlikely destination.

In many large corporations, there are "shadow people" like the Night Director whose role defies a logical explanation. In some cases, because of personal relationships or quirks in the organization structure, their power far exceeds their defined position, and I had the feeling this might be the case with the Night Director and his aide. Whatever they did, it was important enough for them to remain immune from the extensive layoffs that had just taken place.

When I finished my work that Saturday morning the seemingly unlikely pair was still sitting at their post in almost an identical position as when I entered. The only change of scene was a noticeable increase in the level of cigarette smoke hanging over Kapitolena's desk. I smiled and waved to them on my way out, and they waved in return, as they waited patiently for the red telephone to ring and rescue Karpaty from its current dilemma.

Chapter 10

St. John's Day

When the telephone calls began, I was completing the analysis of Karpaty's product line. Sasha and I would go to lunch together at the same time each day. Afterwards, he would go back to his office and I returned to mine. The phone was ringing as I sat down at my desk. Picking it up I heard a woman's voice say "ullo goot mornig." In the past, I had occasionally received calls on my line, but after I spoke to them in English, there would be a long pause and then I would hear the caller hang up. This time, there was the familiar pause, and then the caller began to talk in Russian, and kept talking-and talking-and talking.

I had no idea what she was saying, but she had a rather seductive voice and I enjoyed listening to her. During a rare pause, I would talk about a movie or a book I had read, but only for a few sentences, then my caller would resume her conversation. Finally, I would hear "goot by", as she hung up.

She called again the next day at approximately the same time, and the conversation followed the same one-sided pattern as before. The calls continued almost every other day for three weeks. They would last for approximately fifteen minutes before I would hear "goot by." I sometimes had the impression there were other people with her, but I really had no tangible reason to believe that.

I told Tanya about my mystery caller, and asked if she knew who she might be. Tanya was as perplexed as I was, but offered to come into my office the next day to listen. Of course, there were no calls when she was there.

After three weeks, the calls stopped as suddenly as they had begun, and I never learned what the caller's purpose was or who she might be. It wasn't as if my phone friend was practicing her English; her entire vocabulary consisted of only three words. She was neither lecturing, nor scolding, and would frequently giggle as she spoke. Her calls remained a mystery, but I guess if they were not erotic, I hoped they might have at least been slightly salacious.

I had finished the analysis of Karpaty's commercial product line, and the copies were ready for distribution. Their major commercial products were a series of loudspeakers, which were technically sound and, unlike many Ukrainian produced products, very well made. Their wood cabinets looked as if they could withstand a frontal attack by a Sherman Tank, but all of the corners fit together, and the wood finish was polished and unmarred.

The speaker's audio output was excellent, but the line was too heavily weighted toward the high-end, or the more expensive segment of the market. Because of the difficult economic conditions in the country, high priced speakers had a very limited market, and I recommended additional less expensive models be added to increase sales and expand production volume.

Karpaty also produced other audio equipment consisting of portable "boom boxes," and an audio tape player that was a replica of the Walkman Sony had introduced twenty years earlier. Their product design was antiquated, but the products were well made and provided the company with goods that could be sold within Ukraine and bartered to their Central Asian markets. I recommended they begin to update their line, either by internal development or by obtaining technology transfers from other foreign audio manufacturers. I had been involved with product licensing at Zenith and was able to provide them advice about finding an outside source of technical support.

I tried to make a cohesive grouping of their other products, but it was impossible. The company had begun to make any thing they could with the tooling they already had. This included such diverse products as feed grinders, wood working equipment, electric vibrating devices, meters for taxis, luggage racks for cars, door chimes, baggage carts, hack saws, power supplies, and a remote control for television they were hoping to sell to a European set manufacturer.

I also recommended they eliminate any product that was not selling at least 100 units a year, and concentrate on those that were. In addition, each offering had a group in engineering with a vested interest in the product, and their livelihood was dependent on maintaining the product in the line. Since they had more people than they needed, it wasn't a problem to make so many products, but it did increase their operating costs, and weaken their marketing effort.

I put a copy of the completed analysis, along with a copy of the work plan I had previously presented to General Director Kuvika, in an envelope for the IESC office in Kiev. Kapitolena, Director Kuvika's secretary took it immediately to the company's mailroom. I found later, the reports never made it to the office in Kiev. Nor did any of the other dutifully mailed reports, but I was inclined to attribute this failure to ineffective mail service rather than some other more sinister cause.

My most important project at Karpaty was to prepare a document describing the advantages the company could offer to a foreign investor. This project was dependent on input from the individual departments, and most of them seemed either unwilling, or unable to provide the type of information I needed.

I was becoming increasingly concerned that if I didn't begin to get the necessary information very soon I would not be able to complete the project before I left Ukraine, and my trip would be a failure. It was too early to panic, but considerable apprehension seemed very appropriate.

To see if I could speed things along, I prepared a status report itemizing the information I had already received, compared with information I still required from the individual departments. I reviewed the report with the general director who agreed to talk to the individual vice directors. During the meeting, I used both Valerie and Sasha for my interpreters. Since Valerie had been able to negotiate a raise on his translating abilities, I wanted him to be able to demonstrate he was earning his pay.

Afterwards back in my office, I expressed my surprise the general director was unable to demand more immediate cooperation from his subordinates.

"Have you ever wondered why there is leather padding on the wall between your offices?" Valerie asked.

I had asked Sasha about the padding before, but he had been unable to provide an explanation. "Yes Valerie I have often wondered that. You tell me why it is it so heavily padded?"

"It's for the same reason there are double doors on most of the executive offices. They are there so you can't hear the boss yelling at his subordinates."

Valerie must have been right. I had heard Kuvika bellowing and pounding his huge fists on the desk, even through the thick padding. I was startled at first, but I soon got used to it. Now I paid no attention when I heard the muffled pounding and the piercing shouts.

Listening to the violent anger seeping through the wall, I was often reminded of the television pictures I had seen of Nikita Khrushchev taking off his shoe and pounding on his desk during a speech at the United Nations. Many of the delegates were shocked at his vulgar outburst, but the communist leader acted as if his violent reaction was commonplace. Now I realized it undoubtedly was.

"Why does the general director have to yell so much at his managers?" I asked Valerie. "In forty years of working in American corporations, I don't believe I ever heard anyone yell at his subordinates as much as he does."

"It's the communist style. It is the only way he has of motivating his people" Valerie replied. He can't fire them, and they are not getting paid, so the only thing he can do is yell and threaten them.

"Come here Mr. Miller, look out your window" Valerie directed.

Rising from my desk, I did as he asked.

"See out there." Valerie said pointing to the people working with hoes and spades in their private garden plots given to them by Karpaty. As I peered at their distorted images through the cheap Russian glass, the scene was faintly reminiscent of the old pictures I used to see of peasant life under the czars. The only difference was that the men, instead of wearing baggy homespun trousers, now wore cheap cotton tracksuits. "That's where most of the managers spend their time now" Valerie continued. "They have decided growing vegetables is more productive than what they are doing at the factory.

"Sometimes they don't come into the office for several days. They can't figure out why you come to work every day, and sometimes on Saturday, when you not getting paid either. They think you are doing it to make them look bad."

In the evening I was in my apartment reading when Sasha burst in, "Mr. Miller come with Misha and me. We are going to see St. John's Day."

As we walked along a dirt path I asked, "What is St. John's day, Sasha?"

"Tuk?"

"What is the meaning of St. John to the Ukrainian People?"

I was astonished there would be a religious celebration because religion had been forcefully suppressed under the communists.

Sasha's brow wrinkled as if he was trying hard to understand what I was asking. "John is a Christian name-a Polish name."

His answer surprised me. I knew he disliked the Polish people. One evening as we were walking home from work, Sasha had turned to me and asked if there were many Polish people in Chicago. Not knowing why he asked, I told him there were. "Almost as many in Chicago as there are in Warsaw" I replied.

"They are very stupid lazy people aren't they?" he asked. More as a statement than a question.

"No they are not" I heatedly answered. There were many Polish people working in my department before I retired, and they were some of the best workers I had."

After I had spoken, I regretted I had replied so angrily. Not that what I said wasn't true. I had always found the Polish to be extremely intelligent and hard working people, but Sasha was only repeating what he had been taught. The Soviets had demonized the ethnic-Polish community during the war, and they instilled an anti-Jewish and anti-Polish feeling in the Ukrainian consciousness as a means of promoting loyalty to Moscow.

Misha just grinned, and said nothing as he walked along beside us.

I should have let the subject of St. John's origin drop, but I was still curious. Sasha had told me how the communists had tried very hard to wipe out religion because they believed it was a threat to them. They viewed Christianity as a crime against the state, and the practice of any type of religion was prohibited. According to Sasha, the Christians in the area were forced underground and they would meet secretly at night or in the surrounding woods to hold their religious services. Yet, here we were apparently going to a Christian celebration that seemed to have endured during the anti-religious period.

I continued my questioning of Sasha. "But why do the Ukrainian people celebrate St. John's day?"

He thought for a minute, as he often did before answering. "The Orthodox calendar is two weeks later than the Christian calendar. That is why it is celebrated today and not two weeks ago."

It was an interesting answer, but not to the question I had asked, so I gave up.

More and more people seemed to be joining us as we walked along the path. By the time we reached the park, a large crowd had already gathered. In their center were a group of children and two teachers who were busily forming their wards into two large circles rotating in opposite directions. Two boys were holding a scrubby green tree brightly decorated with white and red ribbons while the children rotated around them.

The boys were dressed in regular street clothes, but many of the girls wore traditional Ukrainian costumes with brightly embroidered white blouses and colorfully flowered skirts. Some of the older girls wore flowing white gowns with a garland of flowers, shaped like a crown, on their heads.

One of the teachers energetically played a concertina, while the other just as vigorously rattled an ancient tambourine. As they played their instruments, the children sang Ukrainian folk songs.

St. John had smiled favorably on the celebration. It was a clear and mild evening, in pleasant contrast to the preceding few days that had been unseasonably wet and cold. Unfortunately, the soft rain-soaked ground was leaving muddy stains on the young girl's long white gowns, but neither they nor their parents seemed concerned.

Later in the evening, the children played a game with two dolls made of sticks and socks, much like many of the dolls they had probably played with growing up. As the music played, the dolls were passed from one laughing child to another. Whenever the music stopped, the two children left holding the dolls were required to enter the middle of the circle and dance together. For many of the dancers, being the center of attention for such a large audience, was a source of considerable embarrassment. In spite of their obvious self-consciousness, the dancers reluctantly and blushingly performed their dance, to the great amusement of the rest of the children, and their beaming parents.

While the happy children danced and sang, their parent's taller profiles were silhouetted in the late light of the summer's night. Each focused their singular attention on their individual offspring. The same men and woman I had seen at the factory looking sullen and depressed now watched the youthful festivities with pleasure and parental pride, taking temporary respite in the carefree pleasures of their children.

As the sun began to set, the ceremony ended with a procession to a small bridge spanning a nearby stream running through the park. At a given signal the older girls removed their crown of flowers and dropped them into the slowly moving water below. They stood for a moment watching their small bouquets float away before the parents collected their reluctant offspring for the walk back to their cramped quarters in their dreary factory housing.

It had been a pleasant evening. The ceremony, with its happy innocent children, had provided an attractive scene and I was pleased Sasha and Misha had asked me to join them.

On our way back, Misha's teen-age daughter left her group of friends and joined us. As we neared our unit Misha asked if we would like to visit their apartment in a nearby building.

The four of us barely fit into the small elevator as we made our jerking and jolting way to the 5th floor. The smelly hallway was dark and badly in need of painting, but Misha's cramped apartment was meticulously clean.

He was obviously proud of his unit, which was decorated in typical Ukrainian style. The walls were pale yellow and the furnishings were bright orange. There was a large set of wood cabinets entirely covering one wall serving as a China cabinet, bookcase, and liquor cabinet. The apartment also contained a large sofa, where he slept, while his daughter occupied a tiny bedroom off the main room. Shortly after we arrived, the young lady told us good night and went to her room.

As he served us coffee and brandy, Misha began to talk about his life. Before coming to Karpaty, Misha had worked on Russian ships in the Black Sea that operated highly sensitive secret listening equipment. He sailed out of Sevastopol and traveled to Dubai, Lebanon, and Somalia. Through Sasha, Misha told how the crew was seldom permitted to go ashore. When they were allowed to visit a foreign port it was only in parties of five, and always accompanied by one of the ship's political officers.

He was very proud of his postcard collection and brought it out for us to admire as he told us about his life at sea. As we listened, I was surprised to see a woman about Misha's age enter the apartment. She had a darker complexion than most Ukrainians, and I thought she might be from the Mediterranean region.

She was apparently in familiar surroundings as she went to the small kitchenette and knew immediately where to find a cup for her coffee. Misha paused briefly as she returned, then continued his story without paying any attention to his new listener.

When he finished his travelogue, Misha began telling how the communists sent his family to Siberia when he was just a child. Because of his early experiences, he lived in fear he would someday be sent back and resented the way the communists had controlled every aspect of Ukrainian life.

Misha had once owned a music video called *I Love Chopin,* which was about the composer's life and featured his music. One evening he made the mistake of showing it to a friend. Later, the friend mentioned the video to someone at the local newspaper, and shortly afterward there was an editorial denouncing Misha and his bourgeois tastes and western tendencies.

The day after the editorial appeared, two men from the KGB pounded on his door. They took a frightened and shaking Misha to their offices where he was detained for two days, and interrogated for hours on end. The KGB finally confiscated the Chopin tape and then let him return to his home. This was the last time Misha listened to any of the Polish composer's music.

While he talked, Misha turned on his favorite television program, *Wild Kingdom.* As the lions devoured their prey, he resumed his favorite topic of conversation. "How much is a 25" television set in the United States? How much are stereo receivers in the stores? How much is a bottle of brandy? How much is a bottle of beer?" I had learned by now it was impossible to answer "I don't know," because he would continue to press until there was an acceptable answer. Now, if I didn't know the price of an item I pretended I did.

When we were leaving, Misha put his arms around the shoulders of the young lady and said in English "my love." It was the first time he had paid any attention to her. After he spoke, Misha gave his lady friend a possessive slap on her rather ample behind. She grinned at him affectionately, and with her dancing dark eyes gave me a conspiratorial wink.

Misha later told me his friend's name was "Aaliyah" which he said proudly "is Arabic for something high, although," he added, "she is really Jewish."

I had enjoyed the children's celebration, and our visit with Misha, but I was tired. I imagined Sasha was more weary than I was after his long day of interpreting. The area between the housing blocks was very dark, but as we neared our building, I could make out the unmistakable silhouette of Medvid "the bear" Tichonovick outlined by the pale yellow light above the apartment house doorway. He was with two friends who had apparently joined him toasting the health of St. John. They were all three "over-wodkaed", as they say in Ukraine, but Medvid was in slightly better shape than his companions. The other two soon tired of our conversation and staggered off into the night, leaving us alone with Medvid.

The Bear was almost as fascinated with things in the United States as Misha. While Misha liked prices, the Bear favored percentages. He asked in rapid succession, "what percentage of people own their own home? What percentage of their income do they spend on food? What percentage of their income do they spend on healthcare? What percentage of Americans are unemployed?" I provided as many percentage responses as he asked questions. If I didn't know the correct answer, I provided one anyway, since I no longer had any fear of contradiction.

Attempting to end my economic interrogation, I shook hands with Medvid, said good night, and headed down the dark corridor to my apartment. Turning the key in the lock, I heard footsteps echoing through the empty hallway. Cursing, I turned and saw Medvid appearing out of the shadows, with Sasha trailing reluctantly behind. The old party-boss apparently wanted to see how the foreign capitalist lived. I was sure his curiosity was not generated by concern for my well being, but to serve as a comparison with his own facilities.

He surveyed my rooms without comment. I was afraid to ask him to sit down for fear I would have "Medvid the night visitor" as an unwanted guest until the next morning. After satisfying himself with my surroundings, the questioning resumed. This time they concerned his son's career. The boy was presently attending Moscow University majoring in higher mathematics.

Medvid asked what percentages of Harvard Business School graduates got jobs, and how much they made. I replied by telling him they all got jobs at very high salaries; but there were many other very good business schools in the United States in addition to Harvard.

He then began asking questions about the job opportunities for mathematicians. I responded that in my opinion the opportunities for them were not as good as they were for business majors. I added math majors usually taught school or were employed in the defense industry where their future was less secure, and the salaries tended to top out at lower levels faster than most business majors. As we talked, Medvid peered at me intently through bloodshot eyes, struggling to absorb everything I said.

I was impressed he even knew about Harvard, and guessed he might be the only one in Ivano Frankivsk that did. I had to give him credit, the wily old devil was already figuring out ways his son could beat the new system. Medvid had told me when I first met him he was a survivor, and he was obviously planning to transfer this characteristic to his son. I could easily imagine the father telling the boy to "throw away your slide rule sonny and buy a pair of wing tips, your now on the verge of a major career change."

When you are sober, a conversation with someone who has had too much to drink can be amusing at first, but then rapidly becomes tedious. This conversation had long passed that point. Sasha looked exhausted and his translations became more labored. I was trying desperately to figure out some way of gracefully getting Medvid out of my apartment when there was a loud knock on the door.

Standing in the hallway were two more of Medvid's friends, "from his former life" he explained laughing. One of the men was very young, the other middle aged. The older of the two resembled Phil Silvers in the Sergeant Bilko series, and kept pointing to himself with great pride saying "Georgia, Georgia." I was reasonably sure he was referring to the Russian Georgia, and I responded by pointing to myself saying "Chicago, Chicago." Everyone found this charade immensely amusing and we repeated our parts several times.

Finally, Medvid decided to join the new arrivals on their way to the next party. As he left, he assured me he could drink all night and still be alert on the job the next day. As I gratefully closed my door, I could see the aging party boss and his cadre, swaying arm in arm, as they silently dissolved into the shadowy corridor.

The next day I asked Tanya if she knew why the Ukrainians celebrated St. John's Day. She had never thought about it, but offered to see if she could find something in the library about its origin.

Two days later she came into the office. "You are going to be surprised by this," she said as she began to recite what she had discovered in a Ukrainian Encyclopedia. She told her story with a halting cadence, and there were frequent pauses while we both attempted to clarify the meaning of many of her words.

She had discovered the celebration of St. John's Day is a combination of pagan and Christian rituals. It began as a Slavic celebration marking the end of the summer solstice and the beginning of the harvest season. It was originally referred to as the Kupalo festival because Kupalo was believed to be the god of love and the harvest, as well as the personification of the earth's fertility. It was thought then that 'Kupalo eve' was the only time of the year when the earth revealed its secrets; and it was the only time when free love was generally accepted.

On the morning of the big day, girls washed themselves with dew that had fallen during the night and which they carefully collected in a bowl left outside their cottage. Afterwards, they ran barefoot through the woods in the belief it would improve their chances to marry.

In the evening, the young women wore scented herbs, and put garlands of flowers in their hair to attract the young men. They also believed they could determine their future by what happened to the garlands they later threw into the water. They hoped the boy downstream who picked them up would prove to be the right one for them to marry.

During Christian times, the church tried to suppress the pagan tradition by substituting the feast day of the Nativity of St. John the Baptist; but most of the rituals of the Kupalo festival remained. After the war, the Soviets tried to turn the celebration into a politicized version of the familiar rituals. In Ukraine, it was designated as the "Day of Soviet Youth" and they attempted unsuccessfully to propagandize it into a communist holiday.

When Tanya finished her story she smiled with pride at what she had been able to find, and was amused at the similarities and contradictions between the festivities I had described and their exotic origin. I agreed with her. It was surprising to me that an apparent simple children's celebration had such a complex history. The conflicting mixture of paganism, atheism, religion, and communism was enough to confuse anyone-even poor old St. John.

After Tanya returned to the library, I looked out my window at the Karpaty employees working in their small vegetable gardens. Watching them work, I wondered if the contrasting philosophies that shaped their folk rituals might still have a profound influence on the contemporary lives of the people I had been with the night before. It began to rain, and I turned away and resumed my work.

Chapter 11

Organization Men

The weather had turned cool again, walking to work that morning I was glad I thought to wear a sweater underneath my jacket. The Voice of America was reporting more floods in the Midwest, and it seemed Europe was experiencing a colder than usual summer as well.

As I passed the small Orthodox Church on my route, I recalled my attempt to attend services there when I first came to Ivano Frankivsk. It was an attractive little church, and with its small onion domes, looked like a cathedral in miniature.

When I attended, the church was packed, and since there were no benches the people stood during the service. I watched with interest as the congregation pinched the first two fingers of their right hand together and crossed themselves in the Eastern Orthodox style, rather than the more open-handed Roman Catholic manner with which I was accustomed. The liturgy of the mass was similar, and even the priest's vestments resembled those worn in my church. At home, I regularly attend Sunday mass, and I thought this would be a way the practice could be continued during my stay in Ukraine.

The service, however, was considerably longer than I expected. When I entered, the other attendees, recognizing I was a stranger, kindly made way for me to pass to the front. As the mass progressed, my back began to ache, and it grew increasingly more difficult for me to stand in the tightly packed crowd. It didn't seem to bother many others in the congregation, however, who looked much older than I.

After thirty minutes, I could tell the service was only beginning, and I knew I would never be able to make it to the end. With considerable embarrassment, I began to squeeze through the assembled staring worshipers to the crowded doorway. Outside, there were many people still standing in the churchyard unable to get into the tiny church. They looked at me with curiosity as I passed, and I smiled sheepishly at them in return.

I again attempted to attend the service the following week. This time, standing in the back, I was able to stay a little longer, but I still couldn't last through the entire mass. Afterwards, I decided my early departure was too much of a distraction to the rest of the worshipers, and gave up trying to attend the Orthodox service.

As I continued trudging up the hill to Karpaty, I could see the company's test vehicle parked in front of the plant. It was a large, camouflaged van with high-powered antennas slowly rotating on the roof. I occasionally had noticed it there before when it was being used for demonstration purposes.

There was a small crowd milling around the vehicle. Some of the men were in military uniform; others appeared to be Karpaty technicians, while still others were Mid-Eastern looking men who appeared to be very uncomfortable in their ill-fitting business suits. I assumed these were the visiting dignitaries.

Russia was no longer able to purchase the amalgamation's military production, but some limited manufacturing activity was continuing for the Ukrainian government. The occasional product demonstrations were for foreign delegations that might also have use for Karpaty's high-tech military products. The company was desperate to find new customers to replace their previous Russian partners, and was willing to do business with anyone that could help fill their vacant factories.

I was aware many of the company's workers continued to believe I was a foreign agent. I could see it in their eyes as I passed them in the hallway. There had been no overt animosity since the incident at the cultural center, but I was always careful not to do anything that would further antagonize them; and I took pains to avoid coming close to their van as I entered the administration building.

On previous occasions when foreign visitors came to Karpaty, lengthy meetings in the General Director's office had followed the product demonstrations. These usually became more raucous as the day wore on. As the noise level grew louder, fueled by ample amounts of vodka, it would eventually penetrate even my padded office wall. I wondered if today would be an exception.

I had begun to prepare a paper for the general director describing how Karpaty could begin marketing their products by supplementing the central government's organization in Kiev. There were several methods that could expand their existing marketing arrangement, and eventually replace it if Karpaty ever became privatized. I intended to describe the alternate approaches and then recommend the ones I believed would be the most appropriate for their market position and product line.

As I concentrated on my analysis, I heard Tanya's timid voice coming from my office doorway. "Mr. Miller?" Smiling, I motioned her to sit down. She took a chair next to my desk and nervously straightened her skirt as she began to describe the reason for her visit.

"Next to my library is the office of the head of the plant's trade union. He has heard about you, and what you are trying to do here, and would like to talk with you sometime."

I was not particularly pleased to hear of his interest in meeting me. None of the vice directors had ever indicated an interest in talking about how companies operated in the United States. It seemed odd the head of the union would now be interested.

The subject of labor organizations was also the one with which I had the least experience. I had never been a member of a trade union, and none of the work performed for the many companies I had been with had ever brought me into contact with the labor movement. Because of my already sensitive position at Karpaty, it was possible that it could become worse by getting caught between management and labor.

It did seem ironic, however, that the vice directors had little interest in what I might be able to tell them, but labor did. Also, I had the feeling the request for the meeting was a personal favor for Tanya. "Yes, sure I will meet with him," I reluctantly told her, "but he should be aware I know very little about labor issues; but tell him to drop by any time."

As our conversation continued, I could hear the familiar sounds of wrangling and haggling seeping through the thick leather-lined walls separating my office and the General Director's. Tanya smiled in embarrassment as we both pretended to not hear the intense commercial conflict occurring in the next room.

Several days later, having heard nothing from the union boss, I asked Tanya if he still wanted a meeting. I learned he was still interested, but he was afraid of the general director and wanted to first clear it through him.

I couldn't blame him for that. My impression of the general director was that he was one tough boss. He was not the type of man to lead by consensus. I constantly heard him pounding on his desk and shouting at his subordinates as he managed them by pure physical intimidation.

He was also what is generally described in business as a "hands on manager." There was a constant flow of people, from all management levels, going in and out of his office. Most mornings began with a noisy staff meeting; and I had the distinct impression no decision was made within the company without first getting his approval.

As tough as he was on his own people, Director Kuvika had always been fair with me. He seemed generally concerned about my well being, and was very conscious of Karpaty's obligation for my food and housing. He also had tried to cooperate with me on any request I made regarding information from his subordinates, even if he was less than enthusiastic about what I was trying to accomplish.

I recognized the Director was in a difficult position trying to manage a failing business whose market, through no fault of his own, had changed dramatically overnight. At the same time, he was responsible for the lives of thousands of people under his employ. Because of this, I didn't want to do anything that might cause him embarrassment, or make my own position more difficult.

I had almost forgotten about my conversations with Tanya, but several days later she called to tell me the union boss would like to meet me in his office that afternoon. When I heard this, I asked "has he cleared the meeting with Director Kuvika?" I already knew my answer by where the meeting was to be held. He would be coming to my office if the meeting had been cleared. There was a brief pause, and then I heard a faint "no" coming from the other end of the noisy interoffice line.

I quickly arranged to meet with the general director myself before the scheduled meeting. As Tanya translated for us, I told him of the Union chief's request, and asked if he had any objections or reservations about my talking with him. After listening to our explanation, he gave me the Ukrainian equivalent of "no problem."

The head of the company union must be treated very well in Ukrainian organizations; his office was as large as mine, and almost as large as the Director Kuvika's. Vladimir Ivanov was a young man, probably in his mid-thirties, with a small build that made him look even smaller as he sat behind his huge desk. He presented himself well, and had prepared for the meeting with a typed list of questions. He used this for a checklist as the meeting progressed.

His assistant sat beside him. He was never introduced, and remained silent during the entire meeting. I presumed his role was serving as a witness if any criticism of our meeting would later arise.

The first question was "what is the basic condition and principles of trade unionism in the United States?" If he was starting with the easy questions, it was going to be a difficult afternoon. I told him "I have no particular knowledge of how unions operate. My experience has all been in marketing and strategic planning."

On the other hand, I thought the union chief didn't know either. His method of operation became obsolete when the Communist Party lost its importance, and he was obviously searching for a new set of rules. I was the only person he had ever met from the "outside" with any perspective on union methods that might be different from those in the USSR.

I gave him credit for asking, and tried to answer his questions as best I could. It was slow going while I searched for answers, formulated a reply, and then had them translated by Tanya. Frequently we would get stuck on a term then have to go back and forth attempting to find an explanation that was understandable to everyone.

In reply to his question I told him "in the United States, after WWII, industry was responding to considerable pent-up consumer demand for products that were unavailable during the war. As industry expanded, unions became stronger and worker's wages and benefits increased. This resulted in expanded purchasing power, which created further increases in consumption. The result was a self-perpetuating upward cycle of demand economics. Later, as this began to level off, foreign manufacturers from lower wage-rate countries entered the American market.

"This increased level of competition put greater pressure on companies to reduce their manufacturing costs, including the cost of labor. While this was occurring, there was also a growing trend toward greater factory automation that negatively impacted the employment level.

"Eventually many companies were forced to move much of their production offshore to achieve lower labor costs and compete with foreign companies. The combination of these factors all reduced the effectiveness of the labor movement in the United States to the point that the percent of employed wage and salary workers who were members of labor unions was now considerably less than before."

Vladimir listened intently while his assistant took notes. I wasn't sure if my answer satisfied him, but he at least put a checkmark beside the question on his list.

He then wanted to know if the unions were able to stop layoffs. It was clear he was asking this because he had been unable to keep Karpaty management from beginning their recent workforce reductions. Vladimir had only recently replaced Bogdan Goodzak as head of the union, and apparently believed he had failed because he was too inexperienced to know how to combat future reductions at the factory. I told Vladimir, " with the current conditions in Ukraine there is very little you can do, other than trying to assure the layoffs are handled fairly. If the company doesn't reduce their number of employees, there is no way they can continue to operate."

If I had been entirely candid, I would have also told him I didn't know if Karpaty would be able to survive even if the company did reduce their operating costs. I had recently heard that Posner, one of the other big defense companies in Ivano Frankivsk had already shut down, and I was sure other companies would soon be forced to follow.

Vladimir made another check mark on his list, while his assistant shook his head.

The next question had to do with how unions operated in government-owned industries in the United States. He was shocked to learn outside of perhaps the US Post Office and a few companies such as the TVA, there were no government-owned businesses in America.

I could understand his surprise. It was still difficult for me to comprehend that the government controlled virtually every business in Ukraine, from the giant amalgamations to the smallest retail stores. I constantly had to remind myself that almost every business and shop in the country was part of a massive serpentine reporting structure leading to the central bureaucracy in Kiev.

Vladimir crossed another question off his list and then asked, "Do American companies pay the membership dues for union members?" This question was quickly followed by "does the government pay the salaries of union leaders as it does in Ukraine?"

"No to both questions", I answered. "Union members pay their own dues out of their salaries, and the union leaders draw their salaries from the members that elect them."

When I finished my answer, he then wanted to know about vacations. "How do the unions in the United States provide for workers vacations? In Ukraine the unions provide discounted and subsidized vacation packages to their workers."

"In the United States, workers pay for their own vacations," I replied.

After that, Vladimir's questions were of a more personal nature.

"Are you an atheist?"

"No, Roman Catholic."

'Are there many atheists in the United States?"

"Not many" I answered, "because of the size of the United States there are many of almost everything, but I believe the number of atheists is relative low."

"Do many of the atheists come from outside of the United States?"

"No" I replied. "I believe that most of them are homegrown. The majority of people entering America now are coming from the Latin American countries where Catholicism is very strong."

Then Vladimir asked, "are Protestants in the minority?"

Again, I told him "no". "The combined Protestant church membership represents a majority in the United States."

"Do many Ukrainians live in your country?"

"There are not as many Ukrainians in the United States as there are some other nationalities such as Italian, German, Polish, or Irish, but there are still a large number of them. In the Chicago area alone, there are over 80,000 living primarily in an area called *Little Ukraine*. They have their own newspapers, and even a Ukrainian language radio station."

"My cousin lives in Chicago" Vladimir replied. "His name is Boris Kutsin. Do you know him?"

I told him I did not, but that seemed to be a good place for us to end our meeting. As I left his large office, I felt sorry for the union boss. He was a sincere, intelligent young man who was interested in doing his job, but found himself in an almost impossible situation. The economic tide in Ukraine was flowing against unionism, as companies were concentrating on merely staying afloat. Vladimir appeared to be a captain who had lost his ship, and had been unable to salvage even his compass.

The meeting ran late, and the sky was growing dark as I picked up Sasha for our evening dinner at the disco. Misha seemed busier than usual, but came to our table to talk with Sasha while we ate. After a lengthy conversation between them, Sasha turned to me. "The disco has been rented by a student group that is finishing its education. They are having a party later tonight to celebrate, and Misha wants to know if you would like to attend?"

"Tell him no Sasha, but thanks for the invitation." It had been a long day, and I was not much of a party person. As I grew older, the idea of large social affairs was rapidly losing its appeal, particularly those where I was the only one unable to speak the language.

"They would like to have you attend, and he has already told them you would come," Sasha responded after conversing with Misha.

I reluctantly agreed. My plan was to arrive early, and find an inconspicuous table at the back of the disco so it would be easier to leave without being noticed.

Later that evening Sasha and I returned to the culture center. Reaching the second floor where the disco was located, I noticed the two old babushkas who regularly occupied two sofas in the hallway were in their usual position. Oblivious to our passing, they were both snoring loudly, stretched out on their individual sofas. I never learned what their job descriptions was, but whatever their responsibilities were I was very envious of them that evening.

We found our table in the rear of the darkened disco. It was set like all the rest. Each table had a bottle of Russian champagne, a bottle of vodka, Spanish brandy, Czechoslovakian beer, Moldavian wine, and Ukrainian mineral water. It was an impressive array of alcoholic internationalism.

The guests began to trickle in. They were a good-looking group of young people. Most of the men were dressed formerly in suit and tie, but a few wore sweaters and slacks. The young women all looked as if they had spent considerable time preparing for the occasion, particularly those accompanying a young man. Some of the ladies wore very short skirts; others preferred the very long.

For the most part, they looked like a group of American college students, pleased to be with one another, and looking forward to the party. They did seem to be a little more serious than I would expect for the occasion but, under the circumstances, they probably had a good deal to be serious about.

The Soviets placed considerable emphasis on education, particularly in the area of the hard sciences and mathematics. Literacy was almost universal in Ukraine, and education was compulsory between the ages of 7 and 16. There were several institutions of higher learning in Ivano Frankivsk producing a large number of graduates, and it seemed most of them were at the disco that night.

As the room began to fill, the disc jockey finished wiring his equipment to a set of very large loudspeakers, and the music began. The speakers worked perfectly as their blaring sounds filled the usually silent disco.

Over the din I heard, "are you the American?"

Before I could answer, a well-dressed, tall, young man sat down between Sasha and me. Leaning close to my ear, he introduced himself as the president of the local chapter of the Brotherhood of Students that was hosting the party. His hair was closely cropped and his English was almost flawless, but I thought I could detect a slight southern accent. He seemed eager to have the opportunity to practice with someone from the United States. From him I learned that the Brotherhood was part of a national organization formed to exert political pressure on the government for improved student benefits.

He described proudly how his chapter was beginning to get involved in local elections and had, he thought, been influential in determining the outcome of the recent voting in Ivano Frankivsk. Even with these successes, his organization had its problems. Their major difficulty was maintaining an acceptable level of membership. After the older students graduated, they lost interest in the Student Brotherhood. While new students would take their place, it was difficult to maintain continuity with an organization that was continually turning over.

When he finished telling me about himself, he asked what I was doing in Ivano Frankivsk. When I told him about the International Executive Service Corps and my assignment at Karpaty, he asked if I would speak to the students.

"What about" I asked?

"Just tell them who you are and where you are from."

"I really don't think they would be interested."

"I think they would be very interested" he replied, and left the table.

During my career, I often spoke to groups as part of my work. That was not the problem. Speaking to a group of students at their graduation celebration was another. I was sure that having some strange geezer stand up on their stage "for just a few words" was the last thing they were interested in doing at their party.

The disk jockey made some announcements in Russian and began the music. A few couples hesitatingly approached the dance floor. As soon as the floor began to fill the master of ceremonies broke in and the couples returned to their tables. After a few welcoming remarks, which Sasha translated for me, the music resumed and the couples again approached the dance floor.

The music stopped once more and a comedian wearing a devil mask came on stage. I had no idea why he wore such a grotesque mask, but as he droned on uninterrupted by laughter I could understand why he might wish to hide his identity. Ten minutes later the comedian left the stage to an unenthusiastic smattering of obligatory applause.

The music resumed. The couples sitting at their tables looked inquiringly at each other. A few of the bolder graduates eventually escorted their dates to the dance floor. The music played, the dancers whirled, and out of the corner of my eye I saw the President of the Student Brotherhood approach the stage.

Oh God not now, I thought, *at least let them dance a little while longer.* My plea went unanswered. I recognized my name inserted in a lengthy Russian introduction, as the president turned to welcome me to the stage. I could imagine how welcome I must be to a group of young party-going graduates.

Glass in hand, and attempting my best Frank Sinatra entrance, I casually sauntered to the stage and accepted the microphone while the remaining dancers resumed their seats. With the Student Brotherhood President functioning as my interpreter, I apologized for interrupting their dancing and promised to be brief. This was probably the best news the graduates had heard that night.

The room grew surprisingly quiet, as the students diverted their attention from their dates to the aging American in the center of the stage. I told them I had been sent to Ivano Frankivsk by the International Executive Service Corps as an advisor to the management of Karpaty. I briefly described the IESC as an organization of retired business managers who volunteered their services to companies in countries around the world.

One of the benefits of talking through an interpreter is it gives the speaker a chance to think about what he is saying while the translation is taking place. My interpreter that evening seemed to be doing a very good job as he substituted his Russian words for mine.

I continued by telling how I had grown up during a depression in a small agricultural community like many around this area. Before I retired I was involved with a job that gave me the opportunity to travel throughout the world, see exotic sites I had only read about, and meet interesting people with cultures vastly different from my own. I even was a member of an organization in America called The Travelers' Century Club, which was composed only of people who had visited over 100 countries. I concluded after a few more brief comments by telling them I hoped their career would be as satisfying to them as mine had been to me. With that I raised my glass in congratulations, returned the microphone to the disc jockey, and left the stage.

I was pleased that I received more applause than either the comedian or the master of ceremonies, but perhaps that wasn't too high a bar to leap. The President of the Student Brotherhood came to our table to thank me, and Misha brought a bottle of vodka I could take back to the apartment.

Sasha and I left shortly afterwards, but Misha told us later that when the dancing finally got started, without interruptions, it went on until two in the morning.

The next day I was telling Tanya about the party the night before. I mentioned that I was impressed with the English capability of the organization's President, and added that he spoke almost like an American citizen.

She looked at me with a wry smile. Arching her eyebrows, Tanya asked, "You know, don't you, that he was trained in *special schools* by the Russians? People like him received intensive training for several years in preparation for very special assignments overseas." With that she collected her papers and, wrinkling her nose, returned to the library, leaving me alone with my thoughts.

Saturday afternoon, I decided to go into town and have dinner in a restaurant, since the disco was closed for the weekend. I dutifully punched my ticket as I boarded the bus, and watched as we went over the bridge spanning the river flowing through Ivano Frankivsk. As usual, there were several fisherman casting their lines from the concrete bank, and a few children swimming in the river's polluted water.

I left the trolley at my usual stop by the central food market, noticing that it was particularly busy that sunny afternoon. Outside of the enclosed market the flower sellers, in their aprons and headscarves, lined the street displaying their daisies, roses, geraniums, and gladiolas for the few people that had enough money to spend for such luxuries.

The open-air fruit market was in the next block. Each stand displayed comparably-sized and similarly-shaped watermelons. I watched curiously as the customers moved from stand-to-stand lifting and thumping the displayed wares. I had no idea how their selection was eventually made, since each striped melon looked identical to the other.

Pausing in front of the Hotel Ukraina, I watched a stream of gaily-decorated automobiles pull to a stop. Saturday was the day for marriages in Ivano Frankivsk. The routine was similar all over the former Soviet states. The nuptials would take place, one ceremony immediately following another, at a designated municipal building. Following the wedding, the bride and groom would leave for a city park. As the wedding party watched and took pictures, the bride would reverently place her bouquet on the local memorial commemorating fallen military heroes that was a standard fixture in all major Soviet parks. The group would then depart for the location where the post-nuptial celebration was to take place. A new bride with her fresh bouquet almost immediately followed the previous flower-laying ritual.

In Ivano Frankivsk, the wedding receptions were most often held at the Hotel Ukraina, which was constructed in the sterile, rectangular style favored by the Soviet leaders during the early 1970's. Its austere architecture was partially relieved by a working fountain placed by the hotel's front entrance. Here, waiting until the sparkling water was fully ejected into the air, many of the couples paused for additional pictures. Inside the hotel was a restaurant and a small bar, along with a number of large banquet rooms that accommodated the many wedding receptions.

Watching the happy couples leave their cars and enter the hotel, I recalled my own wedding over forty-five years before. The weather that day was considerably different than this sunny Carpathian afternoon. Our wedding was held during a blustery December snowstorm on a frigid Iowa day.

The weather was so bad we barely made our train connections in Chicago where we had reserved a compartment on the *City of New Orleans* to transport us in comfort to our brief honeymoon in the "big easy." *Laissez les bon temps roulez.* And usually the good times did roll. Occasionally, however, as with any marriage, particularly in the 60's and 70's, the rain would sometimes reign.

Fortunately, our stormy Iowa beginning was not an omen of things to come. As I walked away from the hotel, I hoped these new marriages would be as happy as ours had been, although I realized these couples faced greater obstacles than we could have ever imagined.

The restaurant where I was planning to eat was a few blocks from the hotel. It was my favorite in Ivano Frankivsk because it had only one thing to offer, which was roasted chicken. This simplified things for the waitress when I performed my cutting pantomime, hopefully indicating I wanted something to eat.

None of the restaurant staffs in Ivano Frankivsk knew English, and the items on the menus remained a mystery to me. In Latin America or Europe I could usually decipher a dish I recognized, but in Ivano Frankivsk, as in China, I was at the mercy of anyone who served me. Some of the waitresses were understanding; others considered me mentally deficient, because I was unable to speak their language. Occasionally the waitress merely walked away leaving me unserved and hungry.

Going up the stairs to the dining room, I thought it was unusually quiet. Entering, I immediately noticed there was only one table occupied, and those people weren't eating. After sitting down I could observe my companions more closely while they studied me. They were four men with two bottles of vodka, and ashtrays overflowing with smoldering cigarettes. All of them were in their thirties, with blond hair, square jaws, and wearing tight-fitting, short-sleeved shirts displaying their muscular arms, and an occasional tattoo.

The man in the center looked across the room at me. "American?" he asked gruffly. His companions chuckled at the question.

"Yes" I replied, in what I hoped was a firm confident voice.

"Where?"

"Chicago" I replied.

With that, he made the familiar crooked thumb and outstretched forefinger gesture crudely replicating a gun that is the universal response to the city of Chicago.

"Bang" he said.

"Bang, Bang" I replied, refusing to be outdone.

Fortunately, they all found this immensely amusing, and I was delighted it was only a game. When you are alone in a foreign country, unable to speak the language, you can feel uncomfortable under good conditions; and I had the strong feeling these were not good conditions. I could feel the hairs on the back of my neck begin to rise, and once again recalled Trevor Gun's warning as we left our plane in Kiev.

Now pointing to himself he said "Igor."

Why hadn't I guessed, he looked like an Igor. Pointing to myself, I said "Russ." Somehow Russ seemed to lack the intimidating timbre of "Igor."

By now Igor fancied himself a linguist. He then pointed to his three companions saying "Ivan, Andrey, Volodymyr."

"Hello there" I said, waving weakly to the menacing three stooges.

"Closed" Igor shouted while making a sweeping gesture with his hand. I hoped he meant the restaurant. If so, it was all right with me; I was hoping to find a way to get out of there gracefully. I waved goodbye and went down the stairs as fast as I could.

Happy to be away from Igor and his group, I went up the street to another restaurant I had also been planning to visit during my stay. It was closed, but there was a small crowd waiting outside for it to open. Shortly after I arrived, so did Igor and friends. Walking to the door he pounded on the glass as an attendant rushed to let him in. Turning he motioned me to come with them. Not knowing what else to do, I did as I was told.

I took a seat at one of the empty tables while Igor spoke to the waitress. He then disappeared into the kitchen. Shortly he reappeared with a bottle of Czech beer in one hand, and a cigarette in the other. Laughingly, he pointed the bottle toward me as if it was a gun, and joined his friends. The waitress quickly came with a plate of chicken, shredded cabbage, and a bottle of beer. Placing the food in front of me, I heard her say "Igor." After I finished I tried to pay for my meal, but the waitress refused the money nodding to the group of muscular men in the front of the restaurant.

When I finished, I waved goodbye and told Igor thank you. He replied "Chicago." I could hear them laughing as I went down the stairs. Outside, the sun was still shining and the people were still lined up waiting to be allowed in.

The next day, I told Sasha and Tanya about Igor and his companions. They looked knowingly at each other and Sasha said, "Mr. Miller, I think you had dinner with the boss of the Russian Mafia here in Ivano Frankivsk."

Throughout the former Soviet states the Russian "Mafiyh" was rapidly filling a social vacuum created by the dissolution of state authority, and the absence of a newly codified and enforceable legal structure. In the early stages of transition, organized crime confined its activities to black-marketing, theft, and providing the protection previously afforded by the police. The need for protection was first limited to the operators of kiosks, restaurants, and nightclubs. It was later so widespread almost all forms of businesses were finding it necessary to form an alliance with a "kryska", or "roof" that provides protection for a fee.

As I left my office that evening, I had to wonder if the generosity extended by Igor was professional courtesy to a presumed member of the "outfit," with Chicago connections.

Later in my apartment, I thought about the men I had met during the last few days. Each, in his own way, was trying to make a life for himself under difficult conditions, while also attempting to work within the same organizational structure with which they were familiar. Of the three, I guessed Igor by abandoning the more traditional route to success would unfortunately, but ultimately prove to be the most successful of the group.

Chapter 12

Fellow Travelers

There was a small multipurpose yard in front of the apartment complex where I lived. It had a few basic items of playground equipment put to good use by the large number of children living in the building. The yard also served as a grazing area for the cows that dined regularly on the strands of grass that had not already been trampled into extinction. An occasional horse, competing for the remaining tufts, could sometimes be seen tethered to a teeter-totter or rusting parallel bars.

What I first thought were clotheslines also occupied a corner of the busy open area next to my apartment window. On closer examination, they proved to be slender iron bars suspended five feet above the ground, placed there for airing rugs rather than laundry. Instead, the newly laundered clothes were strung from the windows to dry. On a dry sunny day, this caused the apartment building to resemble a bulky sailing ship with a crazy collection of oddly shaped, multi-colored pennants wildly flapping in the breeze.

Getting ready for work, I heard the now familiar sound of a rug being strenuously beaten next to my apartment window. This was not unusual since it frequently occurred at almost any time of day or night. It could be seven in the morning, or eleven at night. Time seemed to be of little consequence to my neighborly carpet bangers. I had come to conclude this vigorous activity, in many cases, was providing an emotional release from the cramped quarters afforded most of the other residents.

What was different this morning was the unusual vigor with which this unfortunate rug was being addressed. POW! POW! POW! The sound was loud enough to easily penetrate the thick walls of the apartment building. Suddenly each POW was answered by an equally resounding WHACK!

Quickly finishing tying my tie, and grabbing my briefcase, I rushed outside to see the cause of such commotion so early in the morning. The source was not difficult to identify. Two middle-aged men were standing near one another, each with his individual carpet draped across the iron structure. Apparently, what had begun as a routine household task was turning quickly into a heated competition to see which one could beat the hardest, and last the longest.

As I watched, sweat began to run down the faces of both men, and damp blotches appeared on the backs of their shirts. The children, who were playing on the nearby equipment, left their games to watch the exciting and exhausting new sport. As they cheered on their favorite, they were joined by a straggly group of stray dogs. The dog's barks, mingled with the children's cheers, began to attract an increasing group of parents that came to see what all the noise was about. The growing crowd only served to renew the flagging energy of the carpet competitors who were learning that they were engaging in an exciting but exhausting form of rivalry.

Finally, the older of the two threw his banger high in the air signaling defeat. The crowd cheered, the dogs barked, and I went on my way to work.

Walking up the steep hill to Karpaty, I thought about what I had seen. On the surface, it was an amusing incident, but on greater reflection, I realized they were two very disgruntled men, venting their frustration in one of the few ways that was available to them.

I knew, from experience, the fear that can take control of a person's thoughts and actions when confronted with the possible loss of a job, and the lack of income. This is especially true when it occurs in an environment lacking in alternatives, and there is no prospect of an immediate improvement.

There was much to fear in Ukraine that summer. The country's economic crisis was growing worse. Inflation was spiraling out of control. Russia had reduced its oil and gas supplies, and raised its prices to world levels. About 35% of Ukraine's electricity was produced by nuclear power and, in spite of the serious accident at Chernobyl, this was likely to increase because Russia's resources could be purchased only with a dwindling supply of Ukraine's hard currency. The country's single alternative was an expanded reliance on the antiquated nuclear reactors like those that failed at Chernobyl.

Industrial output was also falling rapidly. This was partly because of a miner's strike that began in the Donbass coalfields, and was beginning to spread to other industries. The striking workers were demanding higher pay, as well as calling for either economic autonomy for the region, or its transfer to Russia.

My own position was also showing little signs of improving. I had finished my analysis of marketing alternatives, and Valerie was working on translating it into Russian for the general director and Bogdan Goodzak the Marketing Director. When this was finished, it was the end of what I could do without further input from the other departments.

The information I requested from the Vice Directors describing their departments' capabilities was trickling in very slowly. When I visited their offices, they were quick to assure me that their portion would soon be completed, but it never was. The worst offender, not surprisingly, was the marketing department.

My major project was completing a document that the company could use to attract outside investment. If the information flow did not improve soon, it would be impossible to complete the project before I left. If this occurred, my trip would be a failure.

Because this was the first thing I had attempted since I retired, failure would be a difficult pill to swallow. On the other hand, I was beginning to wonder if defeat was inevitable if there was any sense in staying in Ukraine for the full term of the assignment. In addition, time was passing more slowly. In the beginning, everything was new, and I was enthusiastic. Two months can be a long time when you are alone, in a different culture, and can't speak the language. Now, time was beginning to drag like a second act in a bad play.

I was still considering my alternatives as I reached my office. While I was hanging up my jacket, Kapitolena came in smiling broadly. "Fax" she said, officiously placing a sheet of paper on my desk and leaving without her usual lengthy Russian commentary.

Miraculously, after all of this time, I was delighted to see that the fax was from my wife. Our two sons, Michael and Paul, had decided to get their mother a fax machine for the home. From his home in Pennsylvania Mike, the son who can fix anything, talked his Mother through the complicated installation process by phone. When they were finished, Elsie was able to get through to Karpaty on her first attempt, using the fax number originally given by the IESC.

Learning that things were all right at home made me feel better about my own situation. I quickly prepared a reply, but it would not go through. Apparently, my wife could contact me, but I could still not communicate with her, other than through my son's office in Bermuda.

While I was considering my communications problem, Valerie came into the office carrying the Russian translation of the recommendations I had prepared for expanding Karpaty's marketing effort. In them I had described how the company could extend its sales effort to foreign markets by using either overseas agents, independent buying groups, catalog companies, or foreign distributors. I also included the relative advantages and disadvantages of each method.

In addition, I discussed in the report how Karpaty could set up their own sales organization making it unnecessary for them to rely solely on the Ukrainian government. Karpaty's marketing and sales organization was still clinging to the old system, but the Soviet Union was no longer there to pump orders from its satellite states into the company's production schedules. The new Russian Federation was funneling its dwindling product requirements into its indigenous companies, hoping to keep them alive, and paying little attention to their former suppliers in the new break-away countries.

The new government in Kiev continued to do business with the administrations in Belarus, Turkmenistan, and Tajikistan, but these countries were economically unable to compensate for the lost military funding that previously flowed from the Soviet Union. What business these countries could provide was allocated by the Ukrainian government to all of its companies, and Karpaty needed a sales organization that would devote its efforts solely to its own interests.

The analysis ran several pages, and had taken Valerie a week to translate and replicate on his computer's printer. As I was paging through the prepared information trying to compare the English words to Russian to see if the content at least seemed the same, Valerie blurted "do you know what the god damned Russians have done now?" (Although Valerie was Russian, his grandfather had come to Ukraine as part of the Russian military and later settled there, so that his family now considered themselves more Ukrainian than Russian.)

"No" I replied.

I kept track of what was going on in Russia by listening to the Voice of America and the BBC on my short wave radio, but I had heard nothing startling during the last few days. The news concerning the two countries was dominated by the dispute over the ownership of the Black Sea Fleet. After Ukraine became independent, the government alleged the Russian fleet of 800 poorly maintained ships, anchored in their homeport of Sevastopol, belonged to them. In July, Russia laid claim to that Crimean City on the grounds it was not included in an earlier treaty. This controversy transcended any other news in the foreign press regarding the two countries.

"What have they done now?" I inquired. I had never seen the usually impassive Valerie so agitated, or heard him swear.

"They devalued the ruble again, after they had just promised they would not."

"Why does that affect you?"

Turning to face the window, he replied, "All my parent's savings are in rubles. They were paid in rubles for most of their lives, and their money is all in rubles. That was how they were preparing for retirement, and it is the same for most of the people here. That's also how they were paying for my living expenses at the University of Moscow."

I could appreciate the effect devaluation can have on people. I had seen it before in other countries. At one time, I did business with two brothers in Spain who had dealt with my company for over twenty years. They were very conscientious, operating their business with a high level of integrity. After so long an association, the brothers were able to buy their components from us on extended credit terms maturing at different intervals.

The Spanish peso traditionally traded at 70 pesos to the dollar. Because of their devaluation it gradually climbed to a level of 120 to the dollar, almost doubling the amount the brothers had to exchange for their dollar denominated debts. They could not meet their inflated financial commitment and eventually went into *concordata,* the Spanish equivalent of Chapter 11 bankruptcy. Their factory was closed by the bank, and later taken over by Spanish gypsies.

"Does this mean you will be unable to return to school?"

Valerie thought for a moment before he replied, "I don't know" he said sadly.

Before we could talk any longer, Svetlana Mizina interrupted us. I had completely forgotten she was coming. Forgetfulness seemed to happen more often as I grew older, and I usually attempted to pass it off as just another "senior moment." Never the less, it was still embarrassing. In this case, my forgetfulness was not obvious, and I acted as if I had been expecting her by looking at my watch as if checking to see if she was on time.

Ms. Mizina was Chief of the Workers and Salary Department, which is the equivalent of the Human Resources Department in an American company. She was one of ten women Chiefs and Vice Chiefs at Karpaty. Valerie's mother was another. Russian companies seem to do a better job than American and European businesses in promoting women into executive positions. There was a limit, however, on how far they could go. I never met one who was the head of a company.

Svetlana was an attractive woman with long brown hair that complimented her angular features. Unfortunately, she had a large mole on her lower lip that would have been removed long ago in western society. In her case, it only served to draw attention to a dazzling array of gold teeth that were displayed prominently each time she smiled. This was not often. I had seen her several times in hallway discussions with other management people, and while I could not understand what they were saying, it was obvious she was easily holding her own.

With the continuing layoffs, Svetlana was very busy and was required to prepare for many meetings with the general director, his vice directors, and the head of the workers union. She did not attempt to conceal the fact she was displeased to have to meet with me as well. Even with her heavy workload, she was the first of the managers to complete the information I had requested, and she had done a good job preparing it.

She flipped coolly through the pages, while Valerie interpreted for us. It was obvious the information was thoroughly prepared, apparently accurate, and displayed a good understanding of what I was attempting to accomplish. Finishing her presentation, she hurried off to still another meeting. The data she left confirmed what I had learned previously from the Chief Engineer, Vice Director Skulsky.

The average monthly salary of an engineer was $14. Management staff's salary was $18 a month, and the average Karpaty employee made $13 a month. These wage rates were approximately half those paid to industry workers in Moscow, and on a dollar basis were some of the lowest in the world. What made the figures even more remarkable was, in most cases, the people involved were well educated, highly trained individuals.

Even when the workers were paid on a regular basis, which they often were not, they still could not acquire many personal items. A small washer or dryer in Ukraine would cost $175 to $225, and a refrigerator or an automobile was out of the question.

Sasha had once told me it would require more than six months pay for him to purchase the two gold rings that were the traditional marriage symbol in Ukraine. Every time he believed he was getting close to the cost of the rings the value of his savings would decline, and the price of the rings would increase, making them even further out of reach. This was another reason Sasha had been postponing the wedding.

A few weeks earlier, when I first came to Ukraine, the exchange rate was 3,200 coupons to the dollar. Later, when I exchanged money at the National Bank of Ukraine the coupon had further depreciated and the rate was 3,600 Ukrainian coupons to the dollar. The value continued to slide, and the last time I had changed money the rate was 4,600 cps to the dollar. This represented a decline in value of approximately 45% in just a few weeks. While the foreign exchange rate had no direct effect on the local residents, their own cost of living was escalating at a comparable rate.

I was beginning to notice a dramatic change in the demeanor of my "staff." Both Tanya and Sasha were becoming more reserved and withdrawn. Before, they had been enthusiastic about our work, and optimistic about the results. They still remained cooperative, but the concern for their own future was apparent. Only Valerie had remained unaffected up to now. But with the ruble devaluation, even his future was murky.

In this type of environment, it was easy to understand why the management of Karpaty was less than enthusiastic about providing information to a foreign advisor for a document that might have only long-term results. But as far as I could determine, it provided their best chance of attracting foreign investment, and without an infusion of funds, the company would be unable to survive.

I knew from my previous experiences that Western businessmen had many opportunities to invest their capital. The markets in China were beginning to expand. Mexico, with its maquiladoras, was offering an attractive location for American companies to locate new operating plants, and Central Europe was providing expanding growth opportunities.

I was often asked what the chances were of acquiring a foreign partner. I would reply candidly that it would depend on how actively they would pursue the opportunity. My belief was while Karpaty management would welcome foreign investment they were not psychologically prepared to seek it out. The communist instinct was still very strong, and it was accompanied by the belief it was degrading to actively solicit new investment. I had been vainly trying to convince them they would never find help unless they took some tangible action.

The logical first step was the preparation of a document describing the advantages the company could provide to a new partner. Without it they had very little chance of convincing a prospective investor such an association would be to his benefit. That was why the project I was attempting to complete would be important to them. Unfortunately, I had not been able to convince them of this, and Karpaty management seemed perfectly willing to wait until the government would bring someone to their door, or a new investor would somehow fall into their lap.

I decided to close up shop for the day, and go into town for a much-needed haircut. The trolley bus was crowded as usual. Sitting next to me was a peasant woman holding a cardboard box providing a temporary residence for a dozen baby ducks. As the trolley jerked and swayed drunkenly along on its uneven tracks the ducklings heads bobbed back and forth in unison, like plastic ornaments on the dashboard of speeding car.

There was a barbershop in the Ukraina hotel. Nearby was a large park I liked to walk through whenever there was time. It had tall trees shading the many benches along its walkways. The park also had the obligatory monument dedicated to some long forgotten military achievement. In an earlier life, the park had been a cemetery. Its many rows of crosses, however, became offensive to the "party of the people." The crosses and markers were mysteriously removed, the ground leveled, and a new park miraculously appeared.

Strolling under the large shade trees, I wondered if the local residents ever thought about their ancestors still entombed under the numerous rusting park benches.

In the lobby outside of the barbershop, a group of women crowded around an old flickering Russian television set. I discovered they represented the entire female staff of the hotel, including the lady barber. The smoke rose around them in dense clouds while they intently watched the latest episode of a Mexican soap opera that was capturing the imagination of an entire generation of woman throughout the former Soviet countries. It was unclear what the attraction was for these women, but I had sense enough to wait until the episode ended before motioning to the lady barber to follow me into her shop.

Sitting in the elevated chair, I made a clipping motion with my fingers across the top of my head, in case there was any doubt about my reason for being there. As she cut away it was pleasing to see that her lavender smock blended nicely with her pink hair and dazzling blue nails. Fortunately, my trim was more conservative than her appearance. She did a good job, and seemed to take an unusual interest in her work. The cost of the haircut was approximately 40 cents, and her effort was rewarded with an American dollar. A prized possession in an economy whose currency continued to plummet.

Leaving the barbershop, the same women still crowded around the television set, deeply engrossed in still another

Mexican soap opera. The only change that had occurred was that the halo of cigarette smoke hanging over them had become more dense as they eagerly watched a scantily clad young woman passionately embrace her handsome Latin lover. My lady barber, in her lavender smock, joined the middle-aged women in their faded housedresses gazing transfixed at a life far removed from their own.

It was still early, and there were only two men seated at a table in the dining room when I entered. Trying to make sense out of a Russian menu, parts of their conversation drifted to my table.

My God! They were speaking English with a distinct American accent. This was the first time I had heard pure English spoken in over five weeks-and they were talking baseball. I quickly laid aside my indecipherable menu and introduced myself.

Barry Durand, the older of the two, was approximately my age. The other, George Collins, was much younger. After they invited me to join them, I found they were both in the Peace Corps.

"Aren't you a little old for the Peace Corps?" I asked Barry.

Before he could answer, a waitress approached the table to take our orders. George could speak a passable restaurant Russian and ordered for all of us. Taking our orders, the waitress displayed the usual indifference that was characteristic of the service workers I had encountered in the country. George stumbled occasionally with the order and, rather than trying to be helpful, she seemed only disdainful of this poor unenlightened person who couldn't even speak Russian very well. So much for the travelers myth that people welcome foreigners who attempt to learn a few words of their language.

As she approached the kitchen, she stopped to light a cigarette. It was still dangling from the corner of her mouth as she slid our cucumber and tomato salad plates across the table as if she was dealing from an old deck of cards.

"Actually" Barry said, ignoring the waitress and picking up the conversation where it had left off, "approximately seven percent of the Peace Corps volunteers are over fifty years old. Recently, they have been attempting to recruit some of us senior citizens to advise companies in former Soviet countries. They believe the older guys inherently enjoy a greater level of respect and authority from the company managers than younger men would - and they are probably right."

After describing what I was doing in Ivano Frankivsk, I asked Barry what caused him to leave home and join the Peace Corps. By now, we had our dinner of cole slaw, pork, potatoes, tomatoes, and an ample supply of crusty, Ukrainian bread, and strong stale coffee.

Barry explained. "I studied engineering on the GI Bill after I got my discharge from the Marines. Following college, I joined Northwestern Bell and spent forty years with them. When they became part of Ameritech I was offered early retirement, and took it. I had my retirement income, but was still looking for a way to remain active and productive. I heard the Peace Corps was recruiting oldsters to assist in the privatization of Soviet industries. It sounded like a way I could make a contribution so, after I talked it over with my wife, I signed up. She decided to stay home, but I went ahead anyway. When I finished a short training program they sent me here for two years."

While Barry was talking, the waitress brought the bottle of Russian champagne we had ordered to go with dinner. The champagne was cheap and reasonably good. The mineral water, on the other hand, was highly saline, and the beer was undrinkable.

In my travels, Ukraine was the only country I ever visited with bad beer. All of the other countries such as China, Colombia, the Philippines, and even Nigeria, at one time recruited German brewmeisters, and developed a universally good product. In Ukraine, the beer tasted like dishwater and, I suspected, was unpasteurized. George poured while Barry continued his story.

"All in all, I'm glad I volunteered, but my Peace Corps career got off to a rocky start. The group that originally requested my assistance here thought I was a banker. Perhaps there is a similarity between the words bell and banks in Ukrainian. When we both found out there was a disconnect it was too late, I was already here.

"I searched around for another company, or organization that needed my help, and I found a management consulting organization trying to get started, so I am working through them."

While he ate, I told them my experience with Karpaty thinking I was coming over to bring them investors from the United States, with bags of money that would immediately solve their financial problems.

Reaching for another cup of coffee, "that's more typical than you think," George offered. "I have heard the same story several times before. Because the government controlled everything in the Soviet Union, the people believe American companies are all part of the United States government and are flush with money. They expect corporate investment to be like lend-lease, and resent it when it is not."

George was more the typical Peace Corps volunteer. He was in his mid-twenties, and while Barry was tall George was short. He had graduated from a Texas University with a business degree. His degree was good but his timing was bad. When he finished school the country was in an economic downturn and jobs were difficult to come by. At least the type of job he was interested in. He thought joining the Peace Corps would be a good career move and volunteered.

During his indoctrination program he had learned some conversational Russian. Barry had been in the same program but it was more difficult for him to pick it up.

"When I got here," George said finishing his coffee, "I was assigned to Pozner, a big military electronics amalgamation. It was like your Karpaty. It was totally involved in Russian military production contracts. After I was with them for six months the company closed, and now I am looking for another posting. It seemed ironic that George had traveled half way around the world because of his inability to find work in the United States, and then lost the first job he had in Ukraine.

"If I can't find another company in Ivano Frankivsk, the Peace Corps will eventually reassign me," George continued. "They expect to have sixty-five volunteers in-country by the end of the year, but most of them will be involved with teaching English."

The two were living at the hotel. We split our bill. Even with the champagne, it came to about $2.00 apiece. I enjoyed talking with them, and we promised to keep in touch. Riding the trolley home, I decided I was very glad I was not going to be in Ivano Frankivsk for two years. The town had turned out to be an interesting place to visit, but as they say, I would not want to live here.

Aside from being confronted by the thugs in front of the cultural center, most of the people had been reasonably friendly, but I missed my family. If the work had been progressing smoothly, and I felt I was doing something the management at Karpaty wanted, perhaps I would have felt better about my assignment. As it was, I was becoming very discouraged.

A few days later, in the office, the telephone rang. Picking it up I halfway expected to hear from my mystery caller with her giggled "ullo goot mornig." To my surprise it was Dave Levine. He and his wife Marlene had finished their assignment and were in town overnight. They were planning to catch the train to Kiev in the morning, and wondered if we could meet for dinner. I was delighted to hear from them. We had no contact since we left the IESC offices, and I often wondered how they were doing.

The Levines were staying at the Hotel Roxolana, which was a charming little hotel that was an Austrian-Ukrainian-American joint venture. It was professionally run in a fully restored 1907 secessionist building, surrounded by small, but well tended flower gardens.

Their room was clean and nicely decorated. The hotel even supplied small bars of soap and large fluffy towels for its guests, an unheard of accommodation in Soviet hotels. The room, however, was very small. We had to either stand, or sit on the beds to speak with each other.

At dinner, I noticed that they were still seamlessly completing each other's sentences as they enthusiastically described how their project had progressed. Their assignment had been in Tlumach, an even smaller town than Ivano Frankivsk. Because of an influential local woman's interest, the town had become extremely active in privatizing its companies, as well as some of its municipal services. They were able to do what Karpaty could not, because none of the organizations involved were considered critical to Ukraine's national defense.

Dave was working with a furniture factory, an agricultural co-op, and a group attempting to establish a stock exchange. The city administration had also petitioned the oblast to become a free-trade zone, but the regional government was not displaying a good deal of interest. The Levines were the third IESC couple assigned to the town, and there was a fourth pair coming after they left.

When we first met, on our drive into Kiev, Marlene had mentioned she also hoped to get an assignment, but this never materialized. However, she had kept busy helping her husband with his work, as well as providing psychological counseling on a volunteer basis to some of the town's residents. Her clients were typically young people whose parents had become aware of her profession, and requested a meeting.

Marlene found that the children she was usually asked to counsel were a little different than their companions, and were acutely concerned about their future. This caused them to be withdrawn from their parents, as well as the other children.

All throughout the Ukraine, the young people were finding it difficult to see any future for themselves, and it was making the process of growing up even harder than usual. It was particularly difficult for those children who felt alienated from their parents and their companions. Marlene did her best at counseling them but there was very little she could do because of the magnitude of the problem, and the limited amount of time available.

We enjoyed each others company as we exchanged our experiences. The Levines were a vital and entertaining couple, dedicated to their project, and helping others. They were just the types of people the International Executive Service Corps wanted to recruit. *They* say, "you are only as old as you feel," but this is a mathematical myth, and an actuarial fallacy. However, the Levines almost made the myth seem real.

It was growing late and we said our good-byes. They took a letter that I had quickly written for my wife, which they promised to mail when they arrived in the United States.

The trolley was less crowded now. As it weaved through the darkened city, I could see lights burning in some of the apartments and thought about my own home so very far away. The possibility of leaving Ukraine early was compelling, but I had agreed to the term of the assignment and I decided I would stay until the time was up, even if the project could not be completed.

Chapter 13

Going to Galicia

Startled out of a sound sleep, I fumbled to shut off my alarm clock—which I soon discovered was not ringing. It was 5:45 AM so it couldn't be the alarm. If it wasn't the clock-then-it-must be-the phone. At that time of day, my thoughts don't flow too swiftly, and the phone had not rung since I arrived. I almost forgot that it hung idly on the wall in the entryway.

Lifting the receiver, I heard a familiar voice repeating "Russ-Russ?" It was my wife. She had been trying to call for weeks, but could never get through the Ukrainian operator. By accident, she had found a young woman from Ukraine who was acting as a nanny for a family in our neighborhood. Lorissa even came from a village close to Ivano Frankivsk. She kindly volunteered to assist Elsie, who picked her up at her apartment at 11:00PM and drove her to our home to make the call.

With Lorissa's help, the call went through almost immediately. It was wonderful to talk to her and to know everything was all-right at home. Telexes' and a fax are fine, but nothing can replace the sound of my wife's voice.

I was too excited to go back to bed so I dressed, made breakfast, and went to work.

Arriving at the office ahead of the rest of Karpaty management, I watched out my window as heavy clouds hid the tops of the Carpathians. It was too early for most of the workers to begin tending to their gardens, but a few hardy souls were already carefully weeding and hoeing their small plots of vegetables.

Turning on the office lights, I began to go through the papers on my desk to see if any new information had come in while I was meeting the Levines the day before. None had. It was becoming increasingly apparent that my time at Karpaty would run out before I could complete the foreign investment project. I was deep in thought, trying to figure out if there was something more I could do to energize the vice directors when Sasha burst into my office with Valerie close behind.

Міністерство зовнішніх економічних зв'язків України Івано-Франківська обласна державна адміністрація **УПРАВЛІННЯ ЗОВНІШНІХ** **ЕКОНОМІЧНИХ ЗВ'ЗКІВ** 284004 м.Івно-Франківськ вул. Грушевського, 21 тел.2-21-01	Ministry for foreign economic relations of Ukraine Ivano-Frankivsk state regional administration **DEPARTMENT OF FOREIGN** **ECONOMIC RELATIONS** 284004, Ivano-Frankivsk 21, Grushevsky str. tel.2-21-01

Chief Manager____________

Karpaty

Mr. Kuvika A. M.

Would you inform The Department of Foreign Economics Relations about defence conversion and provide propositions for attracting foreign investments (hard currency, know how, tooling and engineering) to your enterprise for manufacturing of competitive products.

Your propositions will be sent to Cabinet of Ministries of the Ukraine to include them into National program of attracting foreign investments.

Sincerely yours
Head of the department M. Lisovsky

"Mr. Miller, look what I have" Sasha said waving a letter back and forth over his head in obvious glee. Even impassive Valerie was grinning as the two sat down beside my desk. "It's a letter from the Ministry of Foreign Economic Relations to General Director Kuvika. The Minister in Ivano Frankivsk is instructing him to provide his office with exactly the type information we have been trying to prepare. It came in yesterday afternoon while you were gone, and Kapitolena gave me a copy. Valerie and I stayed late last night making a translation for you. I think now you will certainly get all the cooperation you need."

I couldn't believe it. What a stroke of good luck. The head of the Ministry in Ivano Frankivsk was asking for the same information I had been telling the general director he should be preparing. Apparently, the local minister was complying with a request from his leaders in Kiev, who were now actively attempting to attract foreign investment. They had come to the same realization I had that, before they could talk to foreign businessmen, they would have to have something tangible describing their individual companies.

Ukraine actually has a good deal of advantages that make its companies valuable to foreign investors. It has a large market of fifty million well-educated workers and potential consumers. The country is also geographically well positioned to reach other markets in Central Europe. With a warm water port on the Black Sea, and a reasonable system of roads and railroads, Ukrainian producers are able to reach major industrial and metropolitan areas in both Ukraine and Europe.

The country also has a widely diversified economy with multiple sources of income from agriculture, industry, and natural resources, which provide numerous opportunities for outside investment. The frequent devaluations that made things more difficult for the people would, at the same time, make Ukrainian assets less expensive for a potential investor with hard currency.

Karpaty, with its low labor costs and skilled workforce would be able to provide a foreign organization with numerous advantages. In addition, the company had considerable available facilities, complete with various forms of heavy production equipment, test stations, and cleanrooms that could be converted to new production of appropriate products. It was also located in an attractive and livable area, with a large number of educational institutions and recreational opportunities.

Before these benefits could be evaluated, however, they had to be made known in a readable and comprehensive form. This was the purpose of the document I had been attempting to prepare, and this was the document the Ministry of Foreign Economic Relations was now requesting.

I thought very seriously about pointing out this similarity to General Director Kuvika, but decided against it. It would sound too much like "I told you so." I decided to wait and see what happened.

Before I did anything else, however, I called Tanya to tell her about the young woman from Ukraine my wife had found serving as a nanny in our neighborhood. Tanya was pleased to learn I had heard from home. She knew how concerned I was about the lack of communications with my wife.

She was also interested that the young Ukrainian woman was happy in the United States, and attending a community college in her spare time. Before we finished our conversation Tanya promised to rethink her earlier decision about traveling to America to become a nursemaid for her sister's children.

The next day Sasha and Valerie came into the office holding a translation of the General Director's response to the Ministry. In his answer, Director Kuvika proudly pointed out he already had an advisor from the United States working on just the type of document the Ministry was now requesting. He added it would be available to them on the exact date of my scheduled departure.

I sat back to wait for the flow of information to begin. And begin it did. It was amazing to observe how much power a Ministry's request had on Karpaty management. Even the Marketing Department, that had been the slowest to respond, began sending information.

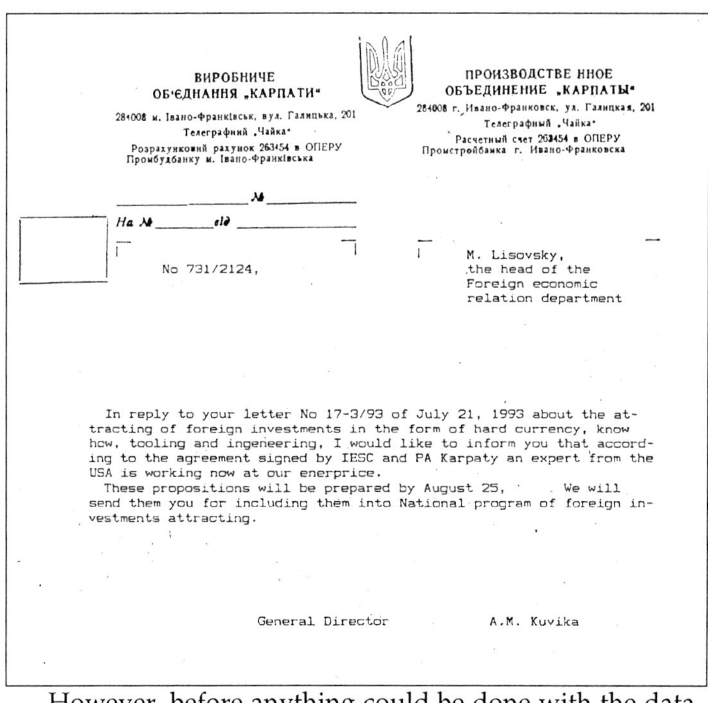

ВИРОБНИЧЕ
ОБ'ЄДНАННЯ „КАРПАТИ"
284008 м. Івано-Франківськ, вул. Галицька, 201
Телеграфний „Чайка"
Розрахунковий рахунок 263454 в ОПЕРУ
Промбудбанку м. Івано-Франківська

ПРОИЗВОДСТВЕННОЕ
ОБЪЕДИНЕНИЕ „КАРПАТЫ"
284008 г. Ивано-Франковск, ул. Галицкая, 201
Телеграфный „Чайка"
Расчетный счет 263454 в ОПЕРУ
Промстройбанка г. Ивано-Франковска

№

На № від

No 731/2124,

M. Lisovsky,
the head of the
Foreign economic
relation department

In reply to your letter No 17-3/93 of July 21, 1993 about the attracting of foreign investments in the form of hard currency, know how, tooling and ingeneering, I would like to inform you that according to the agreement signed by IESC and PA Karpaty an expert from the USA is working now at our enerprice.

These propositions will be prepared by August 25, . We will send them you for including them into National program of foreign investments attracting.

General Director A.M. Kuvika

However, before anything could be done with the data, it had to be first translated into English so I could read and understand it. After that I had to edit it, then assemble the edited copy in a reasonable sequence, and return the edited English version back to Valerie and Tanya to be retranslated into Russian.

Once the retranslating process was completed, it had to be retyped on Valerie's computer. One copy in English, and another copy in Russian. The typed copies then had to be reproduced on Karpaty's monstrous and unreliable copying machine, and finally assembled in a presentable document that the Russian Ministry and English speaking investors could both read and understand.

To establish a workable schedule, I made a simple flow chart of the numerous steps, and assigned a time-line that would produce copies of the finished document to meet Director Kuvika's commitment to the Ministry. Time was short and it was not going to be easy. Even with the improved cooperation of the Directors, I was not certain we would be able to meet the deadline.

As we were working one morning, Sasha came into the office with a proposition. "I think you should go to Lviv with Lydia and me this weekend. It would be sad if you leave Ukraine without ever visiting the old city."

I agreed with him. I had read a good deal about Lviv and its presence in Ukrainian history, and had hoped for an opportunity to see it before I left. Work was proceeding reasonably well, and Valerie and Tanya had all the information they could possibly translate during the next few days.

"Can it be done in a day?" I asked Sasha. I didn't want the trip to turn into another Yaremche weekend that gets stretched out longer than I expected.

Sasha understood my concern. "Lviv is a lovely city. Much to see there. I could arrange for a classmate of mine to act as our guide. It is only 85 miles away. We catch a bus in the morning and back in the evening. Which day would you rather go, Saturday or Sunday?"

"Saturday" I replied. I wanted to go when the shops were open and look for gifts for my family.

Sasha got tickets for us on Sunday.

Lydia, Sasha, and I arrived at the bus depot early. The station terminal was used by both buses and trains, and was always crowded. It was even more crowded on Sundays as workers traveled to visit their families in the outlying villages.

After confirming our departure time, we went to the park across the street to wait. Although it was early in the morning it was beginning to get warm, and I noticed there were people already lining up for the beer truck.

I wondered if this was the same vehicle that occasionally parked by the housing complex. Actually, the beer truck was not really a truck at all, but a flatbed wagon pulled by a tractor. On top of the wagon was a brightly painted yellow tank filled with beer. The large receptacle was fitted with a slender rubber hose with a spigot at one end. People would line up with their mugs, or mason jars, and pay their coins to the vendor who would then draw a slightly sudsy liquid from the large container.

Further down the street was the soft drink vendor. The soda machine was built like a large refrigerator with an opening in the center for a shelf and a small faucet. The vendor sat at a homemade stand displaying the gaily-painted multi-colored words Orange, Mango, Cherry, Cola, and Kiwi. It was the first menu I had been able to read since I came to Ukraine.

I would have to be very thirsty to patronize either stand. The beer in Ukraine was unbelievably bad, and the soft drink vendor had only one glass, which everyone used. Bowing to sanitary concerns, the single tumbler would be swirled in a pail of unknown liquid before it was given to the next waiting customer.

While I watched the lines of drinkers pay their coins and choose their beverage, I heard the distant sound of drums and trumpets. Sasha motioned to Lydia and me. "Let's go. Parade."

As we walked in the direction of the sound, we could see a crowd gathering at a memorial to Soviet soldiers who had died liberating this section of Ukraine from the Nazi army. It was an impressive granite monument, and was one of the few Soviet statues I had seen with "soul." All of the rest depicted fierce looking soldiers, or old political leaders.

This statue was over twenty feet tall, and portrayed a sorrowful mother with hands resting on the shoulders of an equally sad looking little girl, and a defiant young son. It was placed in a well-kept park surrounded by tall pine trees. Markers containing slain soldiers' names lined the walk leading to the monument. Nearby, was one of the few eternal flames that remained burning during the country's critical fuel shortage.

According to Sasha, it was the forty-ninth anniversary of the German defeat by Russian armies. Approaching us was a very unmilitary type of parade led by a small band, followed by a large group of middle aged men in civilian cloths strolling down the street toward the park. Their individual rows of military ribbons glistened brightly in the early morning summer's sun as they walked proudly past the assembled onlookers.

Many of the marchers carried bright banners of different political organizations, but none with the hammer and cycle. Most prominent among the banners was the recently adopted bright yellow and blue bi-colored flag of newly independent Ukraine.

Following close behind was a group proudly displaying the black and red banner of the UPA. This was the partisan army that used Ivano Frankivsk as its base for fighting both the Germans and then the Russians. They believed the defeat of one army by the other represented only a change in the uniforms of the oppressors, and was no cause for celebration. However, they wanted to demonstrate their support for an independent Ukraine.

All the marchers reverently walked by the markers of the dead soldiers and ended by placing a large wreath of flowers at the feet of the granite carved, grieving family. A brief speech by the Mayor followed the wreath laying ceremony, and afterwards the crowd quickly dispersed.

We hurried back to the station, and found our seats on the already crowded bus. Lydia and Sasha sat across the aisle from each other, while I took a seat behind them. Our vehicle resembled a very old, poorly maintained school bus that had been infrequently cleaned. The narrow aisles were filled with leftovers of former lunches on long ago journeys, and the windows were covered with grime accumulated on innumerable past trips.

The strong odors of perspiration, pickles, and cheap Russian cigarettes mingled with faded hopes and fatigue as we bounced along on the narrow, bumpy road in the hot, poorly ventilated bus. The heads of the people in front of me rolled from side to side in unchoreographed unison as the bus swayed from shoulder to shoulder of the poorly defined road.

The 85 mile trip took four hours because of the frequent stops to let passengers on and off at the numerous small villages along the way. Since it was Sunday, the people in the towns were dressed in their best clothes as families walked together to their nearby church. In some places along the way, services had already begun, and crowds of people spilled out of the doorways of their newly reopened churches into the sidewalks, and onto the grassy lawns. The Communist leaders that dominated Ukraine for so long had apparently found what others had discovered before them. Although they were successful at temporarily suppressing organized religion, they obviously had been unable to eliminate it, and it now was reemerging stronger than before.

The gently rolling fields we were passing were larger than I had seen before in Ukraine, and many contained large herds of black and white Holstein dairy cattle. The area looked much like the farms in the area of Wisconsin that my wife and I traveled through on our way to our lake home. As we rode, I thought happily about returning soon to the sound and smell of an outboard motor proclaiming the beginning of another days fishing on our lake. But, that would have to wait for a while longer.

Sasha was born slender and will undoubtedly remain slender until he dies, even though he possesses a fat man's appetite. He had traveled to his village on Saturday and returned generously supplied with food for our journey. The three of us lunched on green apples, wild gooseberries, cherries, and something that his Mother had baked that resembled a heavy biscuit rolled in sugar, with cheese in the center. We washed this down with a liquid made from wild cherries and water, which I fervently hoped had been boiled before it was placed in the bottle.

Lydia was built as a template to Sasha, with an equally hearty appetite. The two of them talked constantly to each other as the trip slowly progressed, interrupted only by my occasional question or anther morsel of food.

Our journey finally came to an end and we joined our sweaty fellow passengers squeezing through the bus's partially stuck doorway. Waiting impatiently on the platform was Sasha's college friend who was to be my guide, and who was to have acquired our return tickets to Ivano Frankivsk. For some inexplicable reason, it is often impossible to obtain round trip tickets in communist countries. This required arrival at your first destination before you can be assured of your ability to return.

The friend immediately disclaimed Sasha's previous assurance that return tickets for the same day would not be a problem. He quickly pointed out the flaw in our schedule, observing that it was now 2:30 and the returning bus left at 4:00. Sasha expressed surprise at this apparent revelation, but I harbored a growing suspicion that it was his plan to spend the night in Lviv with his lovely Lydia all along.

I was not so old that I wasn't sympathetic to Sasha's desires, but believed it was necessary to return that day, and avoid spending any more of my remaining time away from the office.

"Is there a train that goes from Lviv to Ivano Frankivsk?"

"Yes" Sasha's friend Yuriy replied.

"When does it leave?"

"I don't know" was the response.

This conversation was the genesis of a new plan. I was to go with Yuriy while Sasha and Lydia would investigate departure schedules, and hopefully obtain tickets for either a bus or train to return to Ivano Frankivsk that evening. We would then meet at the station at seven to decide what we were going to do. Sasha and Lydia left, walking hand in hand, while Yuriy and I caught a trolley into town.

As we rode, my new guide told me how lucky we were to catch a ride without a long wait, since each day another trolley went out of service. The articulated busses were made many years ago in the Czech Republic, and were now wearing out and badly in need of replacement parts. The Czech company would not accept Ukrainian currency in payment, and the government was unable to provide acceptable hard currency. As a result, more and more trolleys were becoming unfit for further service.

Yuriy was as fat as Sasha was thin, but his English was better. I supposed this was because his instructors were exposed to a more cosmopolitan atmosphere in Lviv, while Sasha's teachers were more isolated in Ivano Frankivsk. The two became close friends while they were studying together at the University. Yuryi had majored in architecture, but had been unable to find a job when he graduated, and was now back in college studying business. He explained that most of his friends were very disillusioned with the situation in Lviv. Not only was it impossible to find work, but all the municipal services were deteriorating, making it difficult merely to live.

"Even the water system is failing" Yuryi complained. If you want to study the history of Lviv, don't go to the library. Go to the water company's headquarters and look at the pipes. They illustrate our history better than any textbook. The first water pipes are over 100 years old and they are a magnificent piece of Habsburg ironwork. Lying next to them are other pipes that were laid under Polish rule, between the two world wars. The third system of pipes was put in only twenty years ago under the Soviets. They are poorly cast in cheap soft iron, and are already full of holes. The city is too poor to replace them, and now most of the households in Lviv have water for only a few hours a day, while others have water only every other day."

Yuriy's apartment, which he shared with his elderly father, was on the fourth floor. It was impossible to draw water past the second level of his building, even on those days when water use was permitted. He and his neighbors had to carry water from the second floor to the fourth floor to bathe or wash dishes, much like you would do if you lived in the country. He was happy, at least, that he didn't live on the seventh floor.

Just as he was finishing his description of his water problems, there was a noise like air rapidly escaping from a large balloon. Our trolley slowly ground to a jerky stop. Throwing up his hands in frustration Yuriy turned to me in disgust and said. "We better walk."

And walk we did. Knowing I was from Ivano Frankivsk, Yuriy took pains to point out the house in which Ivano Franko, the town's namesake once lived. It was at the top of one of Lviv's many hills, on a tree lined street in a neighborhood composed primarily of large brick residential buildings. The houses, prior to the Soviet occupation had been single family residences. When the Russians arrived, they were converted into multi-flat apartment buildings where several families were assigned to a house while sharing kitchen and bathroom facilities.

The son of a blacksmith, before he died in 1916, Franko's work covered a broad range of writing that included drama, prose, poetry, folk tales, and politics written in the house we were now passing. Because he had been considered by Moscow as an "approved" Ukrainian writer, his residence was spared the conversion to multifamily occupancy required by less fortunate, and less prominent occupants.

As we continued on our tour, it was obvious my guidebooks were right. The city of approximately 800,000 people was very attractive, and Yuriy, with his degree in architecture, made a competent guide.

Before WWII the city's residents referred to Lviv as "petit Paree" because of its many churches, narrow cobblestone streets, and wooded parks. Its architectural monuments were more fortunate than those in many other Ukrainian cities. There was no fighting in the streets during the war, and later when the Soviets arrived they didn't have time to raze landmarks or initiate horrendous building projects like those disfiguring Kiev, and other eastern Ukrainian cities.

During its history, Lviv survived twenty fires, and thirty enemy invasions. Some of its fine gothic monuments and architectural achievements have survived and can still be viewed today. We toured the Church of the Assumption, the Armenian Cathedral, and the town arsenal, while I learned more about architectural history from the former student than I really cared to know.

The city's ethnic and religious population was not as fortunate. It was believed that during the Nazi occupation 135,000 people died in the Jewish ghetto and nearly 350,000 more Jews died in German concentration camps.

When Soviet forces occupied Lviv, they imposed severe restrictions on religious activity and the clergy, and their believers were forced underground. Catholics, and especially Greek Catholics, were persecuted and their churches were confiscated and given to authorized Orthodox parishes. After that, many of their priests were sent to Siberia to die.

As Yuriy and I walked through the central district, he described how many of the ancient churches and cathedrals were closed during the Soviet assault on Christianity. Many of them were locked and stood empty. The Soviets described them as "not working."

In others, the religious paintings and icons were removed, and the building were used for grain storage. Another large church had been turned into to a museum of atheism similar to the one I visited in Ivano Frankivsk. Most, however, had survived this callous treatment, and were once again being used as they were originally planned and beautifully intended.

In the center of the old town area is Market Square. In the Middle Ages the nobility built their homes around its center. The present structures surrounding the area were built, according to Yuri, during the 16th century, and rebuilt again during the 18th century. The evolving architectural fashions of the various times can be seen in the 44 buildings presently ringing the square, which now supports a mixture of cafes, bars, and interesting looking shops that, because it was Sunday, were closed and shuttered.

The day grew warm and I grew tired. Finally, I suggested we have an early dinner, partially to repay Yuriy for his tour, but mostly for an opportunity to sit down. I am sure so much walking had been as difficult for my guide as it was for me. He was younger than I was, but he was also heavier.

The restaurant was dingy and uncrowded, but we had to wait till the waiters argued among themselves to see which of them would have to serve us. After a considerable wait we both had our meal of borscht, roast pork, potatoes, tomatoes and cucumbers, bread, and a warm bottle of Czech beer.

After we finished eating there was still time until we met Sasha and Lydia, and Yuriy suggested we go to his apartment and meet his father. The apartment was located in another of the partitioned old residences. There was no elevator, and the climb up the four flights of stairs, on a warm afternoon, was challenging. I was breathing heavily, and sweating profusely, by the time we reached his floor.

A dusty musty odor filled the dim apartment, but I was relieved to have an opportunity to sit and meet Yuri's father who quickly joined us. I mentioned, while Yuri interpreted, that I was very impressed with the variety of religions reflected in the many churches we had seen that day. This comment brought a pleased smile to the retired history professor's face, and he immediately embarked on a lecture regarding the religious diversity of Lviv to his new and captive student.

"Lviv's multi-ethnic history is reflected in its churches that represent the art and architecture of diverse religious influences. This has resulted in buildings in most of the main western architectural styles including Gothic, Renaissance, baroque, rococo, and neoclassical. Each religious movement has left its architectural signature on the historical face of Lviv."

The professor studiously traced the religious history of his Galician Region, beginning with the founding of Lviv in 1256 by Danylo Halytsky, prince of Galicia-Volynia, and the naming of the city after his son Prince Lev. Then the ancient academic tediously proceeded through the 14th century when the invading Polish and Hungarian armies brought Roman Catholicism to the Orthodox peasantry, and droned on to the end of the 19th century when Lviv became the center of Ukrainian nationalism. Finally he described how the independence movement was later centered in the Ukrainian Catholic Church, which was forced underground by Stalin, but reemerged with Gorbachev's *glasnost* in 1980 to play a major role in the new Ukrainian independence movement.

While he lectured, I studied his time-lined face and decided we were almost chronological contemporaries having both grown up during the second world war and its aftermath, matured during the cold war, and now were witness to the dissolution of the once powerful Soviet Union.

Though somewhat similar in age, I concluded that the cultural chasm existing between us was by now unbridgeable. Neither of us could ever imagine what the other's life had been like. He was an academic who had worked in a communist controlled university, while I had earned my living in a series of large corporations that were the bulwark of a capitalistic society.

The only possible bond we might have shared was a strong desire to support and protect our families from the uncertainties that beset our times. But that bond, if it existed, was impossible to explore that warm day in Lviv.

It was with considerable relief that I realized the old man was finishing his lecture, but then to my surprise, he rose unsteadily to his feet and, unlocking a nearby cupboard, brought out his collection of old Ukrainian bills.

Returning to his faded crushed velvet chair, the former professor began to put each one in its proper historic perspective. As he talked I watched his slender, veined hand lovingly extract each bill from its yellowed plastic sleeve; but the stuffy apartment began to have an effect. As the professor droned on over his prized collection, each bill began to look like the one before it while my eyes started to glaze and my mind wander.

It drifted back to Misha's apartment on St. John's day as Misha proudly displayed his postcard collection for Sasha and me to admire. Recalling the evening, I was struck by what people with few possessions consider precious. Misha had his pictorial recollections of past voyages, and the professor valued the currency of past national glories. Much to my chagrin, I was equally disinterested in both, but feigned curiosity about each as best I could.

Finally, I had to suggest to Yuriy we should return to the station to see what progress my traveling companions had made arranging transportation back to Ivano Frankivsk. I thanked the professor for allowing me to share his collection. As we were leaving, I could see the elderly gentleman carefully returning each precious faded bill to its original envelope.

Sasha and Lydia were patiently waiting for us at the station. They had spent the afternoon in the apartment of one of Sasha's university classmates. "We could spend the night there you know" Sasha said, glancing lovingly at Lydia. "We could get the bus to Ivano Frankivsk in the morning."

I knew that we could, but I didn't look forward to spending the night sleeping on the floor, in my clothes, in a stuffy apartment, without running water. I also didn't care to spend another day out of the office.

"What did you find out about the busses Sasha?"

"There is one scheduled to leave in fifteen minutes at 7 o'clock."

"Great."

"But it is not leaving. It has no gas."

"And the train?"

"There is one at 10 o'clock tonight. It gets into Ivano Frankivsk at 2:30 in the morning."

"That's it then. Lets get the tickets now."

Sasha's face fell, and I felt sorry. I could imagine how difficult it must be for a young couple in Ukraine to be alone together. I also looked forward to spending a night on a Russian train with almost the same lack of enthusiasm as I had for sleeping on the floor, but I felt I had to get back to the office and finish my work.

The late night train was packed, and the stops were many. At each station, tired passengers got off while weary travelers got on. Many carried sleeping children, and old peasant ladies carried baskets of produce they were taking to market in nearby towns. The heavy aroma of sweaty people and fresh produce filled the unventilated passenger car, as people tried futiley to raise windows that had become stuck many trips ago.

Lydia slept with her head on Sasha's shoulder, while Sasha dozed between us. The clicking of the rails had a hypnotic effect as the fatigue of the day lulled me into a fitful sleep, only to be awakened with a start at the next station.

At one of the frequent stops, I watched incredulously as a man boarded the train carrying a yellow porcelain bathtub liner on his back. He resembled a sickly saffron turtle, swaying from side to side, as he squeezed past his fellow passengers who were attempting to leave the train at their destination.

He finally found a place to deposit his porcelain shell by setting it upright at the rear of the passenger car. He took an adjacent seat that allowed him to keep the liner from falling on other unsuspecting sleeping fellow riders, sprawled across their cramped passenger seats.

Rather than the expected four hours, the trip lasted six. My feet were swollen and my knees stiff as we finally made our tired way through the flowing crowd at the Ivano Frankivsk station. Light was beginning to crease the dark night sky as we finally got outside and began to walk on the deserted street. We passed waiting taxis, and the empty trolley stand.

My two slender traveling companions began to slowly dissolve into the shadows while I trudged tiredly behind them. Peering at their backs through the darkness, I suddenly had the distinct feeling I was being led through the night by a physical personification of the number 11. "Wait-wait up. Where the hell are you going," I shouted as the two faded from view.

Sasha's voice penetrated the darkness, "The trolley doesn't start service until six in the morning, and we're walking to the apartments,"

I couldn't believe it. It was now 4:30 in the morning, after a 6 1/2-hour train ride, and a night with no sleep, and we were going to walk three miles to the apartment complex. "We are like hell," I said, signaling one of the many waiting taxis. I get very testy without sleep.

As the taxi pulled in front of our building Sasha observed, "you must be very tired." That was putting it mildly. It was years since I had been up all night, and then it was under much more pleasant circumstances.

"You and Lydia must also be tired " I grudgingly acknowledged.

"Yes, but I am a young man." Sasha always had a clever way of stating the obvious.

The next morning "the young man" slept till noon, while "the old man" was in the office by ten.

Chapter 14

The Inbound Leg

It would have been wonderful to sleep late the next morning, but the people in the adjacent apartment began their bathing ritual, as usual, at six. During the two months we were neighbors I had never grown accustomed to the violently intrusive sound of water gushing through their ancient narrow pipes. By now it was not as startling as it was earlier in my stay, and on those days when our building was without water, I almost missed my aquatic alarm clock. At least my neighbors were still working, and I was glad my faceless friends had not joined the growing number of Karpaty employees who were out of work.

Still tired from my trip to Lviv the day before, I pulled the blanket over my head, rolled over, and tried to return to sleep. At one time in my life it was possible to function well with only a few hours rest, but those days had passed many years ago. It was no use, the opportunity for sleep was lost with the cascading waterfall in the next apartment.

My movements were much slower than usual as I showered, shaved, and fixed breakfast. I had abandoned the shirt and tie routine several weeks before and rummaged through the drawers to find a clean sport shirt. Valentina, the laundry lady, must have taken the weekend off, and my supply of clean clothes was running low. The supply of pantyhose that were used as tips was running low as well.

Leaving the apartment, I felt a warning chill in the air. There is something about the coming of fall, even for an old man, that brings back memories of falling leaves, football games, marching bands, and lanky coeds – ah those long-legged young ladies in short plaid skirts. What a time that was – a hundred years ago. I pulled up the collar of my jacket trying to protect against the crisp breeze and what I knew lay ahead.

For someone my age, fall is marked by a sense of melancholy for what it portends and nostalgia for seasons gone by, but it was a good time in Ukraine. The days were mild, and the fruit trees were abundantly blessed with their seasonal offering of apples and pears, while the woods and mountainsides were still providing an ample supply of mushrooms and berries for the more industrious apartment dwellers. The harvest had gone reasonably well. The country's rich black earth had again yielded its traditional supply of grain for the mills and hay for the winter although the large co-operative farms were still considerably less productive than their managers had hoped.

Discussions were continuing between the United States and Ukraine regarding the disposition of the country's strategic nuclear weapons. The Ukrainian Parliament was equivocating on ratifying the START I treaty, and there was extended debate about whether their large 46 SS-24 missiles were even covered by that treaty in the original Lisbon Protocol. All of this, however, had little effect on the residents of Ivano Frankivsk who were more immediately concerned over increasing layoffs and more plant closings.

I nodded to the guard in the lobby, but he was too engrossed in his newspaper to look up. The single remaining elevator had gone out of service again several days before and was still not operating. Hopefully, it was a matter of only getting the maintenance crew to look into the problem. If the elevator was in need of replacement parts, it could be down forever.

The climb up the stairs had not become easier with practice, and by the time I reached my floor, my breath was coming in short, sharp gasps. Entering my office, I was glad to see Valerie and Tanya already at work. Their papers, filled with English or Russian translations, were spread across my table in lengthy columns of documents ordered as playing cards arranged for a game of solitaire in a system that only they seemed to comprehend. It was pleasing to see them so busy without urging.

They both had learned to work independently, and with considerable initiative. This is a quality in short supply among many of the workers - - and managers as well, for that matter. Most of people had lived too long in a system where personal initiative was discouraged and were taught always to defer to the next level of command. Their dedication also demonstrated their confidence in our project, and the importance they attached to what we were attempting to accomplish.

"Mr. Miller what is a resume?" Valerie asked looking up from his papers.

"Good morning Tanya, Good morning Valerie. A resume? why do you ask?"

"I have decided that I would like to get a job with an American company when I finish school. Do you think I could?"

Tanya kept sorting papers while Valerie and I talked, but I could see she was listening closely.

"Sure I do Valerie. Your English is excellent, and you have a good educational background. I also think working on this project may be helpful to you. When we finish, we will make an extra copy you can take with you to show you have worked on a foreign investment study. When you get to Moscow, check in with the commercial section of the American Embassy and let them know of your interest and qualifications. If you like, I will also prepare a letter of recommendation you can take with you."

The corner of Valerie's lips turned upward in what for him passed as a broad smile.

"Now, back to your original question. A resume is a summary of your background and experience showing why you would be well qualified for a particular job. You have to build your experience like a company would build a product, and a resume is a tool that helps you market yourself. Before leaving, I will give you an outline of a resume you can use to construct your own."

In the past, under the Soviet command structure, when someone finished his studies he was assigned to a company and would usually work there the rest of his life. Now things were different, and it was up to individuals to find their own job. The problem was, most of the people had no idea how to go about doing this, and making it even more difficult, there were few jobs to be found.

Sasha had come in while we were talking. It was almost time to go to lunch. "Mr. Miller, will you also give me a copy of the resume form? Lydia and I were talking yesterday. We can't get married. We have no money. It will be a long time until we will be assigned to an apartment, and who knows how long we will have a job at Karpaty. I have been thinking, I would like to see if I can get a visa to work in the United States. If I can do that, Lydia will follow."

At this point Tanya looked up from her work to tell us, "I have written my sister that I would like also to go to the United States and work for her. I am waiting for her reply."

The thought of America as the archenemy apparently had disappeared and the three were now looking toward the United States as a source of their future.

This transformation was not necessarily true of everyone at the factory, however. At lunch Misha joined Sasha and me at our table, as he often did. His duties at the disco were not demanding and, with the exception of an occasional private party, I seemed to be his only responsibility. He never ate with us, except perhaps sharing an occasional desert that was too fattening for my diet, but he often joined our conversation as Sasha interpreted. I had come to think of him as a friend and felt as close to Misha as I did to Sasha, Valerie, or Tanya.

Misha had been talking to Sasha for several minutes while I ate, but I noticed Sasha was not including me in the conversation as he usually did. Finally my curiosity got the better of me and I asked, "what's happening? What are the two of you talking about?"

Shaking his head and looking crossly at Misha, Sasha reluctantly responded. "Misha says you will be leaving in a few days and he is curious, are you really not with the CIA? He says, you understand, he has never thought you were, but some of the less educated people in the factory still wonder. Misha says he really doesn't care if you are or not. It makes no difference to him, but people frequently ask. Since you will soon be gone, and it doesn't make any difference now, he would like to know what he should say."

I was surprised by his question. I had thought that issue had passed long ago. With the exception of the incident at the cultural center, I had never experienced any overt animosity from anyone. Sometimes in town, or on the bus, I would notice people looking at me with curiosity, but with no great anger that I could detect. But suspicion of my motives obviously ran more deeply than I realized. Perhaps this explained why the vice directors were so uncooperative.

I considered my answer carefully before I spoke. "Tell Misha I am absolutely not with the CIA, or any other organization of that type. Hell, I am not even with the UN, or the IFM, or the EBRD, or any other multi-initialed organization except the IESC; and we are all too old to be dangerous," I added with a regretful smile.

Sasha translated my answer for Misha who laughed and shook my hand.

I suppose I could have told them I was occasionally in contact with people from the Central Intelligence Agency while I was working at Zenith. At that time I was traveling frequently to third world countries and would often visit "hot spots" like Columbia, Peru, China, or Sri Lanka. After I returned, I would sometimes get a visit from Agency people in the Chicago office who would ask about what I saw in the countries I visited. Their questions were usually routine. They never asked me to collect information in advance of my trips, and I was glad to provide them with any help I could.

Sometimes their questions were amusing. They were bright people who were dedicated to their agency, but they had no idea how corporations work. Although I would explain to them that my expertise and responsibilities were in marketing, they would often ask questions about very technical subjects that I was unable to answer. I knew they also met with our head of advanced research, who was extremely technical. I presume they asked him about business conditions in the countries he visited, and then would conclude that neither of us were very well informed.

Perhaps I should have told Misha, if "the company" was sending operatives to Ukraine to find out about businesses such as Karpaty, he needn't worry. I decided, however, this would be too difficult for Sasha to translate, and it would be better left unsaid.

When we returned to the office, Sasha told me Medvid "the bear" wanted me to meet with his managers to tell them how American companies handled their international marketing activities. I had often marveled at the lack of curiosity on the part of the vice directors regarding business practices in America. None had ever approached me with questions. Now it was surprising that a request for information was coming at all. Even more surprising to be coming from the vice-director of manufacturing about marketing practices, rather than from Bogdan Goodzak who was head of marketing.

Medvid had said, during our first meeting, that because his department made Karpaty's products, they were the best qualified to market them as well. It was obvious he had not given up on his plan to absorb the marketing function into his own organization.

I was glad I was not the person in the sights of the old party boss. He had been raised on intrigue, and he would be a formidable adversary. It was also interesting that he had no problem adjusting to the demands of a free market system and abandoning communist dogma when it was to his advantage. For Medvid, it appeared, pragmatism transcended ideology. If this crusty old communist could change, whatever his motives, perhaps there was still hope for Ukraine.

I agreed to meet with his manufacturing managers, although there were still major problems finishing the report before I left. The problem now was one of production. The only paper Karpaty had was yellow with age, and unsuitable for a document to be given to the Ministry and to foreign investors. I had brought a supply of paper and pads with me, but my supply was exhausted long ago. Sasha finally located a store in town with much needed supplies, and I gave him money to buy enough paper for the documents we needed.

Once we had the paper, the company's duplicating equipment broke down. It was amazing that a high tech company like Karpaty did not have at its disposal the basic facilities any small shop in the United States would have. We waited several days for the technicians to fix the printing equipment, but they were unable to isolate the problem. Finally one night Valerie sneaked back into the plant, and was able to find the problem and fix it with a soldering iron he kept hidden in his desk.

With all these obstacles, I wasn't eager to take time to speak to the manufacturing department about marketing, but if they were interested I felt obligated to try.

The morning of my presentation, I came into the office early to review an outline of a talk I had originally prepared to give to the marketing people. Bogdan Goodzak had continued his reluctance to meet with me, so I decided to use that outline for my presentation to the manufacturing group.

The telephone rang as I was reviewing my notes. Picking up the crackling line I recognized the young lady's voice saying "ullo goot mornig."

"Hello my friend," I replied. Before I could say anything more there was a short pause, and then I heard "goot by." The line went dead. Somehow, the young lady was aware I would be leaving soon, and this must have been her farewell.

I picked up my notes and went into the conference room where the manufacturing managers had already assembled. There must have been thirty of them, but my mind was not on the faces in front of me; instead it was filled with speculation on who my telephone talker could be, and what she looked like. Did I pass her every day in the hall? Did she see me on my way to work? Why did she feel compelled to tell me good by, when to the best of my knowledge we had never met. At that moment, she seemed to represent all of the Karpaty people that I had casually encountered but would never come to know.

I forced myself to focus on the job at hand, and the people waiting patiently for me to begin. Sasha translated as I talked while a thickening haze of cigarette smoke slowly engulfed the room. His translating ability had improved considerably during my stay, and he and I were now more at ease with each other.

I spoke for twenty minutes, and stopped when I saw eyes glaze and heads nod. It was painfully obvious that the majority of the men had no idea what I was talking about, and cared even less. They had been told by their boss to attend, but even Medvid could not instill interest in his troops for something that had little apparent impact on their everyday lives.

Finished with my prepared notes, I opened up the meeting to questions. After some priming by Medvid, a few of the men began to ask questions on their own. They were the same questions I had received before from other members of the staff.

"How much is a loaf of bread?"

"How much is a bottle of vodka in America?"

"Is it Russian vodka?"

"How much does a factory worker earn?" My answer made their eyes light up"

"What happens when a man is laid off?"

I told them about unemployment insurance.

"How much unemployment insurance does a worker draw?"

When I answered they nudged each other, and one said "Let's all go to the United States. That's more than we made in a year, when we used to get paid."

Finally the questions ended, and I gave a copy of my outline to Medvid. When I planned to give the lecture to the marketing group, I had the outline translated into Russian to leave with Goodzak. Since he wasn't interested, I left it with Medvid. I believe the outline probably represented the most experienced text in free-market techniques that could be found in Ukraine at the time.

The phone was ringing as I entered my office. Half hoping it was my telephone friend, I was surprised to hear George Collins, the young man from the Peace Corps. He was still unable to find another job and wondered if Karpaty would hire him when I left. Since he would work for nothing, I thought the general director might be interested and took the number where he could be reached. I felt badly that George couldn't even find a volunteer job where his talents could be used, but when I told the general director about his offer he was markedly unresponsive.

I spent the evening organizing my belongings, preparing for my departure. While I was working, Valentina brought the rest of my laundry, immaculately cleaned and pressed as usual. I paid her and gave her the two remaining pairs of panty hose that were left. It was still embarrassing to be giving such a personal gift to a woman, but she always seemed immensely pleased to receive them.

Later it occurred to me I had never seen her wearing hose, but even if she couldn't use them herself, they could be of considerable value to her on the underground market. This type of business constituted much of the informal economy that was so prevalent in Ukraine, and in the rest of the former Soviet countries as well. Two pairs of packaged panty hose were equivalent in value to a pair Levi jeans, and would bring more than a factory worker could earn in two or three months.

Before she left, panty hose in hand, Valentina took a going away gift out of her laundry basket. It was a foot long shoe horn made from bone, with a deer's head and antlers at its top. She had tied a blue ribbon around the antlers and said "thank you" in English as she handed it to me.

That night the ringing of the telephone awakened me. Struggling to reach the offending instrument, I stumbled in the dark over a partially packed bag I had left carelessly in the middle of the floor. Expecting to hear my wife, I was surprised to hear the distant voice of a man with a lilting New Delhi accent, repeating "Mr. Miller-is this the American Mr. Miller?"

The call was from the head of a Washington-based international consulting organization with whom I had some previous correspondence. Learning I was on a project in Ukraine, he was now interested in hiring me for a short-term project in Lithuania, under a contract with the World Bank. It was a remarkable offer of $350 a day, plus generous expenses, to do for the Bank what I was presently doing for the International Executive Service Corps for nothing.

Although it meant I would have to leave for Vilnius almost immediately after returning home, the opportunity was too interesting to reject. It was in an area of the world I had never traveled , and I accepted the offer an instant before our connection was broken.

Sasha, Valerie, and Tanya were already at work when I entered my office the next morning. I was excited about my next project, but there was still work to be done on the investment proposal before it could be sent to Minister of Economics. I had asked Valerie to see if he could find covers for the report and was told he had found an Engineering group that could supply them. The finished reports were now stacked on my desk, bound in a heavy brown cover much like a library book. It was more elegant than I expected, or desired, but I had little choice but to accept what had been provided.

There were no similar reservations on the part of my staff, however. They eagerly pored through the documents, looking at the pictures, and checking their translations. Tanya looked up from her copy. "You know Mr. Miller, before you came in we were talking among ourselves and we all agreed that none of us thought we world finish on time. There were obstacles at every point. First, the vice directors wouldn't cooperate. Then when the Ministry ordered them, it looked like it was too late to translate their information. When we finished translations it didn't seem we could get the document printed and bound before you had to leave. But we just kept working, and now here they are all ready to send to the Ministry. We really surprised ourselves at what we accomplished."

I was not sure, at the time, that Tanya and the others fully appreciated what she was saying, but I did. I always believed that perseverance was the hallmark of my generation, and was responsible for whatever success we were able to achieve. During the depression, the war, college, and our careers, whatever obstacles were encountered, we quietly kept working away, and eventually found a solution. By their participation on the project, I hoped my three friends also had learned the value of perseverance, and what can be achieved under very adverse conditions.

I must admit there were many times I also didn't think we could finish our project in time. My three helpers did a wonderful job. It was difficult for them to focus on what they were doing when they were all deeply concerned about their own problems. In spite of this, they managed to put their worries aside, and I told them how much their effort was appreciated.

I spent the rest of the day preparing an outline for the general director suggesting ways he could use the investment document on his own to attract foreign businesses. One approach was directly expressing his interest to the American Embassy in Kiev, another was using the existing network of Ukrainian Embassies in Europe and the United States, and a third was working through the IESC office in Kiev. They had a service available to companies like Karpaty to help them link-up with firms in the United States and develop mutually beneficial business ventures.

It remained obvious that if Karpaty wanted foreign investment they we going to have to actively search it out. What I was providing was merely a tool they could use, and like any tool, it has to be used correctly to be effective. My fear was, however, that the management of the amalgamation was not aggressive enough to do this. Their management capabilities were developed in a system where they were told what to do and judged by their ability to conform to direction. Now they would have to develop strategies on their own, and I was not confident they had the desire, or the ability to do this.

As I was finishing my outline for translation by Valerie, Sasha rushed into the office. "Hurry Mr. Miller-we will be late for the party."

"What party Sasha?"

"Your going away party. I got so involved finishing the investment document I forgot to tell you. Follow me."

We rode the elevator down to the main floor and then took the ramp to the lower level, past the employee grocery store, and into the cavernous factory cafeteria. I tried to keep up with Sasha's long legs as he raced between the now empty tables and chairs into a small private dining room where Misha and his white uniformed helpers were waiting expectantly.

The kitchen staff had one table filled with platters of food, while another was loaded with bottles of Russian champagne, vodka, and the highly saline Ukrainian bottled water. I was astonished to see Medvid and Bogdan Goodzak seated at the table with an open bottle of vodka.

As I looked at the two of them, I thought how mistaken I had been initially. The old party boss who I first thought would be the most dogmatic and difficult to work with proved in the end to be the most adaptable to new ways. On the other hand, the younger marketing manager, who I expected to be the most receptive to change, turned out to be the most intractable.

Sitting opposite the two protagonists were the directors of engineering and accounting. "The general director went on vacation as soon as he had taken a copy of your document to the Ministry" Sasha said, while pouring me a tumbler filled with champagne.

Misha had outdone himself. The food was attractively displayed on the plates and garnished with slices of tomato, cucumbers, and parsley. The dinner began with the obligatory bowl of borscht, followed by platters filled with slices of cold chicken, pork, beef, and assorted cheeses, accompanied by loaves of crusty Ukrainian dark bread.

Looking around the assembled managers, I had no doubt that at least one of them would be delighted to see me leave. I always believed that Bogdan Goodzak was the architect of the resistance I experienced whenever I tried to steer Karpaty in a new direction. If it had not been for the unexpected intervention of the Ministry of Foreign Economic Relations he would have been successful, and my trip would have ended in failure. But that was all behind me now.

The individual directors each made a short speech ending with a toast that Sasha carefully translated. The custom was to drain the glass at the end of each toast, but I found it advisable to only sip mine, claiming my advanced age as an excuse. My temperance didn't inhibit the other partygoers, who seemed pleased at the opportunity for a celebration.

Following the speeches, Bogdan presented me with two of Karpaty's products as gifts. "In appreciation of your work," he said with a wry smile. One product was an electric skin massager Karpaty sold as medical supplies, and another was a piece of audio equipment with a cassette player and detachable speakers. As I was packing the night before I had been comforted by the thought my luggage would weigh considerably less than when I arrived. Now this was definitely not going to be the case.

The dinner ended with a tray of sticky pastries the company baker had labored over the entire day. While I was touched by their gesture, I was glad to finally get back to my apartment, and finish preparations for the following day's departure.

The next morning I went into the office to pick up my own copies of the report, and to say good by to Valerie and Tanya before Sasha and the driver took me to the train. As we said our farewells Valerie shook my hand, and with an uncommon broad grin said, "I will build my background like a product so I will be marketable." I knew I had at least made one capitalist during my stay.

As I was about to leave I was surprised to see Vladimir Ivanov, the company's union boss, trotting down the hallway, gingerly carrying a large gallon jug filled with dark purple liquid. "His famous homemade plum wine" Sasha explained taking the jug from Vladimir, "He made it especially for you, for your journey."

I was astonished and touched by Vladimir's gift. I had believed that my attempt to provide answers to his many questions about unionism in the United States was a disappointment to him, but apparently he appreciated the effort.

Driving through the multi-colored blocks of Ivano Frankivsk, it was comforting to see the churches were now in full operation. We detoured through a side street to avoid the large crowd assembled outside the cathedral. Before the driver turned, I could see the priest passing between two long lines of peasant women crowded together with their baskets of fruit, flowers, and small bundles of grain arrayed at their feet. The priest solemnly strode among them blessing their harvest.

On the train, Sasha helped stow my bags in the luggage compartment above my head. Finishing his task, he turned and put an envelope in my jacket pocket. Later I found it contained a copy of his resume, carefully crafted to the outline I had given him.

You would think that after the many forced farewells, traveling across corporate America, I would have become a professional at saying good-by, but our parting was awkward at best. We shook hands, and Sasha encircled me with his long arms, patting me roughly on the back.

"Good by Mr. Miller."

"Good by Sasha."

With that Sasha left and returned to Karpaty. We both knew from the beginning that my life in Ukraine was temporary and would end with the completion of the assignment. The only question had been if the assignment would be productive; and I believe we both thought that it was. Sasha's English had been troubling in the beginning, but with the help of Valerie and Tanya, the problem was overcome. In the end, I believe we both developed a fondness, and perhaps more importantly, a respect for each other.

I looked about the compartment as the train slowly passed through the outskirts of Ivano Frankivsk. It was a single cubicle, though Sasha thought it would be less dangerous for me to share a compartment with others. Economic conditions in Ukraine were continuing to deteriorate and this was accompanied by an alarming increase in assault and robberies. Passengers traveling alone were considered especially vulnerable. After a moment's thought I decided that the potential risks were insignificant compared with the relative certainty of a long train trip engulfed in cheap Russian cigarette smoke.

Walking through the corridor to my compartment I had noticed the train was less crowded than before. During the two months of my stay the coaches had not got any newer, or cleaner for that matter. The toilets still had no paper and the only water was in puddles on the floor. The red felt seats in my cubicle were worn but more comfortable than those in coach, or the wood benches commonly used on short-haul trains.

As the old engine gained momentum on its narrow gauge tracks, we left Ivano Frankivsk behind. Through the smudged windows I could see the formerly rich golden fields, bereft of grain, were now empty and had turned a drab seasonal brown. Watching the landscape pass, I opened the parcel Misha had given me and removed a sandwich and a bottle of water. There was also a pastry from the night before, wrapped in an old piece of wax paper, and a large pickle.

Soon the sun began to set, and the sky turned to the darkness of a late summer's night. Before climbing into my berth, I placed my valuables inside my pillowcase, and strategically positioned one of my bags by the sliding door to trip any unsuspecting intruder. The rhythmic clicking of the rails and the swaying of the ancient passenger car soon lulled me to sleep.

Very few cities look good through a soiled train window in the early morning light, and Kiev was not one of those that did. The factories, surrounded by the Russian box-like apartment buildings, looked particularly grim and inhospitable starkly silhouetted by the slate gray dawn. However, in spite of the drab surroundings, everything looked good to this homeward bound traveler.

The IESC had sent a driver to meet the train and help wrestle my luggage. While the bags were considerably lighter then when I arrived, they were conspicuously bulky with my gifts from Karpaty. I had wisely left the plum wine with Sasha to share with his apartment mates, along with money to treat Lydia, Valerie, and Tanya to dinner at the Mafia's chicken restaurant, but my luggage still presented a challenge for the driver and me to manage.

It is an unyielding rule of train travel that whoever has the most baggage will be assigned the car positioned furthest from the station. It was comforting to see this principle still prevailed in Ukraine. I was grateful for the assistance provided by the man from the IESC who immediately placed my largest bag on his shoulder. He was a tall fellow with a long stride, and I had difficulty keeping him in sight as he maneuvered confidently through the busy station to the waiting car.

During my stay in Ivano Frankivsk, the offices of the Country Director, Ken Malden, had moved to a new location with more space, and closer to the center of the city. He and his wife had returned to the United States for a short vacation, which also provided them with the opportunity to return with clothes more appropriate for the bitter Ukrainian winter.

In Malden's absence, I met with the assistant manager who was a native of Ukraine. He served as the principal liaison between the IESC and the companies like Karpaty that contracted for volunteer advisors.

We discussed my experiences at length, particularly the difficulties involved in working with an apathetic management through a willing but inexperienced interpreter. Together, we completed my Final Report, and reviewed copies of the earlier reports on product line conversion and marketing reorganization that had been mailed to the IESC office in Kiev, but never received. I also left two copies of the recently completed Karpaty Investment Report with the assistant manager. None of the documents were as professionally produced as I would have liked, but in view of the conditions at Karpaty, they represented a considerable amount of work for a two-month period.

Before leaving the office for a meeting with the local director of the U. S. Agency for International Development

(USAID), I delightedly lightened my burden by presenting the staff with the factory's products I received as gifts, and which were inoperable with U.S. electrical current.

The director of USAID in Kiev was an attractive and knowledgeable middle aged woman, with considerable experience in former communist countries. Her desk was piled high with files and unread reports, and I added Karpaty's to the stack. Over the obligatory coffee, we discussed the political and economic situation in Ukraine and its ultimate impact on the company's future.

We both agreed that the country had considerable capacity for growth. Ukraine had a well educated population, a long established industrial tradition, considerable natural resources, and great agricultural potential as the traditional breadbasket of Central Europe.

Unfortunately, the governing political structure in the country was tenaciously clinging to the practices of the past, while tentatively and very superficially embracing the policies necessary for an independent country in a new economy. These methods were never successful when the USSR was an active participant. Now that the Soviet Union had crumbled, and Russia was concentrating on its own economic problems, Ukraine was spiraling out of control and its bureaucrats were riding an economic carousel to nowhere.

Unless the country was able to improve its financial situation by attracting outside investment, its future would remain murky at best. The global competition for such investment is intense and provided no place for passive participants. In order to realistically attract outside investors it had to stabilize its currency, liberalize investment regulations, and privatize its state-owned co-ops and companies, while at the same time instituting the rule of law. The AID director and I agreed that without these actions there would be no improvement, leaving very little opportunity for individual organizations such as Karpaty that were already caught in a rapidly descending spiral.

Our conversation flowed easily from one subject to another and the time passed rapidly. We both concluded the Ukrainian people had been through worse conditions than they were presently experiencing and managed to survive through their indomitable spirit and resilient character. The hope of the newly independent country now rested squarely on their shoulders.

Soon it was time to leave for Kiev's Boryspil Airport to catch a Swissair flight to Zurich, then on to Chicago and home. Check-in and customs presented the usual pandemonium familiar to any third world traveler. There were too many people in too small a place, administered by willing but poorly trained service attendants, and supervised by sullen guards in ill fitting uniforms.

My journey was ending as it began. Climbing slowly, the plane shuddered slightly as the landing gear retracted into the fuselage. While the flight attendant completed the seatbelt routine the plane banked slightly to attain greater altitude and acquire its bearing toward Switzerland. From my window I could see a few lights begin to shine in Kiev through the early evening dusk. As the 737 disappeared into the gathering clouds, I caught a last glimpse of the broad Ukrainian steppes that were so remindful of the flat Midwestern plains where my original journey began.

Settling into my seat for the long ride ahead, I recalled coming to Ukraine with hopes of making dramatic changes in the company to which I was assigned. Realistically, I doubt if I did anything other than provide a road map for change, if they were so inclined. The transition process is a long and difficult journey into unfamiliar territory, and a good road map can be a valuable tool if properly used. I was not optimistic that mine would. The inertia was too great and had lasted too long.

There will come a time in the future when the old Soviet Empire will be forgotten, and few will mourn its passing. That time, however, had not yet arrived for many in Ukraine. My friends at Karpaty had the bad luck to live in a transitional generation, too soon to acquire the benefits of a new society and too late to bask in the illusory security that the old system appeared to provide. Loosening my seatbelt, I decided it would likely require an entire generational change before the new market system could become entirely effective.

Perhaps more important than altering the operating methods of Karpaty, I hoped I had a role in changing the attitudes of some of the people with whom I worked, particularly their view of Americans and the American system. Whatever the case might be, I regretfully knew I would never again see the people I met in Ivano Frankivsk, but I would also never forget them.

During my stay in Ukraine, I realized there were also changes that occurred in my own attitude. When I first came to the country, I wondered if retirement marked the end of my productive life. Leaving Ukraine, I was less convinced that it did, and was more hopeful it did not. As I looked forward to the journey ahead, retirement seemed less like the end and more like merely a transition to another and equally challenging phase, filled with unknown obstacles but containing new opportunities as well.

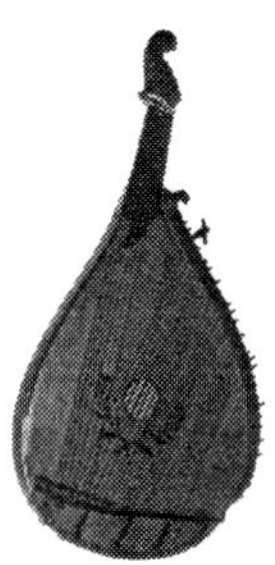

The International Executive Service Corps

Address:

Headquarters	Management and Marketing
333 Ludlow Street	The McPherson Building
PO Box 10005	901 15th Street NW Suite 350
Stamford, CT 06904-2005	Washington, DC 20005

Phone: (203)967-6000

Fax: (203) 324-2531

Email: iesc@iesc.org

Website: http//www.iesc.org

Organization:

President and CEO

Spencer T. King

Executive Vice President

Richard Shriver

Vice President Global Operations

Judy Halleran

Vice President Finance

Herbert Cotter

Director of Communications

Kathleen Failla

Founded:

In 1964 by David Rockefeller, then President of Chase Manhattan Bank, and a group of six prominent American business executives.

Mission:

The mission of the IESC is to contribute to global stability by assisting in the development of free- market economies and democratic societies. The organization provides expertise to strengthen private sector enterprises and government entities to enable self-sufficiency and participation in the worldwide economy. As a consequence, it strengthens the U.S. economy through trade investment and alliances between overseas companies and American businesses.

Funding:

Primarily through the United States Agency for International Development (USAID), but also through individual and corporate contributions.

Human Resources:

The IESC maintains a skill bank of over 12,000 senior level U.S. business executives and professionals supported by a staff of full and part time recruiters residing in the headquarters office.

Program Specialization:

Communications and information technology, industry expert review, export and joint venture development, financial services, management services, marketing services manufacturing services, information systems, E-consulting, market research, environmental services, business planning and others.

Industry Sectors:

Accounting, agriculture and agribusiness, banking, chemicals, communication, construction, governance, education, electronics, engineering, finance, forestry, general management, healthcare, hotels, human resources, information technology, insurance, investments, manufacturing, marketing metals mining, nonprofit organization, petroleum, public administration, real estate, social services, stock bond and commodity exchanges, telecommunications, tourism, transportation, wholesale and retail trade.

Geographic Areas of Operation:

Africa-Ghana, Kenya, Madagascar, Mozambique, Namibia, Nigeria, Rwanda, Senegal, South Africa, Tanzania, Tunisia, Uganda, Zambia.

Asia-China, India, Indonesia, Mongolia, Philippines, South Korea, Thailand.

Europe and Eurasia-Afghanistan, Albania, Armenia, Bosnia, Bulgaria, Croatia, Czech Republic, Hungary, Kazakhstan, Macedonia, Montenegro, Poland, Romania, Serbia, Turkey, Ukraine.

Latin America and Caribbean-Argentina, Brazil, Chile, Costa Rica, Ecuador, El Salvador, Jamaica, Mexico, Panama, Paraguay, Peru, Uruguay, Venezuela.

Near East-Egypt, Jordan, Lebanon.

Areas of Assistance Offered:

Provides technical and managerial assistance for small and medium sized enterprises, non-governmental organizations, trade associations and support organizations. The Public Administration Program conducts training in emerging nations on the role of government in a market economy.

Length of Assignments:

Volunteer assignments will vary from two weeks to three months depending on project requirements, and client needs.

Compensation:

There is no salary involved with the majority of volunteer assignments, but the organization or the client pays all necessary expenses. This includes costs of passport and visas, all required immunization, airfare, lodging and the cost of food and some incidental expenses. Spouse expenses are also usually covered on assignments lasting a month or longer.

To Apply:

The IESC no longer accepts paper application forms. Registration is now accomplished only on-line by filling out the required forms on the organization's website www.iesc.org. Information is then added to the IESC computerized database and when a new requirement corresponds with the posted skills, the volunteer is notified. It may take some time until a desirable match occurs. The volunteer can also periodically scan new postings and skill requirements listed on the website.

About the Author, Russell R. Miller

After completing the project in Ukraine with the International Executive Service Corps, Russ Miller worked on other consulting assignments in association with the World Bank, U.S. Defense Nuclear Agency, the United Nations Development Program, and the United Nations Industrial Development Organization. The projects were conducted in the post Soviet countries of Lithuania, Belarus, Kyrgyzstan, and Kazakhstan.

He also authored two previous books: ***Selling to Newly Emerging Markets,*** and ***Doing Business in Newly Privatized Markets,*** which are published and distributed internationally by the Greenwood Publishing Group.

Miller and his wife, Elsie, have lived for the last 30 years in La Grange, Illinois.

Books from Science & Humanities Press

HOW TO TRAVEL—A Guidebook for Persons with a Disability – Fred Rosen (1997) ISBN 1-888725-05-2, 5½ X 8¼, 120 pp, $9.95 18-point large print edition (1998) ISBN 1-888725-17-6 7X8, 120 pp, $19.95

HOW TO TRAVEL in Canada—A Guidebook for A Visitor with a Disability – Fred Rosen (2000) ISBN 1-888725-26-5, 5½X8¼, 180 pp, $14.95 MacroPrintBooks™ edition (2001) ISBN 1-888725-30-3 7X8, 16 pt, 200 pp, $19.95

AVOIDING Attendants from HELL: A Practical Guide to Finding, Hiring & Keeping Personal Care Attendants 2nd Edn—June Price, (2002), accessible plastic spiral bind, ISBN 1-888725-72-9 8¼X10½, 125 pp, $16.95, School/library edition (2002) ISBN 1-888725-60-5, 8¼X6½, 200 pp, $18.95

The Bridge Never Crossed—A Survivor's Search for Meaning. Captain George A. Burk (1999) The inspiring story of George Burk, lone survivor of a military plane crash, who overcame extensive burn injuries to earn a presidential award and become a highly successful motivational speaker. ISBN 1-888725-16-8, 5½X8¼, 170 pp, illustrated. $16.95 MacroPrintBooks™ Edition (1999) ISBN 1-888725-28-1 $24.95

Value Centered Leadership—A Survivor's Strategy for Personal and Professional Growth—Captain George A. Burk (2003) Principles of Leadership & Total Quality Management applied to all aspects of living. ISBN 1-888725-59-1, 5½X8¼, 120 pp, $16.95

Paul the Peddler or The Fortunes of a Young Street Merchant—Horatio Alger, jr A Classic reprinted in accessible large type, (1998 MacroPrintBooks™ reprint in 24-point type) ISBN 1-888725-02-8, 8¼X10½, 276 pp, $16.95

The Wisdom of Father Brown—G.K. Chesterton (2000) A Classic collection of detective stories reprinted in accessible 22-point type ISBN 1-888725-27-3 8¼X10½, 276 pp, $18.95

24-point Gospel—The Big News for Today – The Gospel according to Matthew, Mark, Luke & John (KJV) in 24-point type-Type is about 1/3 inch high. Now, people with visual disabilities like macular degeneration can still use this important reference. "Giant print" books are usually 18 pt. or less ISBN 1-888725-11-7, 8¼X10½, 512 pp, $24.95

Buttered Side Down - Short Stories by Edna Ferber (BeachHouse Booksreprint 2000) A classic collection of stories by the beloved author of Showboat, Giant, and Cimarron. ISBN 1-888725-43-5, 5½X8¼, 190 pp, $12.95 MacroPrintBooks™ Edition (2000) ISBN 1-888725-40-0 7X8¼,16 pt, 240 pp $18.95

The Four Million: The Gift of the Magi & other favorites. Life in New York City around 1900—O. Henry. MacroPrintBooks™ reprint (2001) ISBN 1-888725-41-9 7X8¼, 16 pt, 270 pp $18.95; ISBN 1-888725-03-6, 8¼X10½, 22 pt, 300pp, $22.95

Bar-20: Hopalong Cassidy's Rustler Roundup— Clarence Mulford (reprint 2000). Classical Western Tale. Not the TV version. ISBN 1-888725-34-6 5½X8¼, 223 pp, $12.95 MacroPrintBooks™ edition ISBN 1-888725-42-7, 8¼X6½, 16 pt, 385pp, $18.95

Nursing Home – Ira Eaton, PhD, (1997) You will be moved and disturbed by this novel. ISBN 1-888725-01-X, 5½X8¼, 300 pp, $12.95 MacroPrintBooks™ edition (1999) ISBN 1-888725-23-0,8¼X10½, 16 pt, 330 pp, $18.95

Perfect Love-A Novel by Mary Harvatich (2000) Love born in an orphanage endures ISBN 1-888725-29-X 5½X8¼, 200 pp, $12.95 MacroPrintBooks™ edition (2000) ISBN 1-888725-15-X, 8¼X10½, 16 pt, 200 pp, $18.95

The Essential Simply Speaking Gold – Susan Fulton, (1998) How to use IBM's popular speech recognition package for dictation rather than keyboarding. Dozens of screen shots and illustrations. ISBN 1-888725-08-7 8¼ X8, 124 pp, $18.95

Begin Dictation Using ViaVoice Gold -2nd Edition– Susan Fulton, (1999), Covers ViaVoice 98 and other versions of IBM's popular continuous speech recognition package for dictation rather than keyboarding. Over a hundred screen shots and illustrations. ISBN 1-888725-22-2, 8¼X8, 260 pp, $28.95

Ropes and Saddles—Andy Polson (2001) Cowboy (and other) poems by Andy Polson. Reminiscences of the Wyoming poet. ISBN 1-888725-39-7, 5½ X 8¼, 100 pp, $9.95

Tales from the Woods of Wisdom - (book I) - Richard Tichenor (2000) In a spirit someplace between The Wizard of Oz and The Celestine Prophecy, this is more than a childrens' fable of life in the deep woods. ISBN 1-888725-37-0, 5½X8¼, 185 pp, $16.95 MacroPrintBooks™ edition (2001) ISBN 1-888725-50-8 6X8¼, 16 pt, 270 pp $24.95

Me and My Shadows—Shadow Puppet Fun for Kids of All Ages - Elizabeth Adams, Revised Edition by Dr. Bud Banis (2000) A thoroughly illustrated guide to the art of shadow puppet entertainment using tools that are always at hand wherever you go. A perfect gift for children and adults. ISBN 1-888725-44-3, 7X8¼, 67 pp, 12.95 MacroPrintBooks™ edition (2002) ISBN 1-888725-78-8 8½X11 lay-flat spiral, 18 pt, 67 pp, $16.95

Growing Up on Route 66 —Michael Lund (2000) ISBN 1-888725-31-1 Novel evoking fond memories of what it was like to grow up alongside "America's Highway" in 20th Century Missouri. (Trade paperback) 5½ X8¼, 260 pp, $14.95 MacroPrintBooks™ edition (2001) ISBN 1-888725-45-1 8¼X6½, 16 pt, 330 pp, $24.95

Route 66 Kids —Michael Lund (2002) ISBN 1-888725-70-2 Sequel to Growing Up on Route 66, continuing memories of what it was like to grow up alongside "America's Highway" in 20th Century Missouri. (Trade paperback) 5½ X8¼, 270 pp, $14.95 MacroPrintBooks™ edition (2002) ISBN 1-888725-71-0 8¼X6½, 16 pt, 350 pp, $24.95

MamaSquad! (2001) Hilarious novel by Clarence Wall about what happens when a group of women from a retirement home get tangled up in Army Special Forces. ISBN 1-888725-13-3 5½ X8¼, 200 pp, $14.95 MacroPrintBooks™ edition (2001) ISBN 1-888725-14-1 8¼X6½ 16 pt, 300 pp, $24.95

Virginia Mayo—The Best Years of My Life (2002) Autobiography of film star Virginia Mayo as told to LC Van Savage. From her early days in Vaudeville and the Muny in St Louis to the dozens of hit motion pictures, with dozens of photographs. ISBN 1-888725-53-2, 5½ X 8¼, 200 pp, $16.95

The Job—Eric Whitfield (2001) A story of self-discovery in the context of the death of a grandfather.. A book to read and share in times of change and Grieving. ISBN 1-888725-68-0, 5½ X 8¼, 100 pp, $12.95 MacroPrintBooks™ edition (2001) ISBN 1-888725-69-9, 8¼X6½, 18 pt, 150 pp, $18.95

Plague Legends: from the Miasmas of Hippocrates to the Microbes of Pasteur-Socrates Litsios D.Sc. (2001) Medical progress from early history through the 19th Century in understanding origins and spread of contagious disease. A thorough but readable and enlightening history of medicine. Illustrated, Bibliography, Index ISBN 1-888725-33-8, 6¼X8¼, 250pp, $24.95

Sexually Transmitted Diseases—Symptoms, Diagnosis, Treatment, Prevention-2nd Edition – NIAID Staff, Assembled and Edited by R.J.Banis, PhD, (2004) Teacher friendly —free to copy for education. Illustrated with more than 50 photographs of lesions, ISBN 1-888725-58-3, 8¼X6½, 200 pp, $18.95

The Stress Myth -Serge Doublet, PhD (2000) A thorough examination of the concept that 'stress' is the source of unexplained afflictions. Debunking mysticism, psychologist Serge Doublet reviews the history of other concepts such as 'demons', 'humors', 'hysteria' and 'neurasthenia' that had been placed in this role in the past, and provides an alternative approach for more success in coping with life's challenges. ISBN 1-888725-36-2, 5½X8¼, 280 pp, $24.95

Behind the Desk Workout – Joan Guccione, OTR/C, CHT (1997) ISBN 1-888725-00-1, Reduce risk of injury by exercising regularly at your desk. Over 200 photos and illustrations. (lay-flat spiral) 8¼X10½, 120 pp, $34.95 Paperback edition, (2000) ISBN 1-888725-25-7 $24.95

Copyright Issues for Librarians, Teachers & Authors–R.J. Banis, PhD, (Ed). 2nd Edn (2001) Protecting your rights, respecting others'. Information condensed from the Library of Congress, copyright registration forms. ISBN 1-888725-62-1, 5¼X8¼, 60 pp, booklet. $4.95 postpaid

Inaugural Addresses: Presidents of the United States from George Washington to 2008 -2nd Edition– Robert J. Banis, PhD, CMA, Ed. (2001) Extensively illustrated, includes election statistics, Vice- presidents, principal opponents, Index. coupons for update supplements for the next two elections. ISBN 1-888725-56-7, 6¼X8¼, 350pp, $18.95

Rhythm of the Sea —Shari Cohen (2001). Delightful collection of heartwarming stories of life relationships set in the context of oceans and lakes. Shari Cohen is a popular author of Womens' magazine articles and contributor to the Chicken Soup for the Soul series. ISBN 1-888725-55-9, 8X6.5 150 pp, $14.95 MacroPrintBooks™ edition (2001) ISBN 1-888725-63-X, 8¼X6½, 16 pt, 250 pp, $24.95

Riverdale Chronicles—Charles F. Rechlin (2003). Life, living and character studies in the setting of the Riverdale Golf Club by Charles F. Rechlin 5½ X 8¼, 100 pp ISBN: 1-888725-84-2 $14.95
MacroPrintBooks™ edition (2003) 16 pt. 8¼X6½, 16 pt, 350 pp ISBN: 1-888725-85-0 $24.95

Once in a Green Room: A Novel—Keri Baker (2001). After being raped and having an abortion while in college, a young woman struggles to deal with her feelings and is ultimately helped by the insights she gains from her special education students. Contact information for help groups throughout the United States.Part of proceeds contributed to RAINN. ISBN 1-888725-38-9, 5½X8¼, 160 pp, $14.95 MacroPrintBooks™ edn (2001) ISBN 1-888725-61-3, 8¼X6½, 16pt, 200 pp, $24.95

To Norma Jeane With Love, Jimmie -Jim Dougherty as told to LC Van Savage (2001) ISBN 1-888725-51-6 The sensitive and touching story of Jim Dougherty's teenage bride who later became Marilyn. Dozens of photographs. "The Marilyn Monroe book of the year!" As seen on TV. 5½X8¼, 200 pp, $16.95 MacroPrintBooks™ edition ISBN 1-888725-52-4, 8¼X6½, 16 pt, 290pp, $24.95

Bloodville — Don Bullis (2002) Fictional adaptation of the Budville, NM murders by New Mexico crime historian, Don Bullis. 5½ X 8¼, 350 pp ISBN: 1-888725-75-3 $14.95 **MacroPrintBooks™** edition (2003) 16 pt. 8¼X11 460pp ISBN: 1-888725-76-1 $24.95

The Cut—John Evans (2003). Football, Mystery and Mayhem in a highschool setting by John Evans ISBN: 1-888725-82-6 5½ X 8¼, 100 pp $14.95 **MacroPrintBooks™** edition (2003) 16 pt. ISBN: 1-888725-83-4 $24.95

Our books are guaranteed:

If a book has a defect, or doesn't hold up under normal use, or if you are unhappy in any way with one of our books, we are interested to know about it and will replace it and credit reasonable return shipping costs. Products with publisher defects (i.e., books with missing pages, etc.) may be returned at any time without authorization. However, we request that you describe the problem, to help us to continuously improve.

The Way It Was-- Nostalgic Tales of Hotrods and Romance Chuck Klein (2003) Series of hotrod stories by author of Circa 1957 in collaboration with noted illustrator Bill Lutz BeachHouse Books edition 5½ X 8¼, 200 pp ISBN: 1-888725-86-9 $14.95 MacroPrintBooks™ edition (2003) 16 pt. 8¼X6½, 350pp ISBN: 1-888725-87-7 $24.95

"...a delightful mix of anecdote, observation, and social history. A book so masterfully written, you can almost smell new upholstery on the street rod. This is definitely the best read..."

Paul Taylor, Publisher. Route 66 Magazine

"...a classic recipe for hours of delightful entertainment.... If this is your first time reading Chuck Klein, it's just like eating chocolate. Once you have the first bite, you know you'll be coming back for more. "

Carl Cartisano, Cruisin' Style Magazine

a new American classic, conjuring up images of good, clean fun for the "hot-rodders" of yesterday and today....a fun, fast read that appeals to the kid in all of us." --

Aaron Lasky, Hot Rod DeLuxe, CK DeLuxe, & Kingpin Magazines

"Your book is great. You have captured the feel and texture of the 'fifties in each story. It's a wonderful read ...which accurately portrays and preserves the magic of the era".

Dusty Rhodes, WSAI Radio, Cincinnati

"As varied as the vehicles --a 1960 Corvette, a '57 Chevy, a 1937 Ford pick-up truck--and the people who drive them--eager teenagers cruisin' for dates, a sailor on furlough, a young woman who understands a "two-eighty-three engine, bored sixty thousandths over"-- these well crafted tales are a veritable potpourri of American road lore." "Bet you can't read just one!"

Michael Lund, Author of the Growing Up on Route 66 Series

Route 66 books by Michael Lund

Growing Up on Route 66 —Michael Lund (2000) ISBN 1-888725-31-1 Novel evoking fond memories of what it was like to grow up alongside "America's Highway" in 20th Century Missouri. (Trade paperback) 5½ X8¼, 260 pp, $14.95 **MacroPrintBooks™** edition (2001) ISBN 1-888725-45-1 8¼X6½, 16 pt, 330 pp, $24.95

Route 66 Kids —Michael Lund (2002) ISBN 1-888725-70-2 Sequel to *Growing Up on Route 66*, continuing memories of what it was like to grow up alongside "America's Highway" in 20th Century Missouri. (Trade paperback) 5½ X8¼, 270 pp, $14.95 **MacroPrintBooks™** edition (2002) ISBN 1-888725-71-0 8¼X6½, 16 pt, 350 pp, $24.95

A Left-hander on Route 66--Michael Lund (2003) ISBN 1-888725-88-5. Twenty years after the fact, left-hander Hugh Noone appeals a wrongful conviction that detoured him from "America's Main Street" and put him in jail. But revealing the details of the past and effecting a resolution of his case mean a dramatic rearrangement of his world, including troubled relationships with three women: Linda Roy, Patty Simpson, and Karen Murphy. (Trade paperback) 5½ X8¼, 270 pp, $14.95 **MacroPrintBooks™** edition (2002) ISBN 1-888725-89-3 8¼X6½, 16 pt, 350 pp, $24.95

Books from Science & Humanities Press by Russ Miller:

Journey to a Closed City With the International Executive Service Corps (2004) Russell R. Miller. One Man's account of what it's like to help build an open capitalistic society in Russia's Breadbasket with the IESC.

ISBN 1-888725-94-X Regular print Science & Humanities Press Edition $16.95
ISBN 1-888725-95-8 large print (16pt) MacroPrintBooks Edition $24.95

Order form			
Item	Each	Quantity	Amount
Missouri (only) sales tax 6.075%			
Priority Shipping			$4.00
	Total		
Ship to Name:			
Address:			
City State Zip:			

Science & Humanities Press
PO Box 7151
Chesterfield, MO 63006
(636) 394-4950
sciencehumanitiespress.com